Social Media Engagement

FOR DUMMIES®
A Wiley Brand

by Aliza Sherman and Danielle Elliott Smith

FOR DUMMIES®
A Wiley Brand

Social Media Engagement For Dummies®

Published by
John Wiley & Sons, Inc.
111 River Street
Hoboken, NJ 07030-5774

www.wiley.com

About the Authors

Aliza Sherman is a pioneer and visionary in the web industry who travels the world to speak to diverse audiences about the Internet, social media, mobile marketing, new technologies and applications, entrepreneurship, and women's issues. She founded the first woman-owned, full-service Internet company — Cybergrrl, Inc. — and the first global organization for women — Webgrrls International. A serial entrepreneur, she also started one of the first social media marketing agencies and one of the first mobile marketing consultancies. *Newsweek* named Aliza one of the "Top 50 People Who Matter Most on the Internet" for her early Internet work, and *Fast Company* named her one of the "Most Powerful Women in Technology." She is the author of ten books, most of them about business and the Internet. She and Danielle co-authored the book *MOM, Incorporated.*

Danielle Elliott Smith is a digital correspondent, host, storyteller, speaker, media trainer, and (most importantly), mom to two sweet and sassy small people — Delaney, 9, and Cooper, 7. In her "free time," Danielle juggles work as the founder of ExtraordinaryMommy.com and DanielleSmithMedia.com, and she hosts and produces her lifestyle series, "Keeping Style in Your Life." She also creates original content for the well-known online magazines *Babble* and *SheKnows* and shares vlogging and media tips for people wanting to jump on camera. An award-winning former television news anchor and reporter, she has covered everything from the red carpet at the Academy of Country Music Awards to the Vancouver Olympics Games and the NFL Pro Bowl in Hawaii. Danielle has been featured on the *CBS Early Show,* NPR, MSNBC, CNN, and Fox News and in *USA Today, Publishers Weekly,* and *Pregnancy & Newborn.* This is her second book; she had the pleasure of co-writing her first one, *Mom, Incorporated,* with Aliza.

Dedication

From Aliza Sherman: To my loving family: Greg, my Renaissance man husband, and Noa Grace, 6, who now knows why Mommy had her nose in a computer — again.

From Danielle Elliott Smith: To my extraordinary husband, Jeff, for holding my hand throughout this process. I couldn't have done it without you. I'm one lucky girl. And to my sweet small people — Punky and Coop — thank you for inspiring me to live my passion and for proving to me that I truly *can* do both: be your mom and live this dream. I'm grateful for you every day.

Authors' Acknowledgments

We'd like to thank our families and good friends, who have been supportive of us throughout the book-writing process.

Thank you to our team at John Wiley & Sons, Inc. — especially Nicole Sholly and Amy Fandrei, who guided us beautifully through this process and held our hands when we needed it. Many thanks also to Kathy Simpson, Rebecca Whitney, Amanda Graham, Joe Waters, and everyone behind the scenes who helped make this book a reality. A monumental thank you as well to Ellen Gerstein, who saw potential in us from the beginning and believed that *this* was our next book. Ellen, you and Amy were right.

We'd also like to thank our book agent, Jessica Faust, of BookEnds LLC.

Special thanks to the many folks from companies, big and small, who shared their stories and thoughts on social media engagement with us so generously, many of whom are now featured in this book. Your input was invaluable and so appreciated.

We'd especially like to thank the members of our communities in our favorite social networks — people who connect with us regularly and make our day. We are grateful for your support.

And you, our readers — thank *you* for choosing this book to guide you on your social media engagement journey. We hope that your journey into this digital space is an exciting one.

From Aliza Sherman: I couldn't have completed this book without my co-author, Danielle, who jumped on this book-writing adventure with me back in 2011 to co-create *MOM, Incorporated*. The book journey was a new challenge for us both and one that I couldn't have tackled without her by my virtual side, to talk me off the ledge and to infuse the contents with her incredible spirit. Cheers to you, my friend!

An extra-special thank you to my husband, Greg, my daughter Noa Grace, to my parents, Lucy and Mike Sherman, and my sister Leah. All five share the title of my Number One Fans and Supporters.

A big thanks to Chelsea, Angeles, Erica, Kelly, Annie, and Heather for keeping me on track from day to day, especially when I was eyebrows-deep in the manuscript for this book.

A heartfelt thanks to Terry Wheatley for her encouragement and sage advice. I'm so lucky to count her as mentor and friend.

From Danielle Elliott Smith: As with our last book, my biggest chunk of gratitude heads northwest, to snow-covered Alaska, where my co-author, Aliza, would sit, "Skype-ing" with me, chatting by phone, hopping into a Google+ hangout, and e-mailing document after document back and forth as we labored over this book. For your willingness to work with me on yet another book, and for more than that — your friendship — I am grateful.

I'm thankful for the many friends who built me up, and talked me down, as I worked my way through this project — especially Alli and Barbara. To the friends who have known me for decades and *still* keep coming back for more: Rose, Karin, Erin, Heather, Taralyn, and Eileen — I adore you deep in my soul. And to Ally, for your patience, hard work, sweet spirit, and ability to keep me on track — I couldn't do it without you.

And finally, to my family. Mum and Dad: A blanket thank-you for being you — two people I love deeply. To Paula and Rick, for your never-ending support, for your ability to make me laugh, and for giving me your son, I'm so thankful. To Jeff, for believing in me when I didn't, for sleeping on the floor of my office so that I'd feel inspired to write, for refusing (against your better judgment) to yell at me for writing all night, and for being the best daddy in the universe: I love you, and I'm forever grateful. Delaney and Cooper, your enthusiasm for everything I do is contagious. I want to be you when I grow up. Every day, you make me better. Thank you for believing in your mommy. You are one of the biggest reasons I now hold this book in my hands!

Publisher's Acknowledgments

We're proud of this book; please send us your comments at http://dummies.custhelp.com. For other comments, please contact our Customer Care Department within the U.S. at 877-762-2974, outside the U.S. at 317-572-3993, or fax 317-572-4002.

Some of the people who helped bring this book to market include the following:

Acquisitions, Editorial

Senior Project Editor: Nicole Sholly

Acquisitions Editor: Amy Fandrei

Copy Editors: Rebecca Whitney, Amanda Graham

Technical Editor: Joe Waters

Editorial Manager: Kevin Kirschner

Editorial Assistant: Anne Sullivan

Sr. Editorial Assistant: Cherie Case

Cover Photo: iStockphoto.com / © Peter Booth

Composition Services

Project Coordinator: Sheree Montgomery

Layout and Graphics: Carrie A. Cesavice, Jennifer Creasey, Christin Swinford

Proofreaders: Lindsay Amones, Shannon Ramsey

Indexer: Valerie Haynes Perry

Publishing and Editorial for Technology Dummies

    Richard Swadley, Vice President and Executive Group Publisher

    Andy Cummings, Vice President and Publisher

    Mary Bednarek, Executive Acquisitions Director

    Mary C. Corder, Editorial Director

Publishing for Consumer Dummies

    Kathleen Nebenhaus, Vice President and Executive Publisher

Composition Services

    Debbie Stailey, Director of Composition Services

Contents at a Glance

Introduction 1

Part I: The Basics of Social Media Engagement 7
Chapter 1: Explaining the Why, Who, and How of Social Media Engagement 9
Chapter 2: Assessing the Impact of Social Media Engagement 25
Chapter 3: Discovering Social Media Engagement Tools 43

Part II: Exploring the Elements of Social Media Engagement 65
Chapter 4: Building Trust and Credibility 67
Chapter 5: Demonstrating Your Online Presence to Maximize Engagement 85
Chapter 6: Creating Connections 105
Chapter 7: Driving Interaction 121

Part III: Examining the Basic Engagement Tools 137
Chapter 8: E-mail, Forums, Blogs, and Websites 139
Chapter 9: Facebook 157
Chapter 10: Twitter 183

Part IV: Engaging Through Additional Social Channels 209
Chapter 11: Pinterest 211
Chapter 12: LinkedIn 241
Chapter 13: Google+ 263
Chapter 14: Location-Based Services 281

Part V: Leveraging Audio and Video for Engagement 301
Chapter 15: Audio and Videocasting 303
Chapter 16: YouTube 317

Part VI: The Part of Tens 335
Chapter 17: Ten Social Media Engagement Mistakes to Avoid 337
Chapter 18: Ten Businesses That Excel at Social Media Engagement 343

Index 353

Table of Contents

Introduction 1

    About This Book...1
    Foolish Assumptions...2
    Conventions Used in This Book..................................3
    What You Don't Have to Read....................................3
    How This Book Is Organized 3
        Part I: The Basics of Social Media Engagement 3
        Part II: Exploring the Elements of Social Media Engagement...........4
        Part III: Examining the Basic Engagement Tools............4
        Part IV: Engaging Through Additional Channels 4
        Part V: Leveraging Audio and Video for Engagement 4
        Part VI: The Part of Tens...4
    Icons Used in This Book 5
    Where to Go from Here...5

Part 1: The Basics of Social Media Engagement 7

    Chapter 1: Explaining the Why, Who, and How of Social Media Engagement 9
        Seeking the Benefits of Social Media Engagement 9
        Keeping up with changing consumer needs....................10
        Humanizing your brand in the marketplace....................12
        Strengthening connections with customers....................14
        Tapping into new markets 15
        Reaping the rewards of an engaged community....................16
        Seeing How People and Organizations Engage with Social Media 17
        Individual consumers..18
        Online communities..18
        Your business...19
        Your employees 20
        Setting Goals for Social Media Engagement 21
        Building trust and credibility 22
        Being present with a human touch.............................22
        Creating connections..23
        Sparking conversations...23
        Driving interaction..24

Chapter 2: Assessing the Impact of Social Media Engagement 25

Considering the Downsides of Social Media Engagement........................ 25
    Managing the "time suck" 26
    Overcoming the barriers to entry... 27
    Surviving information overload 28
    Dealing with potential backlash.. 31
    Avoiding inconsistent messaging 33
Measuring the Value of Your Social Media Engagement 35
    Determining what interactions are valuable 35
    Knowing which numbers to measure.. 36
    Setting benchmarks to evaluate progress 38
    Reassessing to improve engagement 39
    Leveraging success.. 41

Chapter 3: Discovering Social Media Engagement Tools 43

Considering Traditional Online Communications Tools....................... 43
    E-mail.. 44
    Online forums (groups)... 46
    Websites and blogs.. 48
Engaging with Social Networks 50
    Facebook... 51
    Twitter... 53
    Pinterest... 54
    LinkedIn.. 56
    Google+... 58
Incorporating Audio and Video Platforms 59
    Audiocasting or podcasting.. 60
    Videocasting or video podcasts... 61
    YouTube.. 61
Recognizing Other Social Engagement Tools 63
    Mobile applications 63
    Location-based services 64

**Part II: Exploring the Elements of
Social Media Engagement 65**

Chapter 4: Building Trust and Credibility. 67

Earning Trust in Social Media 67
    Making your message clear 67
    Giving your team clear guidelines 68
    Interacting authentically.. 68
    Finding your brand's voice.. 70

Contributing meaningfully to the conversation.............................70
Listening carefully to your community................................74
Responding promptly for greater impact.........................76
Giving the audience what they want..........................76
Building Trust in Traditional Online Marketing.........................78
Engaging appropriately with the media........................78
Adding engagement to press releases 79
Soliciting third-party endorsements the right way 80
Assessing Trust and Credibility........................81
Analyzing sentiment and impact........................81
Measuring the amplification of your messages 83

**Chapter 5: Demonstrating Your Online
Presence to Maximize Engagement.........................85**
Setting Realistic Goals Up Front 85
Assessing your capacity 86
Evaluating the competition 87
Paying Attention to Demonstrate Presence.........................88
Being notified when you need to engage 88
Responding to comments and following up 91
Establishing a Presence Process 92
Creating a messaging map 93
Developing a social media editorial calendar 97
Setting a Schedule 100
Determining how frequently to update........................101
Figuring out the best times to engage........................102
Deciding when to interact........................104

Chapter 6: Creating Connections.........................105
Starting with Your Connection Goals........................105
Setting short-term goals.................................106
Establishing longer-term goals........................108
Identifying Your Audience........................109
Determining who you're trying to reach........................109
Finding your audience online........................109
Figuring out what your audience does online........................110
Creating a Space for Engagement 112
Setting ground rules for participation........................112
Offering a forum for opinions........................112
Showcasing what others know and do........................113
Getting the Engagement Ball Rolling 114
Asking for action........................115
Offering rewards for action 116
Handling negative feedback........................117

Chapter 7: Driving Interaction **121**

Creating the Setting to Stimulate Engagement 122
  Moving past the what's-in-it-for-me? mentality............................ 122
  Building a space where people feel comfortable.......................... 123
  Inspiring others to pay attention and care.................................... 124
Starting Conversations 125
  Tapping in to trending topics.. 126
  Lighting a fire with hot-button issues 126
  Turning to humor.. 128
  Building engagement by way of inspiration 130
Providing Additional Incentives for Sharing...................................... 132
  Offering freebies and discounts.. 133
  Holding contests and sweepstakes 133
  Aligning your company with a cause 135

Part III: Examining the Basic Engagement Tools 137

Chapter 8: E-mail, Forums, Blogs, and Websites **139**

Creating Social-Powered E-mail Newsletters 139
  Choosing an e-mail marketing tool 140
  Putting out the word 142
  Prompting subscribers to become fans.. 142
  Driving more than clicks 144
Participating in Online Communities 145
  Forming and growing an online community................................. 146
  Identifying the people you want to reach 147
  Crafting appropriate messages 148
  Entering conversations effectively 149
Forming Your Own Groups and Forums.. 151
  Evaluating the benefits of a custom group 151
  Choosing a group management tool.. 152
  Building groups in social networks 153
Enhancing Blogs and Websites for Engagement................................ 154
  Facilitating sharing with social network widgets 154
  Expanding commenting with apps 155

Chapter 9: Facebook **157**

Building Deeper Relationships on Facebook 158
Growing Your Page Community 159
  Increasing follower loyalty 160
  Promoting your business page with your personal Timeline 164
Standing Out in the News Feed 165
  Navigating EdgeRank.. 166
  Crafting engaging posts.. 166
  Adding visual elements to draw instant attention...................... 169
  Reaching out to other pages 170

Determining post timing and frequency 170
Driving traffic to your page with cross-posting 171
Leveraging the Advanced Features of Facebook 171
Tagging photos and posts 172
Scheduling posts for the greatest impact 172
Optimizing your page for search engines 174
Graph Search 175
Advertising on Facebook 176
Embedding social widgets 178
Analyzing Facebook interactions 181

Chapter 10: Twitter 183
Engaging in Real-Time via Twitter 184
Understanding how individuals, brands,
and small businesses use Twitter 185
Conveying who you are on Twitter 190
Devising a plan to keep up with fast-moving conversations 193
Measuring Twitter engagement 194
Making an Impact in the Twitter Stream 195
Crafting attention-grabbing tweets 195
Leveraging links to get results 196
Retweeting and @mentioning others 198
Being "present" even when you're not 199
Increasing Engagement via Twitter Features 200
Giving kudos using Favorites 200
Building connections via lists and columns 201
Getting personal with a direct message (DM) 204
Attracting more followers with widgets and buttons 205
Adding Twitter to Facebook (and vice versa) 207
Accessing Twitter on the go 208

Part IV: Engaging Through Additional
Social Channels 209

Chapter 11: Pinterest 211
Creating Connections by Incorporating Visual Elements 212
Preparing your business account 212
Setting up the right boards for your brand 213
Pinning to clearly convey your messages 217
Connecting using pins, repins, likes, and comments 217
Quantifying the value of Pinterest 219
Getting Noticed In People's Pin Feeds 222
Seeking and pinning winning images 223
Honing your repinning strategy 225
Knowing how often and how much to pin 226

Leveraging Pinterest Features to Increase Engagement 228
        Adding hashtags to attract attention 228
        Getting noticed by tagging others 229
        Running a contest to increase interactions 230
        Inviting participants to group boards 232
    Benefitting from Pinterest Integration 233
        Inspiring others to pin your images 233
        Linking Pinterest to Twitter 235
        Integrating Pinterest into Facebook Timelines 237
        Integrating Pinterest into Facebook Pages 238

Chapter 12: LinkedIn **241**
    Setting Up Your LinkedIn Profile 241
        Creating a new public profile 242
        Editing and enhancing your profile 244
    Reaching Out and Connecting with Your Peers 245
        Engaging in reciprocal interactions 246
        Joining LinkedIn Groups 247
    Communicating through Your Company Page 249
        Creating a Company Page 250
        Making the most of your Company Page 251
    Stimulating Interactions through Updates 251
        Posting compelling content 253
        Interacting with others in the feed 254
    Taking Advantage of More LinkedIn Features 254
        Giving and receiving recommendations 255
        Providing endorsements 257
        Forming and managing a LinkedIn Group 258
    Gauging LinkedIn Results 259
        Tracking interactions 259
        Analyzing engagement 260
        Checking the business benefits 260
        Using analytics tools 261

Chapter 13: Google+ **263**
    Checking Out the Benefits of Google+ 263
    Getting Your Feet Wet on Google+ 264
        Building your personal profile 265
        Setting up a Google+ business page 266
        Setting up an effective page 267
    Getting into the Flow of G+ 269
        Leveraging long-form publishing 269
        Posting multimedia 270
        Interacting in the stream 271
        Building your page audience 273

Expanding Your Google+ Engagement 274
    Circling your connections 274
    Connecting with groups in Hangouts 275
    Leveraging the power of +1 278
    Collaborating in Google+ communities 279

Chapter 14: Location-Based Services **281**

Bridging the Real and Online Worlds with LBS 281
    Choosing an LBS (or two) 282
    Setting up an LBS account 283
Making Connections with LBS 284
    Checking in to locations to engage others 285
    Discovering others nearby 286
    Tying images to places through geotagging 286
Using LBS for Promotions 287
    Doing business with Foursquare 288
    Tapping into the power of Instagram 289
    Linking LBS for integrated posts 291
    Offering deals driven by check-ins 292
Adding Mobile to Your Engagement Mix 293
    Reaching customers through SMS marketing 294
    Using QR codes for location-based marketing 295
    Geolocating and geotagging 297
    Creating hybrid online/offline engagement 298

Part V: Leveraging Audio and Video for Engagement ... 301

Chapter 15: Audio and Videocasting **303**

Enhancing Your Marketing with Audio 303
    Using podcasts to build an audience 305
    Publishing audio from a mobile device 308
    Adding audio to your social network 309
Offering Teleseminars and Webinars 310
    Seeing the benefits of webinars and teleseminars 310
    Choosing between webinars and teleseminars 311
    Selecting the right tool 312
Getting More out of Multimedia 313
    Conferencing with video 313
    Engaging with live streaming video 315
    Showing on the go: Mobile video 316

Chapter 16: YouTube 317

   Using Video to Build Community 317
      Capturing your audience's attention.................................318
      Optimizing your YouTube Channel 320
      Creating a playlist 322
      Maximizing your subscriber base......................................323
      Interacting with the YouTube community 323
   Standing Out on YouTube 325
      Producing video content that keeps people watching 325
      Mastering metadata...326
      Using annotations and thumbnails....................................329
   Extending Your Reach with Video..330
      Embedding and integrating your videos............................331
      Taking advantage of video responses 332
      Uploading video on the go..333
      Analyzing your impact 333

Part VI: The Part of Tens *335*

Chapter 17: Ten Social Media Engagement Mistakes to Avoid 337

   Flying by the Seat of Your Pants...337
   Using Too Much Automation 338
   Broadcasting or Sharing Only Your Content 338
   Being Inconsistent 339
   Lacking Personality 339
   Ignoring Feedback 339
   Assuming That Social Media Is Easy 340
   Spamming 340
   Posting the Same Content Everywhere......................................341
   Repeating Mistakes 341

**Chapter 18: Ten Businesses That Excel
at Social Media Engagement** 343

   Wine Sisterhood...343
   Mabel's Labels 344
   Girls Crochet Headbands 345
   Ramon DeLeon, Marketing Mind behind 6-Store
      Domino's Pizza Franchise, Chicago 346
   Cabot Creamery Cooperative...347
   Nylabone..348
   MomBiz 349
   Blendtec..350
   Chobani 351
   AJ Bombers 352

Index *353*

Introduction

You've probably heard that "business as usual" is no more. The way that people communicate, market, and sell has changed dramatically since the advent of social media marketing. We're here to tell you that even though the tools are new and different — and seem to change regularly — you can definitely find out how to master them.

Every step of the way, we coauthors emphasize the best practices of online marketing, customer service, and genuine human communication. As a business owner, you benefit from knowing not only how Internet tools work but also how people use them and how you can leverage them to better reach the customers and prospects who matter the most to you and your business.

About This Book

Social Media Engagement For Dummies starts by shedding light on the fundamental principles of social media engagement — the ingredients that put the *social* in social media marketing. Effective social media engagement (or SME, as we often refer to it throughout this book) should provide tangible and measurable results for your business and boost your bottom line.

By mastering the techniques in this book, you strengthen your connections with potential customers. But don't stop there: Convert potential customers to actual customers, and then use SME tactics to turn customers into active and passionate evangelists for your company.

This book is a practical, hands-on guide to social media engagement, and we speak from experience. We don't only consult and teach others to engage well via social media — we also benefit daily as business owners ourselves, by avidly using social networks and social media tools and platforms. We use these tools to communicate our messages to our respective audiences and to connect with the people who read, listen to, and watch what we publish online.

We build relationships with our audiences and truly care about them. In turn, we are humbled to see that our audiences trust us and respond positively to what we say and do online. We are confident that you, too, can benefit from social media engagement.

Here are some of the things you can do with the information in this book:

- ✔ Understand and apply the elements of social media engagement.
- ✔ Find out how to plan ahead for engagement.
- ✔ Determine which social media tools are right for you.
- ✔ Effectively incorporate engagement into your social media campaigns.
- ✔ Measure your social media engagement efforts.

Social Media Engagement For Dummies isn't meant to sound technical or geeky. We take a down-to-earth approach to the technology and provide a lot of explanations and examples so that you can immediately incorporate SME strategies and tactics into your online marketing efforts. We're results-oriented, and we know you are, too.

Foolish Assumptions

We do our best to be clear and detailed in our explanations of suggested tools and tactics. We assume, however, that you have a basic understanding of several ingredients:

- ✔ You have more than entry-level knowledge of the Internet.
- ✔ You have a website and you know what a blog is, even if you don't personally blog.
- ✔ You're aware of, and familiar with, some of the most popular social networks.
- ✔ You have at least one social networking account for your business.
- ✔ You're engaging in forms of online marketing and even social media marketing, and you're looking to increase the effectiveness of those efforts.
- ✔ You know that your participation is the key to successful social media engagement.
- ✔ More than anything, you value your customers — you want to bring more customers to your business, and you want to turn all your customers into enthusiasts.

Conventions Used in This Book

To be consistent, we use these common *For Dummies* conventions:

- ✔ The first time we use a new term, we define it and *italicize* it.
- ✔ When we tell you to type something (in a box or a field, for example), we put it in **bold.**
- ✔ When we mention a website, a network, a platform, or an online application, we provide the URL for your convenience.
- ✔ When we provide a URL, it looks like this: www.dummies.com.

What You Don't Have to Read

You don't have to read this book sequentially, and you don't even have to read all its sections in any particular chapter. You can skip sidebars and read only the material that helps you complete the task at hand, or you can start by reading only the sidebars, to access information that you can apply immediately to your social media engagement efforts.

How This Book Is Organized

Social Media Engagement For Dummies is split into six parts. Think of the earlier parts of the book as introductions to theories, concepts, and tools; think of the latter parts as plans for turning concepts into actions. In this section, we briefly describe what you'll find in each part.

Part 1: The Basics of Social Media Engagement

We start this book with an overview of social media engagement, from understanding the concepts to using the tools. Part I begins by justifying your investment in social media engagement and explaining the concepts. We explain measurement and the value of engaging, and we introduce a variety of online tools for implementing social media engagement tactics.

Part II: Exploring the Elements of Social Media Engagement

Moving beyond the basics, Part II delves more deeply into the concepts of social media engagement, including building trust and credibility, creating connections, and understanding the importance of being present in social networking. We explain how to start, and participate in, online conversations and drive interactions that help you achieve your business goals.

Part III: Examining the Basic Engagement Tools

In Part III, we review online communications tools that you may already use and others that you may not be using yet. We outline how to use these tools — from the more traditional e-mail, forums, blogs, and websites to Facebook and Twitter — specifically for social media engagement.

Part IV: Engaging Through Additional Social Channels

We don't stop with the popular social networks covered in Part III; in Part IV, we look at a few up-and-coming networks that are changing the way people engage online. We break down the ways that Pinterest, LinkedIn, Google+, and location-based networks (such as Foursquare and Instagram) provide opportunities for engagement in more ways that drive results.

Part V: Leveraging Audio and Video for Engagement

We'd be remiss not to mention multimedia options for social media engagement. In Part V, we cover ways to use audio and video to capture your audience's attention and encourage interactions. We cap this part with a close look at YouTube features that facilitate engagement.

Part VI: The Part of Tens

In typical *For Dummies* fashion, this book includes The Part of Tens to give you quick-reference guides to social media engagement. First, we fill you in on common social media engagement mistakes that you definitely want to avoid. We finish this part with the stories of ten businesses that use social media engagement tactics successfully.

Icons Used in This Book

What's a *For Dummies* book without icons to point you to helpful information that's sure to help you along your way? In this section, we briefly describe each icon we use in this book.

The Tip icon points out helpful information that's likely to make your job easier.

This icon marks an interesting, useful fact that you may want to remember for later use.

The Warning icon highlights pitfalls you should avoid. With this icon, we're telling you to pay attention and proceed with caution.

When you see this icon, you know that there's technical information nearby. If you're not feeling technically minded, you can skip it.

Where to Go from Here

Like any *For Dummies* book, this one is written to ensure that you can dive into any section at any time and find useful information. Parts I and II offer an introduction to theories, concepts, and tools; Parts III, IV, and V lay out distinct road maps for turning concepts into actions. Don't hesitate to skip around this book and refer to it often as a step-by-step guide to completing a task or simply as a refresher. Use the table of contents to find the chapters that can serve you immediately, such as a specific social network, or check the index to key in on a particular concept or task.

Occasionally, John Wiley & Sons, Inc., has updates to its technology books. If this book has technical updates, they'll be posted at www.dummies.com/go/socialmediaengagementfdupdates.

Part I

The Basics of Social Media Engagement

getting started with social media engagement

In this part . . .

- ✔ Find out about the goals of social media engagement and why they matter.

- ✔ Gain insights into the impact and value of engaging via social media.

- ✔ Get a handle on the variety of online tools that you can use to engage effectively with your audience.

Chapter 1

Explaining the Why, Who, and How of Social Media Engagement

In This Chapter

▶ Recognizing the benefits of social media engagement

▶ Identifying the many roles of social media

▶ Deciding how your organization can best use social media

Social media engagement (SME) is the "stuff that happens" during your social media marketing campaigns. SME is an essential part of social media marketing. If you don't connect with others in social networks — and if they don't respond to you — you don't have engagement. Without engagement, you're simply broadcasting messages that fall on deaf ears. Nobody wants that to happen, right?

In this chapter, we help you start thinking about SME, including the benefits of engaging with customers. We outline who participates in SME. *Hint:* It isn't just you. We also introduce concepts that explain how SME happens — or how it should happen — if you're using best practices.

If you're being thoughtful about the way you communicate with — and connect with — others online, you'll have greater success in reaching customers via SME. But first you need to understand what it is, how it works, and what your role is in making it happen.

Seeking the Benefits of Social Media Engagement

When will it ever end? Technology changes constantly and so quickly that it feels like the moment you gain a new skill or figure out how to use a new online tool, everything changes again and your newly acquired skills seem obsolete. Let's face it: Social media engagement seems to change daily.

Simply put, social media engagement (often abbreviated as SME) is the process by which online communications and the content you post online help you build connections with other people within online communities. Social media engagement involves the use of the tools of social media — social networks, for example — to build relationships with others that, ideally, result in some kind of reaction, interaction, or action.

You may be wondering why you should consider using SME. Maybe you're satisfied with your current marketing strategies that involve concrete numbers and set dollar amounts. Maybe you're buying advertising in traditional media such as print, television, or radio and even though you've witnessed its declining effectiveness over the years, it's what you know.

Maybe you're committed to advertising online with banner ads, skyscraper ads, and interstitial *(pop-up)* ads. Sure, the number of click-throughs on your ads has declined, but you chalk it up to people being busy with publishing their own content and being too distracted by Facebook and Twitter activity to pay attention the way they used to do.

You might even be concerned about losing control of your content or copyrights. Nobody fully controls information that's published online. SME acknowledges and encourages not only the consumption of the information you put out there but also lets others interpret, remix (by adding their own ideas), and share it. You can still protect your copyrights and trademarks in social media as you have been doing over the past several years on the Internet. But in SME, you want people to spread your message, and you need to let them do it in their own ways.

Let's face it: This isn't your grandparents' marketing campaign. The world of marketing online as you once knew it has changed drastically since social networks entered the scene, and it's changing even as you read this chapter.

Keeping up with changing consumer needs

Today's consumers are using the Internet for both personal and professional activities, and they're savvier than ever about the way companies like yours are trying to reach them. Though they're inundated and overwhelmed by blatant advertising that tries to pull at their attention, they now tune out most ads, especially the ones that aren't relevant to them.

Finding out how your customers use the Internet

To reach today's consumers online, you must understand how they use the Internet, which sites they visit online, what they're looking for, and how they behave. Spend time pinpointing your ideal customer's online habits. A study in 2012 by Experian shows that more than 91 percent of adults who go online use social networks regularly:

```
http://go.experian.com/forms/experian-digital-
            marketer-2012
```

That number is up from 65 percent from earlier in the year, as reported by Pew Internet Research in April 2012:

```
http://pewinternet.org/Reports/2012/Digital-differences/
            Main-Report/Internet-activities-Those-already-
            online-are-doing-more.aspx
```

Your customers and your prospects want you to be available to them whenever they go online. Just as they expect a search engine to give them instant results for information they're seeking, consumers who go online to search for your company expect that you'll have not only a website but also a presence on at least one of their favorite social networks.

Add social media icons representing the social networks where your company is present and participating, including links directly to each network so that visitors to your website can connect with you in the way they prefer. In Figure 1-1, you can see that The Gap embeds social media icons in the footer of its website so that they appear on every page.

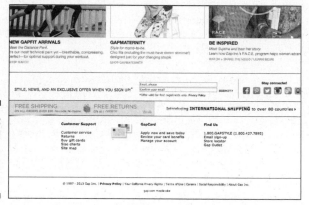

Figure 1-1:
Typical
social media
icons on a
website.

Knowing what customers want from you

Today's consumer takes their expectations a step further than when they were limited in how they could respond to companies marketing to them: They expect you to

✓ **Hear them when they praise you:** People willingly post both positive and negative statements publicly about you, your products, services, or company on their favorite social networks. You need to listen.

✔ **Respond quickly:** If someone comments about a company online, that person expects a response — and may instantly receive responses from *their* friends, fans, and followers. You want to be part of that conversation.

✔ **Provide a forum for them:** Calling a 1-800 customer service line is no longer the way consumers want to ask questions, air grievances, or lavish praise on a company. Your presence on a social network can provide customers with a new way to communicate with you. We realize that it may seem intimidating, but they want to communicate with you publicly.

✔ **Offer communications choices:** Consumers want multiple options for connecting with you. Offer them a variety of options based on their preferences.

In short, the very people whom you're trying to reach — your *target market* — are expecting you to be present in major social networks and not only to lurk there but also to be ready to interact with them.

Humanizing your brand in the marketplace

You may have heard the word *authentic* tossed around in blog posts, articles, workshops, or lectures as an important aspect of social media engagement. We understand the term to mean *real,* as in genuine, honest, and transparent rather than fake, overly commercial, insincere, or shady. We state it this way: Be human.

"Of course, I'm human," you say. "And so is my team. We're *all* human." We know that you're human; however, you need to be human in social networks. Don't subscribe to a regimented formula, set stringent restrictions, or automate every possible action to avoid investing the time and effort it takes to truly engage — and to be engaging — in social networks with your following.

Putting faces to names

Being human in social media engagement starts with people, involves people, and ends with people. No social network functions without people who love to use it connecting with other people through it. For example, the cable television company Charter posts customer service hours on Twitter and shows the people behind the brand. Figure 1-2 shows how Charter features a photograph of its social media specialist (whose Twitter handle is @CharterAbby) as its Twitter icon and a photograph of its customer service team on its Twitter page to come across as friendly and approachable.

Figure 1-2: Charter offers a human touch on its Twitter page.

Your main goal in SME is to be human, real, and responsive so that people want to connect with you and your company in the same networks where they connect with their family and friends.

Attracting and engaging people

You're entering people's inner circles when they let you into their content streams. These content streams are the new online spaces where people are paying attention. To stand out to followers and engage them, you need to:

✔ **Attract their attention.**

News feeds on social networks move quickly, and most people now skim the feeds or reorder them to see only what they want to see from the people they know and like. Use strategic and relevant words and images to get them to notice.

✔ **Entice them to come to you.**

You want people to click on your links or images to move them away from the main news feed and over to the source — your website, your Facebook Page Wall, or another place that you own where you can provide them with more detailed information.

✔ **Compel people to take some kind of action.**

After people notice you and click through to the destination of your choice, give them something to do that is measurable — preferably, something that connects them with you for the longer term, such as sign up for your e-newsletter or like your Facebook Page.

✔ **Give people a reason to return.**

Based on where you've directed them, provide incentive for them to come back to you. If they've signed up for an e-newsletter, draw them in with your messages or invite them to one of your social networks to continue the conversation.

✔ **Convince people to do business with you.**

Continue providing value, be responsive, and interactive, and prove that they should stay in touch with your brand. Close the sale, but don't look at the sale as the end of the road. Converting a fan to a customer is only the beginning of a longer-term relationship.

In the age of information overload online, social media impressions must be even more attractive and more constant and consistent to make a dent in someone's attention. And it all begins with a human touch and with genuine, human connections made via social networks and other social media tools and platforms.

Strengthening connections with customers

Social media engagement requires you to create meaningful impressions to build awareness, gain trust, and increase customer loyalty. Social media engagement also provides your happy customers with the means to spread the word about how great you are to their friends, fans, and followings — all of whom may be potential customers for you. More than anything, well-executed SME helps you close sales and then keeps the conversations going.

Consumers won't be engaged if you give them the impression that you care only about sales. They're interested in having a relationship with the brands they love, not in consuming commercial after commercial. For ongoing engagement, find interesting topics to talk about and share.

When you build your presence in social networks, keep in mind that people aren't only connecting with you and your brand and its representatives by liking your Facebook Fan Page or following you on Pinterest — they're also connecting with other people who like your brand.

By way of social networks, people can display their affinities — the things they like — in their feeds or content streams and on their profiles, pages, timelines, and walls. What they like is a reflection of who they are, and it connects them with like-minded people for online interaction. You want people to show how much they like your brand, to display their connection to you, and, in turn, to expose your brand to their online connections. When a person likes a Facebook Page, the action appears in that person's News Feed, and the Page icons for the brand are displayed on their timeline, as shown in Figure 1-3.

Figure 1-3:
Page likes
displayed on
a Facebook
timeline.

Provide people with a place to connect with you via Facebook, Twitter, YouTube, LinkedIn, and other social networks that are appropriate to your brand. Cultivate communities of engaged fans and followers — wherever you've built your company's social media presences that feel welcoming to customers and prospects alike. By making strong and consistent connections with your customers, you're laying the groundwork for turning customers into evangelists and avid ambassadors for your brand.

Tapping into new markets

Social media engagement includes using online networks and tools for outreach and interactions. The nature of many of the networks you use for engagement provides you with a built-in reach beyond your immediate audience. Some networks have features that amplify your messages and reach better than others.

For example, on Facebook when fans of your Page like, comment on, or share your posts, their friends can see signs of their interaction with your Page. You have the potential to increase your reach exponentially to your fans' friends. On Twitter, if someone retweets your message, it's amplified to people beyond your own following. It's the same principle with Pinterest repins, YouTube thumbs-up votes, and LinkedIn or Google+ shares. Whenever people pass along the information they read, watch, or hear online from you, your content and brand gain more exposure.

One action that's important to successfully expand your outreach is to publish content worth sharing and to regularly remind your followers that they can share the content you've put out there. Even more important to SME is to interact with your immediate audience in meaningful ways so that they're more attentive, responsive, and willing to share.

Figure 1-4 shows how the stationery company TinyPrints hit the engagement jackpot with a post that received numerous likes, comments, and shares — clear signs that it was well-received and amplified by the company's fans. This great content — in this case, promoting a bakery with a beautiful image of cupcakes — produces strong connections and a lot of sharing. This type of engagement activity can translate into exposure for your brand and growth of your fan base, including people you might not be able to easily reach directly.

Figure 1-4:
A post that resonates with its audience.

The most popular social networks offer paid advertising options to reach highly targeted audiences. You can reach the right audience based on not only demographics but also their affinities, and in some cases, their connections to your friends, fans, or followers.

Reaping the rewards of an engaged community

An engaged community is attentive and responsive. That kind of attention and responsiveness can be leveraged for your business in many different ways:

- ✔ **Customer feedback:** Receive immediate input from your customers about their needs to better serve them or to identify business and marketing opportunities.

- ✔ **Market research:** Ask your community to answer questions, take polls or surveys, and fill out questionnaires to produce on-the-fly market research that you can apply to your business.

✔ **Brand evangelism:** Someone who feels connected to your brand often voluntarily talks about you with their friends, fans, and followers.

✔ **Brand ambassadorship:** Provide exclusive perks and incentives to turn your brand evangelists into ambassadors for your company. A brand ambassador program requires a strategic plan and mutual benefit to work, but it starts with identifying your most engaged fans and followers in your social networks and paying attention to them.

Negativity ignored breeds more negativity. Don't focus only on the people who say positive things about your brand and ignore the naysayers and critics. Look for opportunities to address unhappy customers and turn around their opinions.

A natural offshoot of SME and an engaged community is social sharing. When you're interacting with your followers online and you're publishing content that they in turn share with their connections, your content gets distributed within trusted networks.

People who receive your content from their friends are more likely to welcome it than if you push it out to them unsolicited. Spreading information by way of peers is far less commercial and can be much more intimate than using typical online advertising tactics.

Social engagement is not a "quick hit" or short-term folly. The best SME takes place over an extended period, building slowly, evolving as you go (to adapt to the responses from your online community and throughout), and helping achieve mutually beneficial goals.

Seeing How People and Organizations Engage with Social Media

Many people are involved in the exchanges that make up social media engagement. Every person goes online with different needs and different expectations. Knowing what motivates people as they use the Internet helps you better engage with them. Pinpointing your own motivations for being online and using SME to reach customers and prospects is also vital.

Not all roles in SME are set in stone. Both people and entities have presences online and in social networks and all of them contribute to the engagement process in different ways.

Individual consumers

In today's social web, individuals have more power than ever. Consumers are increasingly aware of the power they hold: A person with a blog can review products, build awareness of a brand, and drive sales. Someone can share their opinions about a brand on their favorite social networks and their thoughts can spread exponentially.

New consumers expect more from you and your company, particularly if they're your customer or a prospect. An individual in the mix of SME is looking for these qualities:

- **Respect:** Every person responds well to a respectful approach. A simple thank-you is a good place to start.
- **Response:** Someone who asks a question expects to receive an answer.
- **Rewards:** Though everyone has a different concept of *rewards* or perks, people like to feel appreciated.

If you're worried that you're at the mercy of individuals who can potentially make or break your company by publishing their opinions online, don't panic: Understanding how people online act and react is a lesson in human psychology. Your own actions toward engaging others online should be thoughtful and positive to generate positive results. Throughout the book, we address all of these issues further.

Online communities

Online community is the collective, a virtual place, and the groups of people who fuel social media engagement. Your SME efforts cannot happen in a vacuum. The activities of SME happen within online communities, even communities composed of only two people, such as you and someone else.

Social media platforms and tools convert an individual person into a network of people, interconnected as friends, fans, followers, or other types of connections. Social networks link people to others whom they know personally, but just as often to people they don't know. The connection between individuals in social networks may be another person or even a shared interest. Brought together, they form a community.

To move from broadcasting or publishing online into SME, someone else must be "present" to

- **React:** Reaction differs from network to network and can include superficial responses such as liking or favoriting or clicking the thumbs-up icon. This requires the least amount of effort.

- ✔ **Interact:** Interaction, which takes a little more effort than reaction, shows a certain degree of commitment such as repinning, retweeting, or commenting.

- ✔ **Act:** Action requires a higher level of effort from a fan than reaction or interaction. Action can mean having the confidence to share your content with others or providing detailed responses to your questions, furnishing contact and personal identifying information, or closing a transaction of some kind including a sale.

Without reaction, interaction, or action in response to what you "broadcast," you don't have social media engagement.

Online communities have been around as long as online tools have helped people congregate and communicate among themselves. Understanding the dynamics of online communities is critical to successful SME.

Your business

Any interaction has by definition more than one participant. In social media engagement, your company or organization can be one of the participants. "But a company isn't a person," you might say. True. Therefore, your challenge is to make your company — a corporate entity or the brand that represents it — more human and to understand some basic rules of engagement, both implicit and explicit.

To foster relationships by way of social media — even if you're engaging via your business identity or brand — keep these principles in mind:

- ✔ **People want to connect with people.** You're putting your company or organization on social networks; however, you and other company representatives need to be there interacting, person to person.

- ✔ **Your brand needs a clear voice.** Appropriate and effective communications online starts with basic branding guidelines to ensure that the way you participate in online conversations is consistent and in keeping with your brand personality. A clear brand voice is especially important when multiple people or third-party consultants or agencies are managing your social presences.

- ✔ **You need your own rules of engagement.** Every organization using SME needs both a set of internal guidelines and policies and external community guidelines that spell out which content is allowed and not allowed in the social networks you use.

- ✔ **You need a plan.** For quality interactions, develop a game plan for whom you will engage, where you will reach them, and what you will do regularly, also considering what you want your followers to do. Use tools such as a social media calendar to schedule messaging in advance that dovetails with your overall goals. (See Chapter 5 for how to develop a social media calendar.)

Publish social content that encourages social sharing. Think of the material you post online as the beginning of conversation, not simply content that you broadcast for others to passively consume.

To effectively draw the reactions, interactions, and actions that make SME work for you, get people talking — to you and to each other.

Survey your friends, fans, and followers online to understand why they connect with you, to determine what topics interest them, and to see what they expect to hear from you. Look for the intersections between what you need and what they need and focus on common areas for better engagement.

Your employees

Even if you're the only person engaging via social media for your company, anticipate that employees or team members or assistants or even agencies will, at some point, complete these tasks on your behalf. Spell out your ground rules for online engagement now rather than wait until you need to hand off the duties to someone else.

Your company's internal guidelines for social media engagement will often look similar to the public guidelines you post for your online community to follow. That's because the basic tenets of good community behavior work well regardless of the participants or environment.

This list describes some issues to address to cover the way your employees handle SME for your company:

- ✔ **Frequency of participation:** Even if you already have a posting schedule, you need guidelines to specify how online communities and conversations should be integrated into people's day-to-day work.

- ✔ **Approved content:** Let your social media editorial calendar (see Chapter 5) be your internal guide for developing and publishing approved content.

- ✔ **Tone of conversations:** Your brand guidelines inform your messaging map (detailed in Chapter 5) to provide more than the visual elements of your logo — they also guide the personality, tone, and voice of your brand in social media, down to the key words and phrases to use online and the types of content to post, depending on who you're targeting.

- ✔ **Response style:** Every social network and online communications tool has platform-specific ways to respond and interact. Spell out the way your team needs to respond, such as when to like people's comments on Facebook or how to respond to a retweet on Twitter.

- ✔ **Chain of command:** Establish a clearly defined system to determine who's in charge. If your organization has different team members,

> specify who is an employee's direct supervisor and which activities or actions need to be approved or considered by a manager.
>
> ✔ **Policing process:** Outline steps for removing inappropriate content or comments online, and spell out who has the power to delete material. Many social networks do not provide different levels of administrative access, so your rules and guidelines will dictate roles, responsibilities, and permissions.

To a certain degree, allow employees to use their best judgment when interacting online. As long as everyone is aligned in terms of values, tone, and overall goals, your team should be able to respond and act as needed, especially if you — or their supervisors — aren't available to respond promptly. Delays in responding can create a negative situation in social networks. Attentiveness and responsiveness can help avoid potential problems.

Address the likelihood that your employees use social media in their personal lives. Add to the employee handbook specific rules for content that your company allows and doesn't allow for at-will employees about their behavior in social networks on their own time and within their own, "private" online networks.

We say "private" because nothing that's posted online is truly private. Even the most locked-down Facebook or Twitter account or e-mail message can produce fodder that's distributed across the Internet. After material is released from a secure computer onto the Internet, the reality is that it can potentially be revealed to the online world.

You aren't immune to the dangers of careless online communications and inappropriate exchanges in social media. One mistake can snowball into an avalanche of trouble for your company. Watch what you say and publish online, and be a role model to your employees in terms of appropriate online behavior.

Setting Goals for Social Media Engagement

Social media engagement is an essential part of social media marketing — it's the way you share content online in social networks and the way others respond to that content. SME consists of several parts, like pieces in a puzzle:

✔ **Audience:** The people you want to reach and engage

✔ **Content:** The type of information you put out there

✔ **Reaction, interaction, and action:** The ways people can respond to you

✔ **Outcomes and measurement:** The results of engagement

SME is the "stuff that happens" during your social media marketing campaigns, but also the way you do things to make that stuff happen. We've identified five goals of social media engagement. All these goals involve interactions with people, as we discuss in the following sections.

Building trust and credibility

Online, as in life, you can build better relationships and have more positive outcomes in communications if the people who are communicating trust each other. Trust in the offline world is built over time, and trust in social media engagement is no different.

The need for transparency in SME is huge. More people have greater access to information about anyone and any company because of the Internet. Material that you previously could hide behind your company firewall can now become fodder in social networks in the blink of an eye. Even trusted brands risk tarnishing their reputations with missteps in how they communicate and engage online as much as in how they behave offline.

Both trust and credibility are built on consistency and on follow-through, as we discuss in Chapter 4. Do what you say you're going to do. If you ask for feedback, address head-on whatever you hear. If you "overhear" somebody complaining about your company publicly on a social network, be attentive and responsive. Sincerity and the human touch go a long way toward building trust and credibility and toward laying the foundation for your efforts in SME.

Being present with a human touch

Technology tools exist to automate many tasks, but still no substitute exists for actual human interaction. Even the best artificial intelligence software cannot fully replicate human sentiment, emotion, and sensitivity. Many aspects of social media engagement can be automated, but without the human element — the personality, emotions, reactions, and responses — engagement can fall flat or even utterly fail.

As we mention in Chapter 5, a major challenge of being present online is time. You may feel that you don't have enough time to add engagement via social media to your lengthy to-do list. If you want to turn prospects into customers, build strong and lasting relationships with customers, and convert happy customers into avid evangelists, you — and your team, employees, or representatives — need to personally engage regularly.

Use canned messaging and automated responses sparingly to supplement, not dominate, your presence in social networks. You cannot expect others to be present and to engage with you online if you aren't there as well.

Creating connections

You want more friends, fans, and followers in your social networks, but don't think that amassing sheer numbers gets you closer to achieving your business goals. Bigger numbers may look attractive on the surface, but if the wrong people help you accumulate them — individuals who aren't in your target demographic and who aren't interested in what you have to say — those "connections" are empty and meaningless.

For SME to be successful, you need to be connected with more of the right people — the individuals who willingly align themselves with your brand, who pay attention when you share content online, and who gladly pass along the content you've shared. To attract the right people, start by creating an online presence that reflects your brand and that is focused, attractive, interactive, and intrinsically valuable to the audience with whom you want to connect.

As you begin your outreach to gain friends, fans, and followers, follow the people whom you want to follow you. To boost your outreach, leverage the highly targeted advertising options on the most popular social networks to hone in on the right audience to build your fan base.

Social media engagement works best when you respect your connections and understand that their time and attention are valuable — and often stretched to the limits. Your connections in social media are only as strong as the effort you invest in obtaining and cultivating them over time. Without strong and attentive connections, you can't have real or lasting engagement. For more on the importance of connections, see Chapter 6.

Sparking conversations

We may use the terms *broadcasting* or *publishing* or even *sharing* to describe sending information by e-mail, via the web and social networks, or by using mobile devices. When you're participating in social media engagement, though, you're *conversing*. Everything you post online should be thought of as the beginning of a conversation.

If you want to engage with others via SME, you have to be willing — and able — to be part of the conversation. Your engagement efforts begin, as always, with your business goals, who you're trying to reach, and what you're trying to get them to do. But then your challenge becomes converting your key messages into meaningful conversation starters and maintaining conversations to foster relationships with your connections.

A great way to start a conversation is by telling a story. Storytelling in SME is a powerful tool — you can do it by using words, images, audio, and video. Tell stories that are compelling enough for others to want to pass them along.

Conversations are happening online *all* the time. Some of these conversations involve your brand — whether or not you're part of them. Listen more to what is being said about you, and find appropriate ways to be a part of those conversations.

You can't control all the conversations happening around your brand, but you can engage people who are talking about you outside of your networks, address their comments or concerns, and invite them to continue the conversation in more direct ways including e-mail, website forums, social networks, and even by phone or in person if it makes sense.

Turn to Chapter 7 to see how to start and manage conversations in social media.

Driving interaction

The activity that goes hand in hand with sparking a conversation happens during the conversation and after it ends. You have business goals — we get that. You want people to take action, whether it's to click on your web ad banner, sign up for a prize or content, contact you, or make a purchase. All these actions require deliberate effort — they don't happen automatically. Any telephone salesperson who initiates cold calls can tell you that hang-ups and rejections are much more common than actual sales.

Social media engagement is both the warm-up and the marathon. Attracting more than a passing glance online and making a deliberate action to connect — to like or favorite your content — is only the first step in driving interaction. That one-time action of clicking the Like button doesn't help you reach your goals.

Turn those quick-and-easy liking and favoriting actions into greater commitments of time and trust — into comments and shares. You accomplish this task by executing a well-planned approach to content development and publishing, thoughtful outreach, consistent presence, meaningful conversation, and subtle and not-so-subtle encouragement. Give people a reason to continually interact with you. Understand what motivates your audience to interact. Social engagement starts with you, but interactions aren't only about you. (We dig into this topic in detail in Chapter 7.)

Chapter 2

Assessing the Impact of Social Media Engagement

In This Chapter

▶ Surviving information overload

▶ Dealing with potential backlash

▶ Measuring social media engagement

▶ Assessing and improving engagement

We're the first to admit that social media engagement can be challenging. As with any aspect of marketing, particularly newer ones that haven't weathered the test of time, social media engagement has its pluses and its minuses. You have more opportunities than ever before to reach your customers in new ways and get closer to them, but you need to know about common pitfalls and how to avoid them.

In this chapter, we address the challenges and potential obstacles of social media engagement head on. We also provide an overview of how to measure your engagement activity with your audience, as well as how to assess how you're doing. With careful examination of the results of your social media engagement tactics and campaigns, you will be better equipped to improve what you're doing.

Considering the Downsides of Social Media Engagement

We don't want to sound negative, but the truth is that social media engagement (SME) isn't always easy. From experience, we know that the greatest barriers to engagement can be the concerns and doubts that crop up when you're exploring options. You can easily become caught up in the hype and the naysaying of SME and begin questioning whether you even need to engage with followers.

People commonly question the worthiness of any new concept. Whether it's a new technology or a new strategy that changes the norm, change can be difficult to accept. A common reaction to having to change is resistance or outright rejection.

To nip negativity in the bud, tackle it head-on. Information is the best weapon to counteract naysayers, whether it's a boss, a manager, a client, a colleague, or yourself. Arm yourself with the information you need in order to make sound decisions about incorporating SME into the marketing mix.

Managing the "time suck"

Social media engagement takes time, there's no doubt about it. We wouldn't be honest with you if we didn't admit that fact. There's a difference between making time and wasting time. To prevent the latter, add these components to your SME strategy and process:

- **Goals:** With SME, everything should start and end with your goals, and in your case, your business goals. SME can support many aspects of your business, but if you don't keep your goals in mind, you risk wasting time.

- **A plan:** Social media engagement requires strategic thinking and it benefits from a written plan that outlines how to implement engagement strategies and tactics.

- **Guidelines:** Follow best practices for SME, and craft guidelines tailored to your business. The guidelines should specify how frequently to publish content to your social networks, how much of it to automate, and how often to go online to check in directly with your community. See Chapter 4 for more details on developing SME guidelines.

- **Systems:** Your plan should include the systems you'll implement to streamline messaging and engagement across all your social networks. A system might include the way you link networks — for example, whether you post Facebook updates automatically to Twitter.

- **Tools:** Implementing a system often requires the appropriate tools, such as a social media management (SMM) platform like HootSuite or Sprout Social to gather social networks under a single communications umbrella for efficiency and control.

Distraction is the enemy of social media engagement because it can lead you to wasting time and forgetting your business goals — the underlying reasons why you are engaging online in the first place. You can easily become distracted by all the messages, links, and information that appear in front of you. Stick to your plan, guidelines, and goals. Be disciplined about spending time in social networks.

Overcoming the barriers to entry

"It's too hard." We hear many people say that SME is just too difficult or too overwhelming to bother trying it out. We're convinced that their hesitation stems from the common tendency to fear the unknown or to bite off more social networks than they can chew.

Consume SME in bite-size pieces, and take the time to "chew on" information thoughtfully. Then digest it before you take the next bite. Don't rush into all aspects of SME all at one time.

You don't have to be everywhere all the time. And don't feel compelled to set up a presence on a new social network before you've truly mastered the one (or ones) that you're already using.

In the following list, we highlight common barriers and then suggest sensible ways to overcome them:

- ✔ **"I don't want to listen to people talk about their lunch."** The common misconception about social media engagement is that it consists of people posting online what they had for lunch (or something equally mundane). We'll be honest with you — some people do post about what they're eating. The majority of topics discussed in social networks, however, run the gamut from politics to products to personal moments in people's lives. Publish useful content and connect with others online who do the same and your SME experience will be more valuable.

- ✔ **"I don't have a social media presence."** Although we assume that you already have at least one social networking account, if you don't have one yet, we recommend setting up a Facebook Page as the first platform for your SME because of the variety of ways you can post and the potential for exponential reach via friends and friends of friends. Don't invite anyone to your page at first, to give yourself time to familiarize yourself with its features and to post some initial content. (See Chapter 9 for specific information on preparing for Facebook engagement.)

- ✔ **"I don't have time."** Oh, that elusive 25th hour in the day we always think we need for SME. Social media engagement is about communications, a critical part of marketing and other aspects of doing business. Carve out time to engage in your social networks in the same way you carve out time for (or find help with) handling phone calls, responding to e-mail, or implementing other marketing tactics that require your attention and presence.

- ✔ **"I'm afraid of backlash."** Publishing online for the whole world to see inevitably invites occasional negative responses from individuals ranging from people who have simply "woken up on the wrong side of the bed" to folks with legitimate gripes. Look at these responses as opportunities to "right wrongs" and win people over. See the later section "Dealing with potential backlash" for more tips.

✔ **"I have no images."** Images aren't mandatory components of SME, but they are attention-grabbing, shareable pieces of content. We'd be remiss to let you believe that images aren't vital to engagement. If you sell products, chances are good that you have images, but you may offer services or produce written or audio content. Though a lack of images isn't a deal-breaker for engagement, you should identify or create relevant images that visually illustrate who you are, what you do, and what you want to express. Use a smartphone to take photos that convey a sense of place "in the moment" and showcase your brand personality and company culture. Consumers want to see people behind the brands.

When your own supply of images begins to thin, use stock photography to share with your online community. Stock photos don't have to be stiff, fake, or cheesy. Check resources such as stock.xchng (`www.sxc.hu`), iStockphoto (`www.istockphoto.com`), and Flickr Creative Commons (`flickr.com/creativecommons`) to find appropriate images that you can adapt to your needs. Figure 2-1 shows examples of stock photos that work — you can modify these royalty-free images to use as visual elements in your social networks.

Figure 2-1:
You can incorporate royalty-free images from SXC into your social networks.

Surviving information overload

Social media engagement requires a lot of reading, analyzing, and reporting. On its own, the act of engaging exposes you to a tremendous amount of information that can be overwhelming to digest. We have a few tricks up our sleeves to help you reduce the potential overload and to handle the fire hose of content and conversations coming your way.

Succeeding when SME is restricted

Every barrier to social media engagement can be overcome or circumvented by focusing on strategic thinking and clear goals. Aliza had a client who, because of potential legal concerns, dictated restrictive guidelines for engaging on Facebook, Twitter, and Pinterest. The client provided a narrow list of approved types of Twitter users to follow and restricted on Pinterest the repinning of images owned by other people. All photographs uploaded to Pinterest were required to have copyright notices on the images themselves. On Twitter, messaging had to be related to specific topics, events, and news, and retweets were allowed only when the source was verifiable and on an approved topic.

Aliza followed these initial steps to overcome the client's reservations about SME:

1. Carefully outlined exactly which tactics and messaging were — and weren't — allowed.

2. To build trust, she and her team followed all instructions to the letter.

3. Identified restrictions that could be lifted or at least loosened over time.

Despite initial limitations, the client has been able to leverage Facebook, Twitter, and Pinterest to create content-rich resources and build meaningful connections with its community. They have since expanded their activities as they've received many positive responses from members of their online community.

Develop the habit of using a consistent process of engagement. These steps outline one process we've tested (with time estimates) that works well if you're struggling to handle too much information:

1. **Log in to your social network or social media management tool.**

2. **Peruse your news feeds and messaging streams to see what topics other people are discussing and to gauge the mood of your audience.**

   Average time: 5 minutes. Set a timer, if necessary.

3. **Retweet, share, favorite, or otherwise engage with others as appropriate.**

   Average time: 5 minutes.

4. **Look for public mentions of your brand or direct questions or requests. Respond or forward messages to the appropriate team members or to an assistant to help respond.**

   Average time: 5 to 10 minutes.

5. **Look for direct or private messages that aren't forwarded to your e-mail account, and respond or forward messages to the appropriate team members or to an assistant to help respond.**

   Average time: 5 to 10 minutes.

6. **Log out, and get back to work.**

That's 20 to 30 minutes per session — tops. Repeat these steps two to three times a day. You can get a lot accomplished with SME in about an hour a day.

At times, you may have reasons to deviate from a process. The more active your social networks become and the more your community members interact with you, the more time and attention you should devote to build and maintain momentum.

After you're spending more than an hour every time you monitor and manage your social networks and engage with your audience, look for additional ways to streamline, or turn to others for help. Follow these additional tips for managing information overload:

- **Filter the conversations.** Look for features within the social networks or tools you use to filter conversations so that you see the information that's most important to your business. Use dashboard tools such as HootSuite (www.hootsuite.com), MarketMeSuite (www.marketme suite.com), and SproutSocial (www.sproutsocial.com) to create columns or tabs of specific content streams, searches by hashtags, and other filtered criteria to home in on key conversations. Figure 2-2 shows an example of columns in HootSuite.

- **Stay on top of it.** After you gain momentum from your engagement efforts, maintain consistency and stay on top of the messages and interactions. Develop a plan for covering your channels when you're away so that you don't return to the fallout from a failure to respond or to a glut of messages needing attention.

- **Hire help.** The larger the online community, the less likely one person can spend an hour a day handling the interactions. Spending significantly more time than that can stand in the way of running your business. Consider hiring an intern or a virtual assistant to help you with SME, even if she covers only weekends and evenings or simply directs queries to the appropriate team member.

Figure 2-2: Manage multiple accounts and organize content feeds in HootSuite.

Replace genuine interactions with genuine replies, not timed or canned messaging. Though scheduling precrafted messages can be useful to lessen the burden of participating in your social media channels, you (or someone you've hired and trained) also need to pay attention and respond personally as frequently as possible.

In the end, spending all your time in social networks is unrealistic. When online community members point out your absence or delayed responses, simply admit that you're human and that you're doing the best you can. Thank people for their input and concerns. Then catch up as much as possible, continue to engage well, and identify areas where you can improve.

Dealing with potential backlash

Social media engagement involves humans. You're human. Your team is human. All the people behind the avatars on all the social networks are human. Human beings are complex, emotional beings who can be sensitive and who may not excel at online communications. At some point, you and your company may experience negative, or even hostile, behavior from someone online.

Follow these steps to prepare for potential backlash and then handle it effectively:

1. **Pay attention.**

   Hone your "digital listening" skills by carefully monitoring your social channels and the web at large to hear the positive comments about you and your company — and the negative ones.

2. **Assess thoughtfully.**

   Avoid the urge to panic and respond in a knee-jerk fashion. Instead, evaluate a person's true meaning or motivation versus a person's words. Misinterpreting a snarky comment as criticism, for example, can turn a non-issue into a crisis.

3. **Address negativity quickly.**

   Every minute counts when you're faced with a negative comment in a social network. You may have many responsibilities to tend to, but someone who takes the time to complain about you or your company is often waiting for a response. Have a plan in place for crisis communications so that you know the options for responding. Use a rational, respectful tone in your response. Even an awkward response buys you time to further assess and address the situation.

4. **Acknowledge the person's feelings and perceptions.**

After you review the situation and you're ready to address the comment, understand that strong emotions may have prompted it. Use professional communications skills, and start your response with a statement to defuse those emotions, such as "I hear your frustration" or "We realize that the situation is challenging." Don't invalidate the person's comments defensively — even someone who is incorrect deserves to be heard.

5. **Don't complicate.**

Here's the difference between a well-handled social media engagement situation and a full-blown crisis: The former involves preparedness and sensitivity; the latter, defensiveness and overthinking. Don't run everything past hierarchies and committees in order to put a response on record.

6. **Be human.**

Don't reply unemotionally. Be frank with the other person and all members of your online community who may be watching. People want to see a human response to a crisis, not an overproduced, formulaic, or canned reply. You may have to ask a lawyer or the legal department about admitting fault. But you can at least apologize that something has upset the other person.

7. **Take it offline.**

Don't carry out any crisis control entirely in public. Ask to contact an unhappy individual privately and work to resolve the issue one-to-one.

8. **Be transparent.**

The flip side of going private is not to conduct communications so secretly that people perceive a cover-up. Strike a balance between public and private engagement when the discussion gets heated.

9. **Fix the problem.**

If someone attempts to bring a problem to your attention publicly, and it's truly one that you can solve, admit it, address it, and fix it. If you can't solve it, express empathy with the emotion being expressed. If nothing is truly wrong but someone perceives that it is, don't dismiss those concerns. Take every exchange seriously, and do your best to resolve what you can or provide a resolution or consolation.

10. **Tell your story.**

Telling your own story throughout the "fixing" process can help defuse an issue. Providing updates such as "We're looking into that issue" and "We've taken care of that situation" lets anyone paying attention see that you're attentive and responsive and taking care of the matter even when you're behind the scene.

Avoiding a viral video crisis

A classic example of the challenges of SME crisis control is what happened to the Alaska State Fair in 2010. During the fair, an individual carried a political protest sign on fair property. A video, produced by mobile phone, of the protestor being tackled and removed from fair property, was shown on YouTube. The fair's online community erupted over what appeared to be an excessive use of force and a violation of free speech.

Using respectful, evenhanded tones to respond immediately on the fair's Facebook Page, the fair's social media team explained that fair officials were investigating seriously and consulting law enforcement to determine what happened. This quick response pacified the fair's online community while, behind the scenes, the fair consulted all parties involved — law enforcement officers, members of the media, and the fair's public relations rep and social media agency, carefully revealing only confirmed facts to the public as they gathered details.

As the video reached more people worldwide, fewer of the angry posters on the Facebook Page were even familiar with the details of the event. Some individuals began creating new problems, posting angry, inappropriate comments. The fair banned only a small number of Facebook fans and only those who resorted to foul language or violent threats, both of which were clearly outlined in their existing online community guidelines as violations of community rules.

In time, the fair was able to communicate that the protestor was rightfully removed from the property because posted rules around the fairgrounds stated that picketing wasn't allowed. Neither did the video show the moments preceding the incident, where the protestor antagonized nearby families who had small children. Fair officials emphasized that the safety of families, children, and other fairgoers was of the utmost importance to them.

In a written statement published online, fair officials revealed that the person who was "protesting" had a history of encounters with law enforcement and was carrying a concealed weapon, though it wasn't easily visible in the video. By hearing the facts as they unfolded, most of the fair's online community members were satisfied that their concerns had been addressed. In the end, many fans of the fair praised the organization publicly on Facebook for handling the situation promptly and transparently.

Remember: Negative posts and feedback online are opportunities to address an issue, solve a problem, convert an unhappy customer into a happy one, and conclude a situation in a positive light.

Avoiding inconsistent messaging

Marketers know that it takes at least five impressions before a sale is closed. In cold calling, this rule translates to five calls or meetings. In online marketing, this doesn't necessarily mean five views of a banner ad. Seeing a company's logo on a banner ad could be one of five impressions that etches a company's name into a consumer's mind so they reach for that company's product at the grocery store aisle. Another impression might be a reference from a friend in a social network while another might be a promoted post or tweet. Marketing messages need to be consistent from platform to platform.

Being consistent in your SME efforts is critical to building and maintaining your online reputation and the trust that develops from thoughtful interaction in your social media channels. When you aren't solely responsible for monitoring or managing your channels, you should ensure that the tone and messaging always align with your brand image and personality.

The more people involved in monitoring, messaging, and posting, the more chance for missteps unless you can keep everyone on the same page. This list describes elements to compose or set up and share with your team:

- **Brand documents:** Describe your brand personality, messaging tone, and other details that dictate how your brand is presented in social media channels.

- **Social media engagement guidelines and policies:** Spell out the do's and don'ts of posting and responding online for all members of your team.

- **A written Frequently Asked Questions (FAQ) document:** Strategically answer common questions and situations that are raised in your social media channels and compiled with the help of your team.

- **Terms of service or rules of behavior:** Document these guidelines for your team, and post them publicly for your community members as well. Figure 2-3 shows community guidelines posted to a Facebook Page. You can post guidelines using a Facebook app maker, such as Woobox or Shortstack, or using Facebook Notes.

- **Community policies:** Add a privacy policy and security policy, and post them publicly.

- **A team-oriented, social media management tool:** Look for one that allows teams to work together to manage social channels, to assign tasks to team members, and to record outcomes, such as (on the high end) Radian6 (www.radian6.com) or (the more moderately priced) Sprout Social (www.sproutsocial.com), HootSuite, (www.hootsuite.com), or many others.

When you manage a community online in your social networks, clearly outline how you protect community members' information that's submitted via forms, surveys, registration, shopping cart checkouts, and other communications methods. Search for sample privacy and security policies at your favorite online search engine. Check with a lawyer or the legal department before posting on your website and social channels.

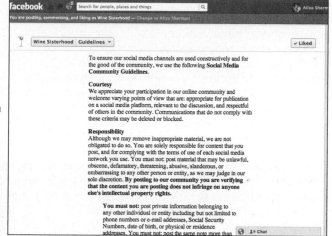

Figure 2-3:
Community guide-
lines text
posted to a
Facebook
Page.

Measuring the Value of Your Social Media Engagement

Consider what matters when measuring SME. We like to say, "It's not quantity, but quality, that matters in social media engagement." Aliza is also fond of saying, "I'd rather have 100 friends, fans, or followers who care than 1,000 who ignore me." Look at everything you do online as a way to build bonds for the long term: Keep an eye on how the relationships start between you or your company and your customers and prospects as well as members of the public at large. When you share content, providing true value helps build a strong foundation for ongoing attention and interactions.

Determining what interactions are valuable

In advertising, costs and measurements are clear-cut, such as paying for an impression (Cost Per Thousand or CPM — the "M" actually stands for the French word for "thousand," *million*) whenever an ad is viewed; paying for a click (Cost Per Click or CPC) whenever a viewer clicks on the ad; and paying for an action or a lead (Cost Per Action or CPA). Social media engagement requires metrics that are different from online advertising, because the mechanics of engagement involve a variety of activities and responses.

With more interactions happening as you engage via social media channels, you have many more numbers to track and even more ways to interpret them. How do you determine which numbers are the most important to you and your company? Go back to your business goals, what you're trying to achieve, and what you hope the target audience does in response to your actions. Then match up the numbers that reflect how people are responding to you and the actions they are taking with your goals. If you're seeing activity in your social networks that you can tie directly to supporting your business goals, you're on the right track. If not, re-evaluate what you're doing. Also consider whether the goals you're focusing on are best supported through SME.

Though the ultimate goal of a business is usually to make a sale or a transaction, SME offers layers of value leading up to, and surrounding, an actual sale. All these seemingly ancillary aspects of engagement in your online channels help to build brand awareness, strengthen customer loyalty, and facilitate brand evangelism.

The benefits of SME may seem difficult to measure or even appear to be intangible, but they eventually lay the groundwork for selling in more personal and lasting ways than advertising ever will. To reach the mobile consumer who's now connected and engaged in social networking, look at the whole picture of how they communicate and how you can reach, and engage with, them.

Social media engagement is not a silver bullet to achieve every marketing objective or solve every communications challenge. Just because you're reaching out to an online audience doesn't mean that they'll respond consistently. Take the time to cultivate relationships and make genuine connections to see more tangible results.

Knowing which numbers to measure

The metrics you use to quantify your social media engagement vary from service to service. However, this list describes some similar types of activities that take place across all of them:

- ✔ **Attraction:** Attracting a qualified, quality following is valuable. You can spend money to push messages to people via ads, but true engagement slowly and steadily builds the audience and connects with them over the long term. Measure the growth of your fan base by counting common metrics such as the number of friends, fans, and followers and by noting actual customers (or even likely prospects) if you can identify them.

- ✔ **Interactions:** You must become part of the conversation online to convert participation by your friends, fans, and followers into interaction. Seek out opportunities to reciprocate participation by liking, commenting on, and sharing comments and by praising others. Pay attention to mentions, requests, and queries, and respond promptly. Keep track of these interactions, particularly the ones that move from social networks to other forms of communication such as e-mail — or even in-person encounters.

✔ **Actions:** Actions are concrete and measurable when marketing online, even in SME, but they require consistent nurturing to take place more than once. Count and track comments and shares as well as likes, retweets, repins, and favorites, and note increases or declines in those activities. Look for potential reasons for the ebbs and flows of these actions, and modify your engagement tactics to account for variables such as time zone differences and changes to social network features.

✔ **Transformations:** The magic of SME happens when your activities transform others, such as turning a dissatisfied customer into a happy one or turning a happy customer into an evangelist for your brand. When these positive transformations happen, the ripple effect of the good news reverberates through your own networks into your customers' networks and beyond. Record the transformations you witness or cause — and archive everything for your records.

✔ **Transactions:** As a marketer, your job is to help close the sale. Customers and prospects can carry out many types of transactions in addition to actual sales. Don't discount activities such as taking polls, filling out surveys, listing contact information (and contact permission), and providing warm leads. Record all types of transactions that are closed throughout each week and month, and watch for trends. Look out for how different SME tactics translate into true transactions, including sales.

Use a tool such as Storify (www.storify.com) to track mentions of your brand in popular social networks, and arrange them chronologically or in an order that tells a story, as shown in Figure 2-4. The resulting visual compilation of tweets and posts is perfect to create reports and to help demonstrate the impact of your SME efforts. Storify lets you compile an organized archive of social media messages from other contributors that are tied together based on a keyword or hashtag.

Figure 2-4: A Storify story.

Setting benchmarks to evaluate progress

As with any measurement process, start with current numbers as benchmarks to establish a baseline or a starting point for analyzing growth in your SME activities. Record not only your numbers in any social networks and other social media tools you're using but also more traditional measurements, including the tools described in this list:

- **Traffic to your website:** When you use the proper messaging, SME can drive traffic to your site.

  Benchmark: The number of visitors to your site

- **Referrers to your website:** One common measurement in web traffic analysis is the number of *referrers,* or sites that refer traffic to your website. Note whether you see an increase in traffic from Facebook or Twitter or another social media tool you use.

  Benchmark: The level of traffic that social networks drive to your site

- **Marketing e-mail subscribers:** If you're using e-mail marketing to reach customers or you're sending a regular e-newsletter, note the current number of subscribers and then the changes based on integrating e-mail marketing into your social media messaging and networks.

  Benchmark: The number of subscribers and even the number of times that your e-mail messages have been opened and shared

- **Customer service inquiries:** Note how many calls or e-mails you're receiving, and then begin tracking how they're handled in social networks. You may even receive fewer calls and e-mails, so be prepared for the shift to the customer relations aspect of SME.

  Benchmark: The number of customer service contacts and where they're taking place

- **Transactions:** Whether a transaction involves people signing up for demos or consultations or actually purchasing products, the numbers should change because of SME. If not, reexamine how you're encouraging people to transact.

  Benchmark: Current sales or other transactions

If you don't set benchmarks that reflect how you're meeting business goals, you cannot accurately measure the impact of your SME activities.

 If you're using a management-and-measurement tool, pay for a professional-level subscription that lets you run reports and save them. Run reports at least monthly to track your progress, and then archive them. Check the numbers weekly if your networks experience a lot of activity or you're altering your engagement tactics. Record your numbers daily, such as an increasing number of fans and followers. Figure 2-5 shows a sample reporting feature in HootSuite that helps you visually quantify the effectiveness of your SME efforts.

Figure 2-5:
A sample report from HootSuite.

Reassessing to improve engagement

Social media engagement isn't an exact science. As you measure your engagement efforts, consider all the variables of being human and interacting with other humans. The core aspects of social media engagement involve human beings, and many variables can affect the interactions between people online, such as

- ✔ **The time of day:** You'll reach different people in different parts of the country or world depending on the time of day you post.

- ✔ **The time zone:** If you are trying to reach your community "in the morning," this could mean posting during your afternoon to reach someone in an earlier time zone.

- ✔ **The day of the week:** Every social network reports that their members use their service more frequently on specific days and usage patterns vary from network to network.

- ✔ **A person's mood:** Not every message you post will be interesting to someone, and there are factors in an individual's day that can make them more or less receptive to your message.

- ✔ **A person's attention span:** Any of your posts might be too long or too complicated for some people.

- ✔ **The level of information overload:** If someone is overwhelmed by their social network news feeds, they may tune out your message.

You will eventually, and inevitably, see the ebb and flow of your engagement reflected in your SME statistics. Though you may be tempted to panic whenever you reach the end of a day with low engagement, be wise and look at data over the longer term, not simply during a single day or even a week.

Look for trends in the engagement numbers, and read online reports about engagement trends on each social network and platform you use to interact with the audience. Don't hold too strictly to the trends you read about — not all trend reports provide consistent figures. Use trends as food for thought, and then test the ones that seem relevant to you and your audience.

An example of inconsistent trend reporting is demonstrated by the difference between URL shortener bit.ly (bitly.com) stating that you should post to Facebook between 1 and 4 p.m. eastern time and especially Wednesdays at 3 p.m. eastern time on Facebook but Buddy Media, on the other hand, stating that Wednesday is the worst day to post and that weekends are better. Who's right? You have to read the entire reports to understand their methodologies. The more important answer is that the ideal posting time depends on your company and your audience.

Pay attention to your own brand's SME trends to see how your particular audience reacts to your posts in social media. Map out optimal posting times, but remain flexible and ready to shift based on the response of your audience over time. Danielle has found mornings between 8 and 11 eastern time to be the time when people are most responsive to her online, but it's more than the time of day that matters — it's also the day of the week. Mondays are more active for her than Saturdays. Aliza discovered inadvertently that her random tweets after work hours draw an attentive and responsive audience as do later-night tweets around 10 p.m. eastern time. Exploring this trend further, she found that many of her followers who respond at those times are from Australia and New Zealand.

What works this month may not work well next month, because of variables that may be beyond your control. Even a slight tweak by Facebook to the display of your Facebook Page updates in other people's news feeds can throw off your previous communications rhythm.

Because of all the shifts and changes in the tools you use for SME, you *must* measure consistently and over long stretches to get the information you need to continually improve how you engage online. Above all, be consistent but flexible to adapt to the constantly changing online landscape.

Don't stress over the numbers as you watch them increase and decrease. These changes are commonplace. Don't let declines bring you down. As in the stock market, your SME numbers will continually increase as long as you use the tools properly and can account for both losses and gains.

Leveraging success

We've said it before, and we'll say it again: Social media engagement starts with knowing your business goals, your audience, and the workings of the social networks you use. Knowing which SME strategies work for your company — and inspire the greatest number of reactions, interactions, and actions — helps you build on your successes.

Pay attention to the types of posts and messaging that work best for your audience. Then do more of what works and less of what doesn't. It sounds simple, doesn't it? It takes practice, but we know it's possible. You can do it!

If you're using several social networks for online marketing and engagement, you might be tempted to put all your eggs into the network basket that returns the best results. Though there's wisdom in using the most powerful network most often, don't ignore other networks outright. Look to leverage the best network by using these additional methods:

- ✔ **Integrating:** Merge your other social networks to post into the most successful one.
- ✔ **Linking:** Connect to your other social networks in posts on the most successful one.
- ✔ **Converting:** Implement an advertising budget on your best network.

Promote all your social networks on the most successful one, and enhance the best one by using the others. For example, if Facebook is your main social network, you can still use Instagram and set it up to post photos to your Facebook Page to add visual interest. Connecting social networks so that they feed into one another in an orchestrated way can make them all more effective.

Success with SME relies on not only your own actions but also the actions of others. Pay attention to the participants in your online community because their activities fuel the conversations and the amplification of your messaging. Pay attention to what works well for them, and do more of it.

People like to be appreciated and recognized. Offer online community perks, discounts, or other benefits for engaging with you and to show appreciation of their attention and interactions. Don't attempt to bribe your community — buying loyalty is a short-term fix to inattentiveness or apathy. Instead, express genuine concern about community members and recognize their contributions.

Chapter 3

Discovering Social Media Engagement Tools

In This Chapter

▶ Evaluating online communications tools

▶ Examining social networks for engagement

▶ Using multimedia tools to engage

▶ Introducing social mobile engagement

*T*hrowing out the old tools you've been using and jumping onto the band-wagon to use a new and exciting communications and marketing technology can be tempting. You may feel like you have the capacity for only so many tools, so eliminating the old seems like a way to make room for the new.

This chapter lays the groundwork for our assertion that not all of the older communications tools you are using are broken. Even though it is common-place to consider social networks as the main tools for social media engagement, understand that many of the tools you've been using online are part of the overall landscape of SME.

Considering Traditional Online Communications Tools

Before social networks existed, people communicated online in different ways. *Electronic mail (e-mail)* was used for sending direct messages to one person or to many people. Messages that could be read by groups of people morphed into forums, known as *Usenet newsgroups,* and eventually became the current form of online web-based forums.

Throughout these fast technological changes, the way people communicate has changed in major ways. Social networks and other multimedia and social media tools and platforms are incredibly popular, but the use of traditional online communications tools still has a lot of value. E-mail, online forums, and websites can — and should — all be incorporated into your strategy for social media engagement (SME).

SME doesn't take place on social networks solely on the web. Social engagement aspects in a myriad of online and even mobile apps, tools, and networks should work in concert to help you connect and interact with the target market.

E-mail

You probably use either e-mail software on your computer, such as Microsoft Outlook, or web-based e-mail applications, such as Yahoo! Mail, Hotmail, or Gmail. For business communications, you might use a service, such as Google Apps, that includes e-mail.

Though e-mail doesn't seem flashy or modern, it's still the most important engagement tool now in use, and it can tie in with social networks more easily than ever. Figure 3-1 shows an example of an e-mail message with social media links or graphics in the signature file, which were embedded using the WiseStamp app (www.wisestamp.com).

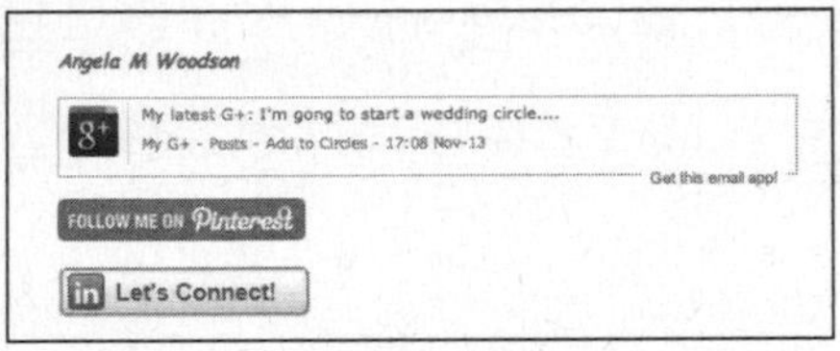

Figure 3-1:
Use social media links or graphics in an e-mail signature.

Far more people have e-mail accounts and use e-mail daily to communicate than use social networks. By some counts, more than 3.1 billion people have e-mail accounts (The Radicati Group, Inc., 2011; www.radicati.com). Compare that number to the largest social network, Facebook, and its billion or so users. Social networks are catching up to e-mail but, so far, haven't eliminated the need for more direct correspondence that's separate and apart from social networks.

If SME consists of reactions, interactions, and actions, e-mail clearly fits the bill. When you send out an e-mail, you and others can react, respond, interact, and take actions such as these:

✔ Pass along the e-mail to others.

✔ Download a file attached to an e-mail.

✔ Click a link to visit a website.

✔ Play an embedded audio or video file.

✔ Fill out a form embedded into the body of the e-mail.

✔ Take a poll or survey embedded in the e-mail.

✔ Connect to someone's social networking accounts.

✔ Click a link to begin an online purchase.

E-mail is more than a message carrier: It's a conversation starter as well as a multimedia and multifeatured communications tool to engage others beyond simple back-and-forth communications.

Even as you set up your social networking presences, don't discount e-mail marketing. Any marketer can tell you that a database of fully vetted e-mail addresses is a valuable marketing asset. Many online marketing professionals report that e-mail is still the most effective way to connect and engage with others because of the contained nature of e-mail messages in an inbox and people's habitual use of e-mail.

Do not force people to *opt out of* (or have to take a specific action to remove themselves from) your e-mails because you've subscribed them without their knowledge or permission, which can lead to negative feelings about your brand. The well-established e-mail marketing best practice of allowing people to opt in by giving express permission is still alive and well.

E-mail marketing tools of the past were intended to *broadcast* (in one direction only) messages to many recipients. E-mail marketing platforms now integrate social media features to let recipients easily connect with you on social networks and not simply read your e-mail, delete it, and then forget about you. E-mail marketing tools also let you announce when you've sent a marketing e-mail or an electronic newsletter by autopublishing an update to your friends, fans, and followers on social networks.

You may already have an e-mail sign-up form on your website or blog. Add ways for people to provide you with their e-mail addresses in your social networks. For example, integrate an e-mail sign-up app into your Facebook Page using any of the popular e-mail marketing tools, such as Constant Contact (www.constantcontact.com) or MailChimp (www.mailchimp.com). Figure 3-2 shows you how MailChimp does it.

Figure 3-2:
Using
MailChimp
to allow
fans to
sign up to
receive your
e-mails.

Online forums (groups)

When you have people gathering online to discuss common topics, you have the seeds for building online community. Where you have online community, you have the potential for actions, reactions, and interactions. None of these activities is exclusively an aspect of SME, but they're common to all online communities where people gather, including web-based online forums or groups.

Though people still congregate and interact within web-based forums, they now have these community-building options that are powered by social media:

- ✔ **Facebook Groups, shown in Figure 3-3:** Focus on discussions among members (despite their similar appearance to Facebook Pages and Timelines) and can feature members at the top of the page.

- ✔ **LinkedIn Groups, shown in Figure 3-4:** Facilitate information exchange, and networking among LinkedIn members — usually, professionals.

- ✔ **Google+ Communities, shown in Figure 3-5:** Build your audience on G+ through their Communities feature similar to LinkedIn Groups.

Most social networks provide you with the tools to create more contained, or even private, members-only forums for ongoing discussions. Facebook Groups offers two privacy levels: Private (others can see your group listing but you must approve requests to join) and Secret (your group isn't listed publicly so you must invite others). LinkedIn has a single private level; you approve requests to join. In early 2013, Google+ introduced Communities that offer a privacy level for member approval. See Chapter 13 for more information on Google+ Communities. Twitter lets you make your Twitter account private but does not offer a group feature.

Figure 3-3:
Facebook Groups focus on discussion among members.

Figure 3-4:
LinkedIn Groups enable networking and exchanging information.

Figure 3-5:
Google+ Communities bring together like-minded individuals.

Whether public or private, online forums and groups work well when several factors are present:

- ✔ **A focused topic area or theme:** Conversations in the best forums remain on topic.

- ✔ **Like-minded or interested people:** People join groups voluntarily based on their interests and needs.

- ✔ **Strong community leadership:** A good moderator keeps the discussion going with a light touch so that everyone feels welcome to the conversation.

- ✔ **Clear community rules:** Every group needs publicly posted guidelines that define proper behavior and spell out bad behavior.

- ✔ **Fair policing:** Many online communities police themselves, admonishing or removing individuals who post inappropriately, and others let moderators ban people.

See *Online Community Management For Dummies* by Deborah Ng (John Wiley & Sons, Inc.) to get the nitty-gritty on managing an online community, whether it's based within a social network or not.

A benefit of setting up a group in a social network such as Facebook or LinkedIn is that you can build an online space for people to gather that feels like a cohesive community. Building a community on a Facebook Page, for example, is challenging because of the way Facebook limits people from seeing your messages and from seeing other people's posts on your Page. The limitations of Facebook Pages hinder group-wide discussions. On a Page, most community conversations take place in a disjointed manner within the comments of various Page updates.

People tend to Like a Facebook Page to show their affinity for a brand, though they may also want to interact. They join a Facebook Group specifically for the interaction among members. People connect with you on LinkedIn to add you to their contacts and likely don't interact with you regularly. They join your LinkedIn Group to engage in dialogue — with you and with other members of the group. People are more likely to look forward to the conversations and respond in more depth when they join groups with the intention of participation.

Websites and blogs

You may not think of websites in relation to online community and social media engagement, because websites are often considered static destinations and repositories of information rather than engagement tools.

Engagement isn't only a means of attracting someone's interest and attention, though a website can be attractive and attracting. To make a website more interactive, you have to add features to it beyond static HTML pages in order to turn a site visitor or reader into an active community member or customer.

To understand what drives people to interact and to know how the tools you have at your disposal provide for engagement, you should understand a little of the history of the tools we now use for SME. In the early days of the web, "interacting" on a website was limited to clicking an e-mail link.

Then came the *guest book,* a web-based submission form that posted a message publicly on a web page under the guise of signing a guest book for the website owner. In some cases, people realized that others were signing the same website's guest book at nearly the same time.

Even in those primitive days, people wanted to make contact and communicate with one another, so they began talking to each other by leaving comments to each other on web-based guest books and refreshing the pages until they saw responses.

Early on, people could share an article from a website with a friend via e-mail. Soon they could leave comments on articles. Then came blogs, and with built-in features such as comments. People commented on not only a blogger's content but also on one another's comments. Blog comments weren't feature-rich, but they turned websites into online communities.

Now you can build your website on a blog platform and instantly have an easier way to manage content and updates as well as embed more social features into your site.

Comments on blogs are no longer confined to websites. Social commenting tools, such as Facebook Connect comments, and third-party software add-ons, such as Disqus (www.disqus.com) and Livefyre (www.livefyre.com), let people log in to your website to comment using their social media accounts or identities. Add social networking triggers to your site to increase the likelihood of people engaging with you — and with each other — when they visit.

Table 3-1 breaks down various ways to engage through websites and blogs.

Table 3-1	Basic Engagement on Websites	
One Way	*Two Ways*	*Multiple Ways*
Signing up for an offer	N/A	N/A
Filling out a feedback form	Finding live help	Supporting the community
Sharing with a friend	N/A	Clicking a Like or Favorite widget
Answering polls (private results)	Answering polls (public results)	Answering polls with sharing
E-mailing site owner	Adding comments to site	Adding social comments

No matter how many interactive tools and features you place on your website or blog, people are increasingly inclined to move the conversation to their favorite social networks. That's why we encourage you to embrace social networking for stronger and more consistent engagement than your website can provide and to integrate your social networks into your site to make the transition to those networks easy and seamless. We talk more about how to make e-mail, forums, websites, and blogs even more engaging in Chapter 8.

Your website content may be interesting, and people might return to read it, but if you cannot engage site visitors in dialogue, they're less likely to convert to prospects — they'll be avid but inactive readers.

Engaging with Social Networks

Technology developments over the past decade have played a significant role in moving websites from static pages to basic online community hosts to full-blown, interactive, and interconnected social networks. A *social network* is a website with technology on the back end and features on the front end that give people ways to connect to one another by acting, interacting, and reacting.

Investing a lot of time, attention, effort, and money into building presences and communities on social networks has glaring downsides. You're competing for the time and attention of individuals whose attention is already fractured. Today's consumers, customers, and prospects can publish and build an audience and online community as easily as you can. All this publishing adds to the glut of information and messages that are already out there, often translating into noise. You're trying to get the attention of individuals who may also be publishers, broadcasters, and leaders of their own communities. You're also competing against all the other businesses clamoring to reach those same individuals. Worst of all, individual tech companies — with their own agendas, business models, and goals — own the social networks.

Every social network has different rules or terms of service dictating which behaviors the company behind the network allows. Pay attention to the rules as you plan how to use each network to achieve your own business goals.

The upside of participating in social networks is that a lot of people use them, so you have the potential to reach a great many customers and prospects — and the general public at large. If you use social networks well, you have an inside track to people's interests and affinities. You have the chance to reach them and communicate with them on mutual ground and in the environment where they're most comfortable. You can build and strengthen your brand and your relationships with the very people who can keep your company in business. You can also reach even more people — *exponentially* more people — when your own connections share your information with their connections.

Facebook

Facebook claims to have a billion monthly active users (as of October 2012), and it has become one of the largest social networks in the world. Facebook offers several layers of public and private information depending on which features members use and on how members configure their privacy settings.

Interactions and conversations happen on Facebook in a number of ways:

- ✔ **Status update:** Post to the Wall of a Page, the personal Timeline, or a Group using text, photos, videos, or links.

- ✔ **Comment, Likes, and Shares:** React to posts by clicking Like, posting a comment, or sharing the post.

- ✔ **E-mail:** Private message one individual or many Facebook friends. Pages and Groups are limited in terms of how they can message individuals to prevent spamming.

- ✔ **Checkins:** Use a smartphone to check into a Place on Facebook if a Page has been set up with an actual location, or to a Facebook public event within three hours of the event's start time.

- ✔ **Facebook chat:** Instant message one individual or groups of people.

If you're using your personal Timeline on Facebook to market your business, you may be blurring the lines between your personal communications and business marketing. Facebook states in its Terms of Service that you cannot create a personal Timeline for a business and cannot use your personal Timeline for commercial purposes.

We recommend that you create a Facebook Page for your professional presence on the network, and keep your personal Timeline, well, personal. We each have a personal Timeline and a Facebook Page, and we use them in different ways. Danielle is comfortable using her personal Facebook Timeline to share images and news from her personal life with her Facebook friends. As a media personality, she is in the public eye, and a portion of her brand is about family. Still, she doesn't accept friend requests from everyone who asks. Figure 3-6 shows Danielle's Facebook Timeline, where she shares with a wide audience (several times a day) a blend of family-related posts and work-related posts.

Danielle maintains two separate Pages for both her main sites but dedicates the bulk of her attention to her personal Timeline because it integrates both sides of her brand. Danielle's Page for her website, Extraordinary Mommy, centers on the content from her blog at ExtraordinaryMommy.com. (See the leftmost image in Figure 3-7.) Danielle's company page, Danielle Smith Media, focuses on industry-related news — social media, media training, and video tips. (See the rightmost image in Figure 3-7.)

Figure 3-6:
Danielle posts several times a day to her Facebook Timeline.

Figure 3-7:
You can maintain separate Facebook Pages for your blog and your company.

Aliza joined Facebook before Pages were available, so she initially used her personal account as her professional Facebook presence. As more of her friends and family joined the network, she soon realized the value of using it to share more personal information; by that time, however, her Facebook friends consisted of many people she did not know personally. When Facebook introduced Pages, Aliza set one up to post her business news and technical tips. She finds it challenging to maintain both presences. Over time, she has tried to make her Timeline more personal and is now careful about accepting friend requests.

How you use Facebook should be a combination of your personal preferences and best practices and an understanding of how others use Facebook and Facebook's Terms of Service. You also have to consider the tools that Facebook provides for you to use, and how you use the components for engagement. See Chapter 9 for details on how Facebook features work to help you better engage with others.

Read and understand the Facebook Terms of Service (www.facebook.com/legal/terms). The site prohibits using a personal account or personal Timeline for commercial gain. The company created Facebook Pages to give businesspeople another option. Though many people violate these rules and haven't gotten caught — yet — we recommend not taking chances.

Facebook has been known to close down personal accounts that violate its rules. Per Facebook: "You will not use your personal timeline for your own commercial gain (such as selling your status update to an advertiser)." Neither are you allowed to hold contests that require participants to use Facebook features as part of the contest.

Twitter

With more than 140 million users, Twitter is smaller than Facebook but has fundamentally changed how people communicate with one another. Twitter has impacted not only how individuals and companies communicate but also how people consume and report news. Nobody ever imagined that a service that limits messages to 140 characters could cause such enormous changes around the world.

Unlike Facebook, Twitter conversations are predominantly open to the public, unless you choose to make your Twitter account private. Most people go with the default public setting to share their updates — or tweets — with the world. Although private Twitter accounts are available, in order to engage easily and widely with others, your account must be public.

Twitter has its own way of organizing conversations and interactions on its network that can be confusing to new users. You can communicate on Twitter by posting one of these elements:

- **Tweet:** A publicly posted message to your Twitter stream that also appears in the streams of your followers.
- **Retweet:** A publicly posted message that repeats or restates an existing tweet from someone else that credits the originator and can be seen by your followers.
- **@mention:** A tweet directed to someone specifically that appears in their stream.
- **Direct message (DM):** A message sent to someone else privately if you follow them and they follow you back.

We both love Twitter and use it often. The shorter tweet lengths may not appeal to you, but they force you to be more concise and specific in your messaging. In this day and age of text messaging and smartphone use, being able to adapt your communications style to accommodate the smaller screens of mobile devices is a good skill to have.

From its early days, Twitter has allowed programmers to use its application programming interface (API), the behind-the-scenes code that makes up the network. This openness allows applications to integrate easily with Twitter, including tools to monitor it, manage it, measure activity on it, and post creatively to it. The same cannot be said about all social networks.

We both connect some of our other favorite social networks to Twitter, including Instagram and Foursquare. The image on the left in Figure 3-8 shows a tweet from Danielle using Instagram; her Instagram account connects to Twitter, so she has the option to tweet to her Instagram account the photos she posts via her smartphone. The rightmost image in the figure shows a tweet from Aliza using Foursquare; Aliza tweets her Foursquare check-ins sparingly, and she carefully provides context so that her Twitter followers have more to read than simply a place name with a link. (You can read more about Instagram, Foursquare, and other location-based services later in this chapter, in the "Location-based services" section, and also in Chapter 14.) We talk more about enhancing Twitter in Chapter 10.

Pinterest

Pinterest was touted as the fastest-growing social network of all time when it surpassed 10 million monthly unique visitors in January 2012. (ComScore, Feb. 2012) By October 2012, Pinterest was receiving nearly 25 million monthly unique visitors (Compete, Oct. 2012), surpassing the popular microblogging site Tumblr. Pinterest is hot!

Denotes the tweet came from Instagram

Figure 3-8: Tweets from an Instagram account and a Foursquare account.

Like Twitter, Pinterest is also changing the way we communicate, focusing far more on images than on text. Though Twitter challenges you to publish messages in 140 characters or fewer, Pinterest pushes you to find more visual ways to convey your messages and position your brand. There's no denying that Pinterest is all about the visuals.

If you prefer to publish text content, Pinterest can work as a gateway to content residing on your website or blog or other sites. If you prefer to communicate with your audience using only text, Pinterest may hold you back based on how most people prefer to use the network — looking at and sharing visuals.

Even though Pinterest users can comment on pins in a similar way to commenting on updates and photos on Facebook, fewer than 1 percent of Pinterest users (according to Repinly, a Pinterest directory) choose to comment. Knowing the limitations of certain social networks, and how people prefer to use them, are important factors in choosing which networks are right for you.

You can communicate and interact on Pinterest using these actions:

- ✔ **Pin:** A post of an image and video to the Pinterest stream and to your topic-specific boards with descriptions.
- ✔ **Like:** A favorable reaction to other people's pins.
- ✔ **Repin:** Sharing other people's pins to your followers.
- ✔ **Comment:** A response to pins, but used less often than Likes and Repins.
- ✔ **Collaborate:** Pinning with others using Pinterest's group boards or secret boards.

Pinterest introduced business accounts in late 2012 for brands. The implied intention of these accounts was to eventually provide companies with metrics, advertising, and monetization options. In early 2013, Pinterest introduced metrics strictly for business accounts.

We both enjoy pinning, and we appreciate the power of Pinterest. We tend to focus most of our online marketing time and energy, however, on networks where we can engage more conversationally. Regardless, Danielle has many videos that are ready-made for pinning. Aliza likes to use Pinterest to publish bite-size pieces of advice culled from her many articles and blog posts that lead to the content source.

We're both firm believers that pictures speak louder than words — but we would add that *great-looking* pictures speak louder than words. A poor image or video is a hindrance, and not at all helpful when it comes to Pinterest.

Figure 3-9 shows how Aliza uses a Pinterest board as a résumé specifically to highlight her work and related articles. Figure 3-10 shows a board of inspirational quotes that perfectly complement Danielle's overall mission and message.

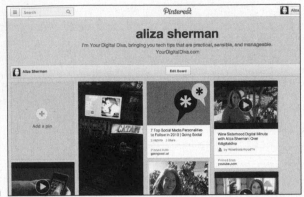

Figure 3-9:
Compiling
a board to
serve as a
résumé.

Figure 3-10:
Pinning
images with
inspirational
quotes.

LinkedIn

LinkedIn has been around since 2003 — several years before Twitter was launched, and available to the public several years before Facebook. In August 2012, LinkedIn reached 175 million users. A laser focus on professionals and businesspeople sets LinkedIn apart from all other major social networks.

If you're looking to reach a more business-minded audience — particularly for B2B marketing — LinkedIn is a useful tool. We go into a lot more depth in Chapter 12 about engaging via LinkedIn.

As with many social networks, LinkedIn has a number of basic ways to engage with others with a slant toward professional networking. You interact on LinkedIn using these methods:

✔ **News feed:** Post information in your own feed with text, images, and attached files.

✔ **Like, comment, share:** Respond to posts from your connections, and they can do the same on your posts.

✔ **Company Page:** Publish and share corporate news to your Page followers.

✔ **LinkedIn e-mail:** Send a message between connections.

✔ **LinkedIn inMail:** Reach non-connections by sending messages using this paid membership feature.

✔ **LinkedIn Groups:** Public or private discussion forums for like-minded individuals or organization members.

✔ **LinkedIn Polls:** Publish or respond to quick polls that can be shared on through your news feed.

We authors have LinkedIn profiles, and we recommend that every professional person should set one up. LinkedIn is excellent for personal brand building and business networking. Figure 3-11 shows Danielle's LinkedIn profile and Aliza's company page on LinkedIn. LinkedIn also offers company pages to build a presence for your business as well as LinkedIn groups to help you build an online community.

Figure 3-11:
Danielle's LinkedIn profile and Aliza's company page on LinkedIn.

Google+

Google+ (often abbreviated as G+) hit 400 million users in September 2012, according to Vic Gundrota at Google. Even though Wikipedia reports that only 100 million Google+ users are active, that's still a lot of users.

Despite its large user base, Google+ can feel much more intimate than other major social networks. Google+ has a fast-moving stream, similar to Twitter, and it offers many of the same multimedia and interactive features as Facebook Pages. Yet Google+ conversations somehow manage to feel more interconnected than on Twitter and more cohesive than on Facebook.

Members of Google+ can communicate in a number of ways:

- Post to their G+ streams, whether the posts consist of text, photos, videos, or links.
- Add a +1 rating (similar to a Facebook Like) to posts or photos.
- Share a post from someone else in your stream.
- Comment on posts.
- Text-chat within Circles.
- Video-chat in Google Hangouts.
- Live-stream video by chatting in Google Hangouts on Air.

You can also target messages to specific groups by using Google+ Circles or groupings of connections and create as many circles as you want. Figure 3-12 shows a circle consisting of writers and reporters using G+.

Figure 3-12:
An example
of a G+
Circle.

To become familiar with the features, try out Google+, and start with a personal account before expanding to a Google+ Business Page. Definitely reserve your G+ Page name now even if you don't start updating it. In Figure 3-13, you can see that Red Bull posts photos and videos of extreme sports to its Google+ Business Page. See Chapter 13 for different ways to engage using Google+ including G+ Communities.

Figure 3-13:
A brand's
G+ Business
Page.

Incorporating Audio and Video Platforms

When you evaluate tools for social media engagement, you might not immediately consider audio or video. Listening to audio or watching video may seem at first glance to be passive activities. Granted, listening or watching doesn't involve the typical two-way or multiple-way conversations of SME. Still, audio and video can play an important role in stimulating engagement.

As we've stated elsewhere in this book, actions, reactions, and interactions make up engagement. Both audio and video involve publishing content — in this case, multimedia files uploaded to or embedded into websites, blogs, or social networks. Most places where you can post or view digital audio or video online usually include ways for people to Like, Favorite, comment on, or share what they listen to or watch. These interactions happen either in a multimedia player or on the site where the content is uploaded.

Where you have content and where you have tools in place for responding to that content, you have the potential for engagement. Audio or video can attract attention and provide content to start a conversation — so audio and video cannot be left out of the SME equation.

Audiocasting or podcasting

Audiocasts are digital audio broadcasts on the Internet. You may also hear them referred to as *podcasts* because they're often played on iPods. In 2012, 29 percent of Americans had listened to a podcast (Edison Research).

Podcasts can refer to video in addition to audio. In this book, *podcast* refers to digital audio online, and *video podcast* refers to, well, digital video online.

Most podcasts are available for listening or for download entirely for free. Radio stations and radio production companies can produce podcasts in professional studios with professional audio editors. Just as often, independent producers, marketers, and audio enthusiasts can produce podcasts too with varying degrees of production quality.

Some popular podcasts on the Apple iTunes store are *This American Life* and *Freakonomics Radio* and a number of NPR shows.

A podcast can be delivered on G+ by using these methods:

- ✔ **Live streaming:** Usually recorded
- ✔ **Recording:** Generally followed by broadcasting
- ✔ **Embedding on a site, blog, or social network:** For instant or on-demand play
- ✔ **Archived on a network:** For individual download or subscription

Podcasts are recorded in many lengths and styles. Some podcasts are produced similarly to radio shows with recorded intros and outros edited in after the content is recorded and even with music added. Sometimes, podcasts contain commercials. Podcasts can also be streamed or recorded live, even from a mobile device, and uploaded on the fly with no editing.

Aliza is a big fan of podcasting. Several years ago, she recorded nearly 100 episodes of *Digital Marketer* for the Quick and Dirty Tips Network. Since then, she has self-produced various podcasts including *Zen of Being Digital*. Danielle, with her strong background in television news, gravitates toward video. A large portion of her brand revolves around self-produced videos hosted on her sites and her YouTube channel and around professionally produced pieces when she is hired as an on-site correspondent. That video, too, ends up on all her channels.

Don't underestimate the power and portability of audio to connect with your audience. You can also engage your audience in audio conversations online, as we explain in Chapter 15.

Videocasting or video podcasts

A mere handful of years ago, we couldn't confidently recommend using online video for digital marketing and SME. Bandwidth was still an issue for many people, and even with the fast-growing popularity of YouTube, consumers were unable to easily watch video on their Internet connections. Oh, how things have changed in the past few years!

Millions of people now watch videos online daily. By the end of 2011, 182 million U.S. Internet users watched online video content and viewed 43.5 billion videos. Google sites — YouTube in particular — was the number-one video site at that time, followed by Vevo and Yahoo! Sites (comScore). That's a lot of video being watched and a lot of video being uploaded.

This list describes a few ways in which digital video that's hosted online can benefit your engagement. You can use a well-produced video to

- ✔ **Grab the attention of your audience:** Video attracts attention. The Play button graphic on an image immediately compels action. (Click!)
- ✔ **Enhance content:** Video adds a dynamic dimension and an enhanced visual appeal to the content you publish.
- ✔ **Embed content in other formats:** Video can be easily embedded into websites, blogs, and social networks, providing richer content to consume.
- ✔ **Inspire audience reaction:** Most online video players incorporate social features, including the ability to Like or Favorite and comment.
- ✔ **Share:** Digital video is easy to share, especially when someone shares a link to the video online or within social networks. Gone are the days of e-mailing large video files to share with connections.

Also gone are the days of having to spend tens of thousands or hundreds of thousands of dollars to produce highly polished, professional videos. These days, a minimally produced video can be as popular as (or even more popular than) videos with expensive video production.

Don't set out to produce a *viral video* (a video that is shared organically by thousands or millions of people). Too many factors are at work when a video *goes viral* to be able to plan an entire marketing strategy around producing one. Using video for SME is one tactic in a more complex online communications plan.

YouTube

The Grand Poobah of online video is undoubtedly YouTube. The latest statistics on its website state that more than 800 million unique users visit

YouTube every month and watch more than 4 billion hours of video. Users upload 72 hours of video to YouTube every minute. In 2011, YouTube had more than 1 trillion views, or around 140 views for every person on Earth. And on and on it goes.

This list describes several winning features that make YouTube useful for SME:

- ✔ **It's free.** You can't beat free for hosting video files online, especially when files can be large and cumbersome.

- ✔ **It attracts numbers.** The sheer volume of members and viewers makes YouTube a natural choice for video hosting and engagement.

- ✔ **It benefits from search engine optimization (SEO).** The added benefit of how YouTube videos show up in Google searches makes your videos hosted there potentially much more accessible.

- ✔ **It has tools that are easy to use.** Editing and embedding video can seem complicated until you use basic tools such as the ones offered on YouTube.

- ✔ **It has a number of community features.** YouTube incorporates engagement features into its site and video player, including the ability for anyone to Like, comment on, embed, e-mail, and share videos (as long as they're signed into their Google account). The site also offers a video commenting option.

- ✔ **It offers advertising options.** YouTube offers a number of paid advertising options to give your videos a boost and exposure to more people for potential engagement.

YouTube isn't the only free video-hosting site on the block. Vimeo, for example, offers a free membership level and provides good-quality video playback and an elegant video player. If you're looking for the highest number of eyeballs on your video message — and potentially the highest number of interactions and shares for your video — YouTube is undeniably the right tool.

YouTube is considered the second-largest search engine in the world. (Google is first.) It doesn't hurt that Google owns YouTube. Your videos on YouTube may therefore have a better chance of visibility than if they're hosted on other video sites.

Aliza is just getting started with online video as a tool for social media engagement, but several of her clients use it regularly. Danielle has been using video successfully for a number of years in her own business. She has a large enough viewership that she can monetize her videos. Because her entire business revolves around content production — particularly video — and engagement with her audience via her multimedia content, making money from her videos on YouTube makes sense. You may not make money directly from your videos on YouTube; you can, however, achieve tangible business goals and boost SME by incorporating YouTube-hosted videos into your online marketing mix. See Chapter 16 for different ways to effectively leverage YouTube.

Recognizing Other Social Engagement Tools

Let's face it: The world has gone mobile. Statistics from ComScore indicate that 234 million U.S. residents now use mobile devices. Smartphone use has increased 4 percent to 110 million (more than 1 billion worldwide, believe it or not). That means 47 percent of Americans are using smartphones.

Tablet computers are also becoming more commonplace. According to Pew Research Center, as of early 2012, 58 percent of American adults have desktop computers, 61 percent have laptops, 18 percent own e-book readers, and 18 percent have tablet computers. Tablet computer ownership has increased more than 16 percent in less than two years.

The increase in mobile device use for accessing the Internet also changes the way people access websites. Check your website stats, and you'll see an uptick in visits to your site from mobile devices and mobile versions of social networks such as Facebook.

The way people communicate changes continually with the rapid rise in smartphone use and the increasing popularity of tablet computers. Communications tools are more portable than ever, and social networks are all going mobile. People now have unprecedented access to the tools and platforms to reach out to, and engage with, their audiences, customers, and prospects — which means that they can be reached anywhere and at any time.

Mobile applications

A mobile application, or *app,* is a compact piece of software that runs on a mobile device — a table computer, a smartphone, or even a gaming device. The app can be a mobile version of a website or another online content or be a self-contained application with content that resides entirely on a mobile device. Mobile apps pack features and functionality into relatively small files with interfaces that fit the smaller screens of tablet computers, smartphones, and the like.

All the most popular web-based social networks have mobile versions that appear legible and clear on the smaller mobile screen. Many social networks offer their own mobile apps so that you can easily access their networks from your Android or iOS mobile device. Some web-based social networks with apps include Facebook, Google+, LinkedIn, Pinterest, Twitter, and YouTube.

Some of these popular social networks can also be accessed from third-party mobile apps such as HootSuite (www.hootsuite.com) that let you post to many of your networks from a single mobile device. All these dashboard tools for managing your social media also have web-based versions, and some even have desktop versions to make access to your social networks conveniently cross-platform. Without the mobile aspect, however, they would be missing a large and growing share of users as more people turn to their mobile devices to access and communicate online.

Mobile continues to grow at an astronomical pace. According to YouTube, its traffic from mobile alone tripled in 2011. More than 3 hours of video is uploaded to YouTube from mobile devices every minute. That's *powerful*.

Location-based services

A subset of mobile applications are *location-based services (LBSs)*. LBSs are social networks that are focused around places — actual physical locations — and they tap into the GPS in a smartphone or mobile device to offer features and functionality. *Mobile* is the operative word in LBSs — they offer ways to turn social *media* engagement on the web into social *mobile* engagement.

Though many LBSs are available, we mostly focus on Foursquare and Instagram because they have options and features either geared toward or useful for companies and brands. We both use Foursquare and Instagram practically daily in our own SME efforts. Danielle is especially adept at connecting with her community via Instagram. Aliza has helped numerous clients incorporate these and other LBSs into their day-to-day engagement activities and to enhance offline events with online conversations. We go into more detail about LBS engagement in Chapter 14.

Part II
Exploring the Elements of Social Media Engagement

TIP

Five Ways to Be Present for Social Media Engagement

- ✔ Watch and analyze the best of what your competitors are doing, to evaluate where you stack up when it comes to **online reach, conversation, and engagement.**

- ✔ Respond to comments and follow up to **provide timely customer service** to your audience.

- ✔ Implement a social media engagement messaging map that encourages **conversations between your brand and your audience.**

- ✔ Create a social media editorial calendar to accomplish your goals and **meet the needs, wants, and desires of your audience.**

- ✔ Determine the best times to engage in active and reactive interactions with your audience.

web extras

Go to www.dummies.com/extras/socialmediaengagement to dive deeply into trust-building tactics for social media engagement.

In this part . . .

- See how to build trust with your audience to win them over.

- Discover the best ways to pay attention to your online communities so that they know you care.

- Find your audience, connect with them, and build better customer relationships.

- Get the conversation started to drive real interactions and results.

Chapter 4

Building Trust and Credibility

In This Chapter

▶ Choosing messages that win followers

▶ Harnessing the power of listening and responding to your audience

▶ Constructing the foundation for a trusting relationship with your community

▶ Measuring the response to your messages

*W*ithout trust online, you have nothing. In fact, you might have less than nothing. It's better for you to have zero social media engagement (SME) than to have massive but untrustworthy engagement. If building trust and credibility online isn't on your agenda, slowly close this book now and prepare for your social networks to begin gathering digital dust.

Earning Trust in Social Media

Trust can develop in two ways:

✔ Your audience engages with you, already believing that you're worthy of their trust. If this is the case, you're in the clear unless or until you break that bond of trust.

✔ Your audience demands that you earn their faith.

If your following is the former, lucky you. Aim to continue building — not breaking — their trust. To deal with the latter, read the tips in the next few sections.

Making your message clear

Diving in to engage in the social media sphere without ever having given thought to how your brand should be viewed or the messages you should convey is dangerous — and even more so if your brand uses social media publicly as a team. Take the time to flesh out your messaging — not simply its content but also how you express it.

Giving your team clear guidelines

Putting in place your official social media engagement guidelines presents a unified voice and begins the process of engineering the foundation of your audience's conviction that you're worth their time, energy, and — eventually — their dollars.

To set up SME guidelines, follow these suggestions:

- **Do your homework.** Dig a little. Find out who your audience is, where they spend their time, and what they're already talking about. The more you know about them, the easier it is to tailor your message directly to them.

- **State your mission.** As a brand or a business, you should have already developed a mission statement. Now it's time to make that statement relevant to your social media approach to guide your team as they begin to share your message publicly online. USA.gov calls its approach the "guiding principle" and reminds everyone working on its social media team that everything it does is "motivated by this principle."

- **Make them short and sweet.** Your team doesn't need guidelines the size of a novel. If your written guidelines are too long and complicated, your team won't understand them, process them, remember them, or use them to engage. Guidelines that are succinct are easier to commit to memory and to follow with ease.

- **Allow for experimentation.** You can follow your guidelines — and you can also "color outside the lines." Trusting that your team can effectively use the information you give them, and expand on it, pushes your message to the next level of engagement.

Interacting authentically

We suspect that the word *authentic* raises your buzzword hackles, if you've heard it (as we have) time and time again in reference to social media. Yet the words *real* and *genuine,* though they mean the same thing, don't seem to carry the same punch to relay the importance of the qualities of your brand when engaging with your community online. This list describes the brand qualities that create authenticity (and build trust) in social media engagement:

- **Personality:** Show some. Your audience engages because they feel invested in who you are as a brand or company. Are you fun and fearless or serious and savvy — or the one who brightens their day? Showing personality gives a glimpse of the people behind the brand.

✔ **Honesty:** Nurture it. Honesty goes hand in hand with the trust you're trying to build. When someone in your community asks a question, respond to the best of your ability — and be truthful. If you don't know an answer, promise to find out. Trusting you, they'll come back to learn more. Return with an honest answer.

✔ **Transparency:** Give your SME teams names and faces to create personal connections. The Kodak account on Twitter, for example, is run by the company's chief blogger and social media manager, Jenny Cisney. It's her face you see when you communicate with Kodak on Twitter, as shown in Figure 4-1. When people know that they can connect with an individual behind your brand, your brand becomes personalized.

✔ **Ownership:** Take responsibility for your mistakes — they happen. Your community will judge you far more harshly if you attempt to act as though they don't. Owning up to praise is easy. Also respond openly to your customers' questions, concerns, and criticisms. Your greatest critics can become your most outspoken fans when they trust that you hear them and respond honestly and transparently.

Use the word *you* when engaging in social media rather than refer to generic *customers* or *people*. Your audience prefers that you speak with them, not about them or at them. Make it personal.

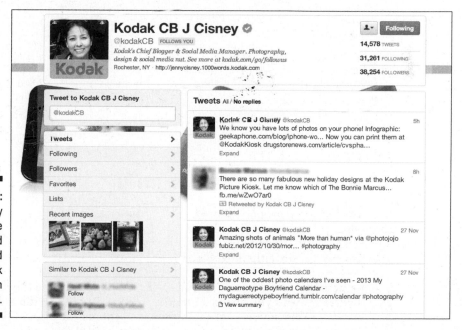

Figure 4-1: Jenny Cisney is the name and face behind the Kodak account on Twitter.

Finding your brand's voice

One step in conveying your personality online is finding your brand's voice. If you're building a bigger brand that involves many people behind the brand, you still need a unifying voice that everyone who posts online for your brand can use.

Figure 4-2 shows how CoverGirl uses Instagram to reveal its unique personality, by showcasing new makeup, trends, and events in keeping with its followers' expectations.

Not every attitude translates well online, and yours may not be perceived the way you intend. If you personally are the brand, be careful about the personality you convey when interacting with others online. As you can see in Table 4-1, there's a fine line between the quality you're aiming for and how others might see it.

Table 4-1		Minding Your Tone	
What You Might Say	*Your Intent*	*How You Might Be Perceived*	*A Better Approach*
Hi, beautiful.	Friendly	Fresh	Hi, there! or Hi, friend!
Do it this way, now!	Knowledgeable	Know-It-All	Here's an idea. . .
Ha! You're SO smart!	Witty	Snarky	Well played, friend.
Did you see what happened to Sarah in this video?	Humorous	Mocking	Can't miss fun — have you seen Sarah's new video?

Contributing meaningfully to the conversation

Conversations are happening everywhere online, and many of them take place in social networks. Become part of those conversations in a way that makes sense to your brand and your business goals *and* to your audience.

Recommendations from friends and family, and even those from social networks, are referred to as *earned media* in the advertising world. According to Nielsen, of the consumers who were interviewed worldwide, 92 percent say that they trust earned media more than all other forms of advertising (www. contentcurationmarketing.com/consumers-trust-earned-media-more-than-paid-media-according-to-nielsen/).

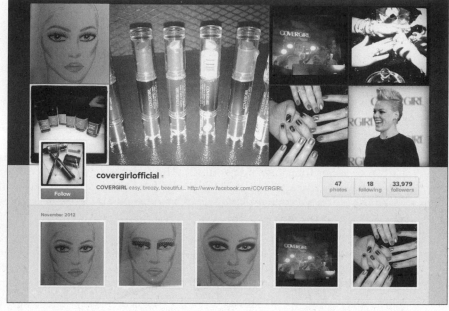

Figure 4-2:
CoverGirl
expresses
its brand
identity
on its
Instagram
page.

According to ROI Research, of the users who were interviewed, 58 percent of Twitter users and 53 percent of Facebook users who were interviewed said that they're likely to purchase a product after following a company or product in social media. Trust in a brand, and interaction with it in social networks, can translate into sales.

We cover online interaction in much more detail in Chapter 7. For now, follow these tips to start entering conversations in the right places and in the right ways:

- **Investigate the topics that matter to your audience.** Research to find out where they spend their time and what topics they care most about. See whether you can reach them on Facebook or Twitter, and whether they're willing to read your content or respond to beautiful pictures, for example, on Pinterest or Instagram. A tool such as Followerwonk (www.followerwonk.com) assesses your followers' interests and creates a *word cloud*, a visualized series of words compiled of the most popular user-generated words or tags. The word cloud is for you to showcase those interests on your website or other social media platform. You can also ask current customers and prospects where they spend their time online and what they're comfortable doing there.

- **Build your social media presence.** After you know where your audience interacts, go there. Create a Facebook Fan Page or sign up for Twitter or start a Pinterest account. Hire a writer to compose content for your blog or even for your social networks. Listen, respond, and start *engaging*. Let your audience know that they matter to you from the moment they connect with you.

✓ **Continue asking questions.** After you have established a presence in suitable networks and you're building an audience, continue asking them questions. Prove to your audience that their thoughts and opinions matter to you by asking them what they think and by listening to what they have to say.

Mabel's Labels, a small business based in Toronto, Canada, established its footing firmly in the social media space by interacting daily with its customers. The company knew that, to be successful, its representatives had to discuss topics other than Mabel's products. The business regularly asks questions of its followers, answers questions, and follows up on discussions the same as in face-to-face conversations. See an example in Figure 4-3 of how Mabel's Labels asks questions.

Figure 4-3:
Mabel's
Labels asks
questions
of followers
every day
and then fol-
lows up with
comments
as the com-
pany's fans
reply.

A *meaningful* conversation is one where the parties involved gain value from the exchange. Not every conversation is easy. Sometimes, events that are beyond your company's control affect your business and your customers. Use your social networks to maintain the dialogue about what is happening as it happens so that your customers feel acknowledged and important.

Create an incentive

Asking questions isn't the only way to inspire people in your online community to start talking. Sometimes, you need to do a little more to keep your customers curious, engaged, and interested in coming back to your online presence — and to keep them talking about you publicly to their friends, fans, and followings. Sure, people are often happy to describe their plans for New Year's Eve, the foods they're eating for breakfast, their favorite restaurants in San Diego, or the best parts of their day, but after they answer, they have no incentive to come back.

Make your audience feel like an important part of your brand, like they're part of the family or part of your team.

Share quality content — yours and others'

Blasting content about your company, products, or services 24-7 is the same behavior exhibited by the kid in the front row in third grade, who continually raises his hand and shouts, "Me! Me! Me!" Surely your followers like you for a reason, but they want to know that you're more than a one-trick pony. Here's the key question to ask: Do you share quality content about any topics other than yourself or your brand?

To do so, move outside your brand sphere and look for compatible brands and individuals who can help you educate, inspire, and entertain your community. Take a look at Chipotle, for example — a chain restaurant that has quite a following. At this writing, the company has more than 2 million Likes on its Facebook Fan Page. Chipotle works with chefs who provide audiences with recipes and cooking instructions at events and align with organizations such as the Farmer Veteran Coalition to support good causes such as helping mobilize veterans to feed those in need across America (see Figure 4-4). The company posts updates to Facebook with content about these other individuals and organizations.

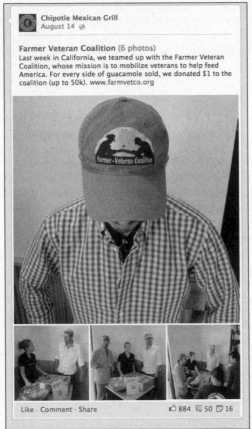

Chipotle Mexican Grill
August 14

Farmer Veteran Coalition (6 photos)
Last week in California, we teamed up with the Farmer Veteran Coalition, whose mission is to mobilize veterans to help feed America. For every side of guacamole sold, we donated $1 to the coalition (up to 50k). www.farmvetco.org

Like · Comment · Share   884   50   16

Figure 4-4:
Chipotle posts information about individuals and organizations it works with to supplement content about itself.

Listening carefully to your community

Broadcasting to your community and never stopping to listen to what they have to say in return makes it impossible, in the long run, for others to trust you. Think about the times you've had conversations with friends or colleagues and suddenly realized that they weren't even listening to you. "Listening" online usually requires reading. Finding the most relevant information to read — in this case, people's opinions about your brand — starts by monitoring online conversations. Though we advise you throughout this book to be attentive and responsive in your own social networks, you also have to listen beyond them.

A variety of tools can help you better listen to your community and to the online community at large. In Parts III and IV of this book, we discuss the listening tools and techniques that are unique to the social networks Facebook, Twitter, LinkedIn, and Pinterest.

Checking out conversations about you

Begin with one of the easiest and most comprehensive methods to monitor what is being said about you and your brand by setting up Google Alerts. To do so, go to www.google.com/alerts (see the figure), and then follow these steps:

1. **Fill in the query field with the term you want to search for.**

   Type your business name, a common misspelling of your business name, the name of your company's CEO, or the names of its products, for example. You can set up more than one alert.

2. **Enter the result type for the term you're searching for.**

   For the most comprehensive results, choose Everything. You can always hone in later.

3. **Choose how often to notify you about a matching alert: as it happens, once a day, or once a week.**

4. **Specify the number of results you want: all of them or only the best.**

5. **Include your e-mail address so that you can receive alerts in your inbox.**

6. **Click the red Create Alert button.**

Responding promptly for greater impact

We know that it's impossible for you to be online and monitoring your social networks 24 hours a day. Set a schedule for regular checks of your online communities to manage the conversations in an organized fashion. More important, in addition to setting alerts to hear what the online community is saying about you (see the nearby sidebar "Checking out conversations about you"), make the time to pay attention to your community so that you can hear what they're saying to you and respond in a timely manner.

Check in regularly throughout the day to catch what is being said that doesn't reach you by way of alerts. Go online during the periods when the largest number of people — including your customers and prospects — are present: early in the morning, midmorning, early afternoon, and early evening. Knowing your audience and interacting with them often can help you determine the best times to reach your own online community.

If you live and work on the east coast but your target market and most of your audience is based in California, adjust your timing for online content publishing and interacting accordingly.

The timeliness of your responses is an important part of trust-building online. Leaving questions unanswered for days, weeks, or even longer leaves a bad taste in a customer's mouth and can dissolve that person's trust in you.

A timely response is even more important when you (or someone posting for you) make a mistake. Address mistakes as quickly as possible — it can mean the difference between a positive and negative impression of your brand.

Ramon de Leon owns several Domino's Pizza franchises in the Chicago area. When a customer tweeted a complaint about receiving the wrong pizza, De Leon did more than fix the problem — he posted a tweet, as shown in Figure 4-5, to explain that the correct order was en route *and* that the store would "wow" her. Then he created a personalized video apology with his store manager. This video, which has been viewed more than 160,000 times, is a stellar example of social media follow-through.

Giving the audience what they want

After you have drawn your audience's attention, you're faced with the million-dollar question: how to keep their attention and compel them to action? Crucial to solving this puzzle is how you follow through, though the answer starts with the foundation you lay. This list explains several reasons that people stay connected with you in social networks — why they click the Like button or share your posts:

- ✔ **The content resonates with them.** Your content makes them smile or laugh or moves them emotionally.

- ✔ **The content originates from a source they trust.** The content was shared by you, a friend or connection on a social network.

- ✔ **The content reflects something about themselves.** You may have published the information, but they agree and react to it and share it to reveal a part of themselves.

- ✔ **The content puts them in-the-know.** People like to be the "first to know" or to have insider information on special promotions, contests, and other offers. Some also like to be the first of their friends to share this news within their own circles.

- ✔ **Others respond.** People like to have things in common with others, and when other people respond to your content, it invites even more responses that continue the conversation and build bonds.

- ✔ **You respond.** If people know that you're right there to acknowledge them when they like or comment on your content, it's incentive to respond again. People love to be noticed and to feel that they matter.

- ✔ **You give perks.** People like to be part of the "in crowd," and beyond information, you can offer them discounts, coupons, and deals that they receive because they're connected with you. Plus, they can pass along offers to friends to spread the good feeling all around.

Figure 4-5: This franchise manager and his store manager apologized online for a customer's bad experience.

The better you know your audience, the more likely you are to post content that people feel connected to — and that they'll respond to and engage in. Then it's your turn to be responsive, to engage, and to follow through to build a stronger relationship and give others good reasons to trust you.

Building Trust in Traditional Online Marketing

Before Twitter, there was the e-mail newsletter. Before Facebook Fan Pages, businesses ran online banner ads. Traditional online marketing — like newsletters, banner ads, and e-mail marketing — still exists and also requires a level of trust. Building a rapport between your brand and your customers and prospects builds your business and helps your brand thrive.

Engaging appropriately with the media

Emphasizing social media engagement doesn't mean that you ignore the importance of the role of traditional media. Being mentioned in the media is still an important part of marketing, and press pages on company websites are filled, for good reason, with the logos representing media outlets such as *Wall Street Journal, The New York Times, Oprah, Fast Company, Today,* and CNN. Television, print magazines, and newspapers still exist and are still powerful.

These days, these media hits often happen because brands do more than send press releases and make cold calls to members of the press. Reporters and producers pay attention to social networks for potential news stories and to find news sources organically. Savvy brands can position themselves in social media to attract the media's attention, and they can engage with members of the press by following them in social networks to engage them in dialogue, draw their attention to potential news stories, and provide resources including links.

Nurture relationships with your local media and even with national or international media. Find creative ways to suggest story ideas and to position yourself or someone from your team as a topical expert. Incorporate images and video into your online pitches via social media to attract attention. Work to build a reputation as a trustworthy and reliable source for quotes and news leads.

 Strongly consider media training for whoever might be appearing on camera or acting as a company spokesperson. Being knowledgeable about your topic doesn't compensate for a lack of polished media presence. Displaying poor skills in front of the camera can hurt your credibility and even make you look untrustworthy.

Adding engagement to press releases

Traditional press releases are taking new forms because of social media. They can no longer simply make announcements and spew marketing language. A press release must now be part of the conversation in social networks.

With the growth of social media and publishing tools at everyone's fingertips, the days of editors and producers serving as the gatekeepers of news have passed. Anyone can be a citizen reporter, creating and sharing news with friends, fans, and followers. This situation places reporters — and PR people — in precarious positions if they fail to adapt to the new ways of disseminating news.

Making your press release social is another way to become transparent. The more accessible your company news and information are to the general public, the greater level of trust and credibility you build. To give your press releases a better chance of being seen, and of bypassing the traditional channels of news publishing, you can

- ✔ **Include links to your social networks:** These links allow members of the media to engage with your company online. Include links within the press releases that lead to additional content, to even more multimedia, and especially to all the major social sharing networks.

- ✔ **Share them on your blog and social networks:** Putting this information on your platforms increases the opportunity for it being seen by your community and spread to other sources who might want to cover it.

- ✔ **Add social sharing tools to every release:** That way, readers can share them easily with their connections.

- ✔ **Host them on the web:** Most social-media–powered releases are now hosted on the web rather than e-mailed or faxed.

- ✔ **Use short, catchy headlines:** Headlines in press releases should make sense, be relevant to readers, and be crafted with search engine optimization (SEO) in mind. A headline often becomes the content for your tweet or update with a link to the rest of the release.

- ✔ **Make it multimedia:** A press release should contain images (perfect for Facebook and Pinterest) and even embedded audio and video files. Since the releases are hosted on the web, embedding multimedia like this to enhance them is a breeze.

- ✔ **Provide "tweetable" quotes:** Content is consumed at a fast pace online. Pull out quotes and excerpts of your releases that have a maximum of 120 characters so that they're easily shared on social networks, especially Twitter.

When writing a press release, consider the story you're trying to tell. Storytelling is an important part of engaging in social media. Start there and use the elements of storytelling to convert a press release from a static document into a dynamic start of a conversation.

Press releases: Not just for the Big News

David Meerman Scott, the author of *The New Rules of Marketing & PR* (John Wiley & Sons, Inc.), suggests that the rules for the modern press release have changed and encourages you to adjust right along with it. One piece of advice he gives is "Don't just send press releases when 'big news' is happening; find good reasons to send them all the time."

We agree with David that the formal press release, sent only occasionally to announce a company's big news, is now defunct. Look for ways to tell your story often and to keep your stories "out there" as part of your daily online conversations. Your conversations with the media in social networks should be ongoing, not monthly or quarterly, when your calendar indicates that it's time to send a release.

Just because your release is more "social" doesn't mean that you should disregard the best practices of press release writing. Good grammar, proper punctuation, and addressing "the six W's" of information-gathering — who, what, when, where, why, and how — are still essential parts of any well-written press release regardless of the distribution method.

Use social media release (SMR) tools such as PitchEngine (http://new.pitch engine.com) and PressDoc (www.pressdoc.com) to easily build press releases on the web with embedded social features at an affordable price. These tools are specifically designed to bring journalists and social media together and offer stats so you can determine who has seen your press release.

Soliciting third-party endorsements the right way

Satisfied customers represent gold that's waiting to be mined. The best way to have them endorse your brand? Ask. Don't be afraid to request online reviews about you or ratings of your business, product, or service.

Make it worth the effort for people to praise you publicly. When a happy customer raves about you on a social network, be sure to express your gratitude. Share their kind words with your larger fan base. Find a creative way to say thank you.

Lead people to popular review sites so that their praise finds even more exposure, such as

- ✔ Yelp: www.yelp.com
- ✔ Google Places for Business: www.google.com/places
- ✔ Angie's List: www.angieslist.com

- Citysearch: www.citysearch.com
- Yahoo! Local: http://local.yahoo.com

Positive, unsolicited reviews from consumers at these review sites go a long way toward building your brand's credibility. Controlling the content of reviews on public sites, however, is impossible.

Never fake a positive review for your own business in a social network or review site. If you get caught and called out publicly, you can instantly lose your credibility and the public's trust. On a review site, you can be banned; on a social network, you can't be banned for pretending to be a satisfied customer, but the loss of trust isn't even remotely worth any perceived benefit.

Assessing Trust and Credibility

You know that you're trustworthy. You believe that you're credible. But how does your community feel about you? Having a lot of friends, fans, and followers as well as likes, follows, and repins may seem to be tangible measurements of how people feel about your brand, but they may not tell the full story.

Be sure that the people who are connecting with your brand via social media are truly connecting with you — and will stay connected over the long haul.

Analyzing sentiment and impact

Understanding whether your community has a positive, negative, or neutral response to you and your brand can help you determine how to continually hone your social media engagement approach. How you measure up against competitors in the minds of your online audience is another important factor to assess. You can also benefit from identifying the key influencers who are driving the bulk of the online conversation about you and the general consensus among the most vocal members of your community.

Many tools (either free versions or paid versions that offer free trials or free levels) can help you measure some less obvious aspects of social media engagement. Here are a few that we like:

- **Sysomos** (www.sysomos.com) has a social media monitoring tool, Heartbeat, that measures sentiment and helps track conversations by country, city, or state or by profession or gender. (Pricey.)
- **SalesForceMarketingCloud** (www.salesforcemarketingcloud.com) Formerly Radian6, SalesForce ties in to Google Analytics, Webtrends, and Omniture to gather statistics and determine which online thought

leaders are generating the most chatter about you and driving the greatest amount of traffic to your sites. (Pricey.)

✔ **PeopleBrowsr** (`http://rs.peoplebrowsr.com`), a lower-cost alternative to the paid services, lets you search by topic, brand, or name. Use it to highlight as many as 1,000 days of Twitter conversations, and filter results by gender, sentiment, community, or location. In Figure 4-6, you can see sample search results for Danielle's Twitter handle — @DanielleSmithTV. (Affordable with a 14-day free trial.)

✔ **Simply Measured** (`http://simplymeasured.com`) is fee-based, but you can have free reports e-mailed to you, including a free Facebook Competitive Analysis Report to see what other brands are doing well and a free Klout Audience Report to see how effectively you're engaging with your followers on Twitter. (Paid but offers free reports.)

✔ **Social Mention** (`www.socialmention.com`) uses the tagline *Like Google Alerts, but for social media.* In seconds, this service measures the likelihood that your brand is being discussed in social media and whether the general sentiment is positive, negative, or neutral. The results also indicate the possibility that the people who are talking about you will do so repeatedly and list the keywords being used in connection with your brand or name. (Free.)

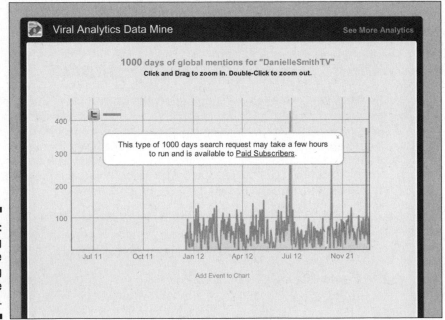

Figure 4-6:
Evaluating how people are referring to Danielle on Twitter.

Measuring the amplification of your messages

Hidden behind the noise of social media, competing for attention, is amazing content — *your* amazing content. Occasionally, you may feel as if you're standing at the edge of the Grand Canyon, shouting your message, asking questions, and sharing an extraordinary story with only this response: an empty echo.

As we discuss earlier in this chapter, the key to hearing more than an echo is to listen. As you move from one social platform to another, as you share an image, as you ask a question, or as you dole out a slice of content that you know is special, you gauge the results.

Did your community like an image 84 times, comment 24 times, and share it 2 times — yet no one responded when you asked whether they had plans for the weekend? The solution is easy: Share another image and try a different type of question.

Though some social networks provide you with insights into how well people are responding to your social media engagement efforts, a myriad of third-party tools can help you measure response rates across your social networks or on the ones that lack built-in tools. Here are a few that we like:

URL shorteners

bitly (`https://bitly.com/`)

Google URL Shortener (`http://goo.gl/`)

Ow.ly (`http://ow.ly/url/shorten-url`)

su.pr (`http://su.pr/`)

Social media management tools

Buffer: `http://bufferapp.com`

HootSuite: `http://hootsuite.com`

Sprout Social: `http://sproutsocial.com`

Other tools with useful analytics

dlvr.it: `http://dlvr.it`

PeerIndex: `www.peerindex.com`

Klout: `http://klout.com`

To avoid having to simply notice the ebbs and flows of responses when you're trying to engage, invest in the appropriate analytics tools to more accurately and consistently read how well you're engaging. These tools can help you determine how to improve the way you engage and in turn improve the results of your engagement efforts.

As you respond, engage, and talk, your customers will see you as an individual, not an entity. You're humanized. You gain credibility and trust. You win.

Chapter 5

Demonstrating Your Online Presence to Maximize Engagement

In This Chapter

▶ Specifying manageable objectives

▶ Paying attention to online events

▶ Developing a process with a messaging map and calendar

▶ Deciding what to do and when to do it

Your presence in this online space determines your purpose, at least in the eyes of your audience. In this chapter, we discuss the many ways you can manage your online existence, set the expectations of your community, follow up on a regular basis, and create true connections.

A human touch, pushing beyond the logo that defines so many brands and businesses to engage with the audience, captures the feeling that identifies you.

Setting Realistic Goals Up Front

"The start is what stops most people."

—Don Shula

We suspect that Don Shula, the former Miami Dolphins football coach, might well have been referring to social media engagement (SME) when he spoke of the challenge of getting started. Faced with the head-spinning efforts of maneuvering a blog or Facebook, Twitter, LinkedIn, Pinterest, Instagram, or another of the seemingly unlimited social media websites, being tackled by an offensive lineman might somehow sound more appealing.

In football, no player can quarterback the team, tackle players, and receive passes all at the same time. In social media, certainly, neither you nor your team can master all the engagement skills and participate in all your social networks at one time. You need careful planning and a process to juggle all the activities of SME.

Regardless of human limitations, being present in social networks is critical to your success at engaging via social media. You — or your team members or representatives — should actively and directly engage with your online community members, friends, fans, and followers.

To see how to be not only present but also effective online, start by assessing your capacity and studying the competition, as we discuss in the following sections.

Assessing your capacity

When Danielle was following her first passion, television reporting, she accepted a job in a small market — Yuma, Arizona. A reporter embarking in this career usually operates as a "one-man-band." Danielle had to play the role of reporter, photographer, producer, and news anchor. Her ability to truly master each of these jobs was limited not by lack of skill or desire but by being only one person with only so much talent or ability. But she learned over time exactly which tasks she could master and which ones to complete only acceptably so that she didn't "burn out" on her profession.

Honestly evaluating your company's capacity to handle every aspect of SME is important early on so that you don't set yourself up for failure — *and* everyone who works with you. If you're a one-person band for your brand's SME, you have to be smart and selective about the tools you use, the way you use them, and the way you engage.

To set realistic expectations about your aptitude for engaging with customers and prospects in social media, consider these factors:

- **Time:** Determine how much time — daily, weekly, or monthly — you can invest in engaging in social networks.

- **Resources:** Outline the support system you have in place to do the work. *Resources* in SME usually refers to

   - *People* who handle the work

   - *Tools and services* you use to streamline the work

- **Skills:** Even if you have the people and the tools to engage, without the right skills or the capacity to develop those skills via training, no amount of resources will put you on the right track toward properly engaging with your audience online.

Maintaining a poor social media presence is worse than having no presence. With an inactive presence, your audience assumes you are listening, but will fault you for the days and weeks of silence when their thoughts and questions go unanswered. Avoid the temptation to let tools that maintain your presence in social networks substitute for using them well based on best practices. Additionally, if you don't know how to properly engage, your presence in your networks can fall flat or — worse — create a social media crisis. Research how best to use the resources at your disposal — or make time for proper training.

Evaluating the competition

You can learn a lot from watching and analyzing the best behaviors of competitors. You need to know where you stack up in online reach, conversation, and engagement. Looking toward competitors for benchmarks is a common business practice.

Services such as Simply Measured (`http://simplymeasured.com`) compare and analyze you and your competition to determine who has the competitive edge. Simply Measured incorporates Facebook, Google+, Google Analytics, Instagram, Klout, Twitter, Vimeo, and YouTube. The analytics tool provides benchmarks for, and analysis of, how you and your competitors are faring across social networks in these areas:

- **Engagement rate:** This metric looks at your overall engagement and your competitor's engagement, and at which percentage of the conversation is original from your brand versus an @reply to an existing conversation. The difference here is important in order to measure true engagement and not simply broadcast messages.

- **Responsiveness:** Members of your community want to know that they can trust you. (See Chapter 4 to gain their trust.) Gauge your level of responsiveness in relation to the other businesses in your industry. We don't have to tell you that your customers expect you to reply when they reach out. You can generate reports that measure timeliness, response rate (as in the percentage of time you respond to an inbound tweet), and the length of the conversation.

- **Reach:** This term refers to the size and strength of your overall social presence in social networks, your fans and following, and their comments and likes, as compared to your competition.

Using a tool such as Simply Measured can help you identify realistic goals for your company's responsiveness as an essential part of SME. The manner and timeframe of your responses to queries in your social networks can clearly reveal your commitment to being present.

Note how present the competition is in their social networks and how engaged they are within their online communities. Learn from their successes *and* their failures. Improve on what they do well, and avoid what clearly isn't working.

Recording your own statistics over time is important; however, don't do it in a vacuum. Measure your engagement efforts against your competitors at least quarterly. Evaluating the competition isn't a one-time endeavor.

Search online to find ratings or reports on your industry's progress in SME. For example, the Vintank Brand Index measures how wineries are engaging on Facebook and Twitter and ranks them based on a number of factors, such as fan growth and interaction. Use these numbers to set goals for your own engagement activities.

Paying Attention to Demonstrate Presence

If you're paying attention, you know when your brand is being talked about online. When you listen to what is being said, you know what your next steps should be to properly engage.

Too many companies allow comments and questions to remain unanswered or unacknowledged on their pages. Dozens of comments per day may seem close to impossible to handle, but making a commitment and demonstrating presence goes a long way toward proving to customers and prospects that you value them.

Being notified when you need to engage

To stay on top of those mentions or conversations that need your attention or review, put monitoring tools and practices into place. Even when you aren't online, you need to be aware of what is being said to, and about, you.

We talk about the importance of listening in Chapter 4. You "listen" in social networks mostly by reading. You can read the streams of content that you see when you log in to social channels, but when you're not there, set up alerts and notifications to let you know when you need to respond.

Setting alerts and notifications

Follow the strategies described in this list to set up alerts and notifications:

✔ **Google Alerts** (www.google.com/alerts): As we describe in a sidebar in Chapter 4, these free alerts notify you anytime a name or keyword you've chosen is found in news articles, on blogs, or in the Google search engine (so it includes some public posts from forums and social networks). Simply fill out the alerts as we describe to make notifications arrive in your inbox.

- ✔ **Twitter** (`https://twitter.com`): The microblogging site allows snippets of conversation to happen 24 hours a day — 140 characters at a time. Your community will often use this tool to reach out with questions, thoughts, and concerns.

  You can use several tools to access Twitter. You can set some of these tools to notify you when designated keywords are mentioned in tweets, such as Echofon (`www.echofon.com`), TweetDeck (`www.tweetdeck.com`), and HootSuite (`http://hootsuite.com`). You can customize columns in TweetDeck and HootSuite to keep track of other people, trending topics, and even groups.

- ✔ **Facebook** (`https://www.facebook.com`): This site has both a personal and professional use, allowing you to engage with your audience at any time to hear feedback, share news, and have conversations.

  Use the Pages Manager app for iOS to receive notifications for all pages you manage. You can also receive notifications of mentions and interactions on your Facebook Page via e-mail and on your mobile device.

From your Facebook Page, go to Account Settings and select Notifications, and then choose ways to be notified (in addition to on Facebook, where you receive *all* notifications). You can also choose to be notified by e-mail, with numerous options; by push notification (as described in the following section), depending on which mobile app you're using to monitor Facebook; or by text, with additional breakdowns such as types of activities that trigger notifications and time frames for receiving them. You can read more about optimizing your SME on Facebook in Chapter 9.

See Chapter 4 for more options for listening tools that notify you and let you manage responses.

Set up multiple alerts so that you're notified whenever your brand name is mentioned — even if someone misspells it or uses your Twitter handle or any other variable to mention you, your company, team members, products, services, or related brands. Check out the nearby sidebar for more about setting and monitoring alerts.

Avoid falling behind or having to play catch-up. Missing important mentions exhibits weak customer relationships and a poor understanding of SME. Staying on top of alerts gives you time to respond and, if necessary, address team members to ensure that everyone is on the same page to properly respond.

Monitor this!

Set up alerts to monitor these items:

Name of your company

Common misspellings of your company's name

Names of key employees

Main product names

Website name (if it's different from the company's name)

Other brand names associated with your company

Company's Twitter handles

Company-specific keywords and hashtags

Industry-specific terms

Industry (or other) relevant keywords and hashtags

Names of primary competitors

Increasing efficiency with push notifications

A *push notification* is the friendly signal that new interactions have taken place on one of your social platforms. These notifications typically arrive via mobile device and, depending on the settings, announce that you've been mentioned on Twitter or that someone has liked, or commented on, an update on your Facebook Page, for example. These notifications can also come from social media management (SMM) tools such as HootSuite.

A push notification prompts you to respond. To turn these notifications on or off on your iPhone, iPod Touch, or iPad, follow these steps:

1. **Tap the Settings button on the Home screen.**

   Small gears appear on the button.

2. **Tap the Notifications button.**

   It looks like a red circle in the middle of a black square.

3. **Scroll down and tap the applications that you want to place in the Notifications Center.**

   Apps in the Notifications Center are listed at the top, with others below them. You can toggle this setting on or off by tapping each app.

To turn on push notifications on an Android device, you manage them in an individual app's settings. (An app may have notifications turned on by default.) In newer versions of the Android operating system, to disable unnecessary notifications so that you can focus on the ones that matter, simply tap and hold your finger on the notification the next time it pops up. From there, you'll be directed to the app management screen to deselect the Show Notifications option.

To be effective in SME and to demonstrate presence, avoid the impulse to respond immediately to every single notification. You should be able to see at least part of any comment being made in order to quickly assess its urgency and either respond quickly or put it aside to view later.

Responding to comments and following up

When you call a customer service line, you expect someone to answer the phone — even when you know that many customer service numbers are not manned 24/7. Even though the focus of SME is not to provide friendly phone calls or face-to-face interaction, your fans increasingly expect responsiveness. Somehow, SME promises more than a customer service call can deliver.

Because many companies are now responding effectively, consumers have increasingly high expectations. Rather than take traditional routes to praise and complain, they take to their social channels of choice — often, just to register frustrations about response times.

One brand that excels at "hearing" its customers in social networks and responding in a timely manner is Jockey. If you stop by its Facebook Page on any given day, you can see that questions, comments, and critiques are addressed individually — *all* of them.

Does Jockey have a perfect response or solution every time? No, but its customers definitely value being heard. As you can see in Figure 5-1, a customer thanked the company for its response, even though it wasn't the one she was seeking.

Figure 5-1: Openly expressing gratitude for a response.

Four Canadian moms, determined to label every item that their children might ever lose — from clothing to sippy cups, and from school supplies to stationery — founded the company Mabel's Labels. They relied heavily on social media engagement to build their brand and customer base.

From sponsoring giveaways to highlighting individual customers to inspiring Wow-I'm-a-mommy! moments (see Figure 5-2), the founders make it more than their job to connect, respond to, and reconnect with their more than 64,000 Facebook fans and more than 22,000 Twitter followers — it's their way of life. They receive more than 60 comments to a single question, and 20 comments deep, they respond to keep the conversation going.

Each connection, response, and follow-up you can make in your social channels solidifies your brand in a consumer's mind.

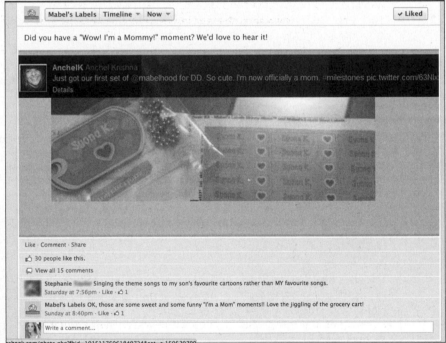

Figure 5-2: Posing questions and following up in the comments.

Establishing a Presence Process

Listening, responding, following up — all these activities take a lot of time, but they also demonstrate your commitment to being present in your social channels. We know that being present around the clock isn't a realistic option, so put in place strategic processes to ensure that your brand has presence even when the humans behind the brand aren't sitting behind their computers or holding their mobile devices.

Your presence process can include messaging that's precrafted *and* scheduled. When developing a plan that best serves your audience, allow your business goals to be your compass — and build from there. Whether you aim to increase brand awareness, build your audience, or sell a product, having a goal is only a start — you need a map to go along with that compass.

Before you embark on a vacation, you probably research to find the information you need and study some maps. As you embark on SME activities, you can benefit from doing similar research and developing a road map to guide your communications in your social channels.

In the beginning stages, the process for maintaining a visible social presence includes these steps:

1. **Identify your goals, the audience, and the actions you want to drive.**

2. **Assess your assets, such as the content you have (or that you can create) and the images and video at your disposal.**

3. **Locate your audience online wherever they congregate, communicate, and connect.**

4. **Choose the networks where you can best reach your audience.**

5. **Build and design your presence (possibly in multiple locations), and create any additional assets to properly benefit from each network.**

6. **Begin engaging strategically, by reaching out in the right way to the right people with the right messages.**

To get the engagement right, you have to do some planning, by answering these basic questions: How will you engage with others? What will you say? How will you say it? Who will you address? Where and when?

Before you start engaging online, your planning process should include two components: a social media messaging map and a social media editorial calendar. Those two tools serve as guides to maintaining messaging that's consistent, on-brand, and targeted while you're in the midst of communicating across social channels.

Creating a messaging map

As a business, you should have already established your brand and defined your voice and personality. Having a clear brand identity that informs all your messaging is part of both traditional marketing and online marketing.

With SME, a distinct character and an intrinsic understanding of the qualities of your brand guide the way you present yourself online. The words you use, the tone you adopt, the images you upload, and the way you respond to and interact with others defines the *you* that your audience knows and loves.

If you represent a brand, clearly specify the "personality" you use online. In most instances, companies use a brand personality that expresses a unified voice. Everyone on a company's social media team adopts that same identity for consistency. In some cases, allowing individual team members to be identified or to stand out is part of an overarching strategy to convey the brand's image.

A social media messaging map differs a little from other documents or tools that may be referred to as message maps. The document known as a *social media messaging map* is based on your brand qualities but also maps out these elements:

- ✓ Who you're trying to reach
- ✓ What you want to say to them
- ✓ How to attract their attention and engage them in conversation
- ✓ What actions you want to drive

A messaging map that's thoughtfully developed and clearly organized encourages conversations between your brand and your audience while acting as the North Star to keep your messaging on track. The messaging map then leads into the development of a social media editorial calendar, where you and your team craft posts and tweets that can help you start, and continue, conversations in your social channels. Together, these tools keep you and your brand present, consistent, and engaged.

Rather than rehash PR messages, look for ways to be conversational, share valuable information, tell stories, and inspire followers to respond because what you're saying in social networks is relevant to them. You can include marketing messages, but serve up more than commercials.

Developing a messaging map

Follow these steps to develop a social media messaging map:

1. **Describe your target market, audience, and tribe.**

   Specify who you're trying to reach. Suppose that you're a personal chef whose target is moms in their 40s. They're working, they're busy, they're harried, and they want to save time — but they don't want to sacrifice the health and needs of their families.

2. **Break out the segments of your target audience.**

Social networks have multilayered audiences. If they're relevant to you, be sure to address them or at least acknowledge them. Vendors, the media, and other stakeholders are all separate categories, for example. If your main target is moms in their 40s, secondary targets might be their partners, women's professional organizations, or websites and publications geared toward working moms and older moms.

3. **Get granular, by spelling out the demographics and psychographics of your core audiences.**

Describe the market segments in detail. (What do they like? How do they spend their days? What are their personality characteristics?) A target mom in her 40s is likely a working mom who is juggling work and life issues, and who may be struggling with healthy eating and fitness or with not spending enough time taking care of herself. She is solutions-oriented. She knows the 'what' when it comes to her problems, but struggles with the 'how to fix it' — this is where your brand enters with the answers.

4. **Identify the key interests of people in your market segments — the topics that resonate with them.**

The typical mom in her 40s seeks bite-size content, a supportive community, and time-saving tips, and she could use a little humor to brighten her day. She loves wine. She dreams of travel.

Taking a closer look at your target market is the first step in developing your social media messaging map.

Avoid making biased assumptions about your audience. You're not trying to stereotype as you develop your social media messaging map. Instead, flesh out your version of the ideal customer. Ask questions every step of the way to get to know your audience better and to refine your messaging.

Crafting messages to achieve your goals

After you identify your audience and the topics they're interested in, the next step in developing your social media messaging map is to craft some sample messaging, to refine its tone and wording. Follow these steps:

1. **Circle back to your goals.**

Knowing and serving the audience is useful, but staying close to your goals is also important as you craft messages. To continue the example in the preceding section, suppose that you're a personal chef targeting moms in their 40s. You want customers to hire you to prepare healthy, custom meals for themselves and their families. You also want satisfied customers to encourage their friends to hire you.

2. **Establish what types of posts to use.**

   You can develop many types of messages based on the audience and on your goals. A mix of the following elements maintains fresh and relevant content: *Announcements, Events, News, Special offers, Inspiration, and How to.*

3. **Come up with specific topic themes for messages that serve both your audience and your goals.**

   Combine everything that you've already considered, and then get *more* creative. Review your message types to home in on content themes geared toward moms in their 40s, such as

   a. *Announcements: This week's menu*

   b. *Events: Healthy food and wine tasting*

   c. *News: Online articles about women and their health issues*

   d. *Special offers: Refer-a-friend discounts*

   e. *Inspiration: Inspiring quotes*

   f. *How to: Quick time-savers*

4. **Craft sample messages geared toward each audience and goal.**

   a. *Announcements: Pinterest Menu Plan: 7 Meals in 30 Minutes or Less*

   b. *Events: Tweet: Join us for a Healthy food and wine tasting Thursday Evening from 6-8 (Include link to Facebook Event)*

   c. *News: Blog Post: 3 On-the-Go Breakfasts To Start Your Day Off Right (Can link from Facebook and Twitter)*

   d. *Special offers: VIP Refer-a-friend discounts for Facebook Friends only*

   e. *Inspiration: Quote: "Life is not merely being alive, but being well." ~ Marcus Valerius Martialis*

   f. *How to: Video: Prepare healthy Snacks for your Kid's Lunches (link on Blog, Facebook, Twitter and Pinterest)*

The content that results forms a grid specifying who you're trying to reach and the types of messaging you'll develop and post to reach them. Detail themes and topics that you'll incorporate each week in order to show consistency.

When you're consistent, your audience knows what to expect and becomes more inclined to participate. In fact, they'll look forward to upcoming content. The sample messaging should indicate tone and voice, down to specific wording, as shown in the social media messaging map in Figure 5-3, which we created by using an Excel spreadsheet.

Audiences:	Coach	Swimmer	Parent	Sponsor
Motivations & Interests	Looking to improve team skills. Set their team apart	Looking to do something cool, get inspired, meet celebrities, braggin rights	Looking to provide opportunities for their child, life lessons, lasting benefits	Looking to reach the next generation of customers, looking to reach parents
Types of Posts	Calls to Action	Conversation Starters	Testimonials	
Book the Event	SEND LAUNCH EMAIL (Create Facebook Event, Plancast, Eventful, submit to local online calendars)			
3 months out	FEATURE CHAMPION AND CELEBRITY SWIM INSTRUCTORS			
	Inspire your team	Get inspired	Treat your kid to inspiration and use this discount code today.	Be part of an inspiring event
2 months out	PROMOTE PRIZES FROM SPONSORS			
	Get free gear for your team	Win free gear	Your kid can win free gear	Get your gear in the hands of your next customers
6 weeks out	BUILD EXCITEMENT AND ENCOURAGE SHARING			
	Your team will gain powerful skills - encourage them to participate	You'll have an awesome time - let your friends know you're going	Your kid will have an experience of a lifetime. Share the inspiration.	Thanks to our sponsors X, Y & Z. Get buzz for your brand by being a part of this event.
4 weeks out	CREATE A SENSE OF URGENCY			
	Just 6 weeks left	Are you going?	Time is running out	It's time to get your brand in front of your ideal customers.
2 weeks out	FINAL PUSH			

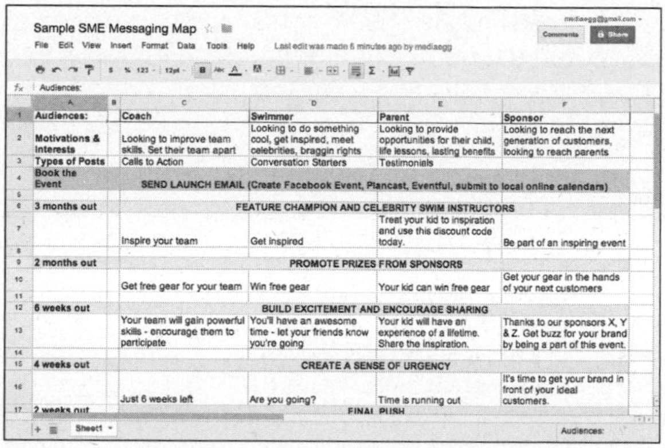

Figure 5-3: A sample social media messaging map.

REMEMBER

Tie your messaging to your goals. Flexibility (rather than rigidity) is important, and being responsive to conversations in real-time is critical. Just don't lose your overall focus.

A messaging map helps you build out a framework for an editorial calendar that includes specific types of messages — and the messages themselves. This calendar is the foundation of (and your guide to) communicating in your social networks.

Embracing the core themes of your social media messaging map gives you the perfect place to start when crafting the messages you share every day or week. Listening plays a major role in your daily engagement activities as well. Find a balance between marketing messages, responses, outreach, and interactions.

Developing a social media editorial calendar

Keeping up with the breakneck pace of social media can run you ragged. Is it time to tweet? Post to Google+? Pin a great-looking image? Publish a blog post? The social media editorial calendar is built on your goals *and* on the needs and desires of your audience. Working in tandem with the messaging map, the editorial calendar guides you to compose content that you'll publish and share in your social networks, and some of this content can be scheduled.

We're not recommending that you create formulaic or canned posts. We're encouraging you to be strategic, remain on-message, and clearly focus so that your messaging is more effective. We're giving you permission to schedule some messaging in advance to help alleviate the time pressures of being continually bound to your computer.

Experiment with easy-to-use and affordable social media management tools that let you schedule posts and tweets to a number of popular social networks, such as HootSuite, Buffer (`http://bufferapp.com`), and SproutSocial (`www.SproutSocial.com`).

Creating a calendar

You can use a number of tools to develop an editorial calendar. Start simple with an Excel spreadsheet or, if you're familiar with Google Docs (`http://docs.google.com`), a Google spreadsheet (our favorite). Then you can easily share with others and collaborate. Another online shared option is Zoho Docs (`https://www.zoho.com/docs`).

Populating the calendar

Follow these steps to populate your social media editorial calendar:

1. **Create a quarterly (3-month) spreadsheet.**

   Adding more months to the spreadsheet can become unwieldy; using fewer than three months creates more documents to manage.

2. **Create weekly tabs to cover the months you've specified.**

   Give the tabs names to help you recognize the week, such as Dec10-16, Dec17-23, and so on.

3. **Make a Template tab for weekly messaging.**

   This template serves as a baseline guide for subsequent weekly pages, to remind you of key topics and messaging.

4. **Add content columns.**

   Add these columns:

   a. *Day/Date:* The day of the week (Monday, Tuesday, Wednesday, and so on).

   b. *Events:* Online or offline events that also trigger messaging.

   c. *Post Topic:* Custom topics that you've created and types of posts that you've identified as interesting to your audience. In the example above, Crafting messages to achieve your goals, you would distribute the following topics in this column (not all in a single day, but repeatable weekly):

   This week's menu (every Monday)

   Healthy food and wine tasting (leading up to the event)

   Online articles about women and their health (one a day)

   Refer-a-friend discounts (a few times a week)

Inspiring quotes (one a day)

Quick time-savers (one a day)

    d. *Link:* The location where you want to drive traffic. Most posts should have links — to your own content or to others' content you're sharing.

    e. *Twitter/Facebook:* Rows for precrafting a number of tweets per day and a spot for a post based on that day's topic.

    f. *Other Channels:* Columns for additional channels as needed. Each channel has its own rhythm and content needs. If you're publishing regular video, for example, add YouTube. If you're trying to reach a more professional audience, add LinkedIn.

5. **Add repeatable messages to the Template tab.**

These messages are vital to helping you achieve your goals, and they can be time sensitive, such as an upcoming or ongoing Hire Us event. Even if you're repeating a message, revise the wording so that you don't sound like a broken record. Also note how topics in the Post Topics column repeat weekly.

6. **Copy and paste the template into each week's tab.**

Add the base template before filling in new content for each week so that you don't accidentally paste over your work.

7. **Begin filling in the blanks with conversational messages.**

Don't rely solely on the core topics and messaging in your calendar. Come up with additional messaging that is complementary and relevant.

Managing the calendar

We recommend filling in the editorial calendar *at least* a week in advance. Repeatable topics and messaging can be carried out over weeks at a time. Evergreen content (or content that is always interesting to readers because it isn't tied to a timeframe) can be moved around to accommodate more pressing messages. Look forward to what is happening, or to what you want to happen months from now. Keep holidays, special events, and seasons in mind if they affect your business.

Events that have fixed dates can immediately trigger messaging that leads up to the events and encourages people to register or to buy tickets. Craft this messaging as soon as you confirm the date, to ensure that they're added to your calendar. Come up with 15 different ways to say, "Come to our event in September," and then schedule those messages across your SME platforms during the weeks leading up to the event. This saves you from trying to remember every week and prompts your community to remember, purchase tickets if necessary, and then attend.

Taking the time to plan strategically around the core content you will publish during the next few months or the next year supplies you with a roadmap. Stay flexible in order to adapt to your roadmap and improve it. Having a social media messaging map and a social media editorial calendar in hand gives you more of a framework for establishing your presence in your social media channels. These tools keep that presence consistent and fresh.

Over the past few years, we've developed a social media editorial calendar, in the form of a spreadsheet. You can access the starter template at `http://bit.ly/smesmcal`. In Figure 5-4, you can see a section of a calendar that shows tweets and Facebook updates optimized for each social network.

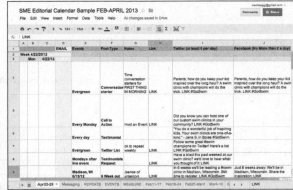

Figure 5-4:
A sample section of a social media editorial calendar.

Maintaining an editorial calendar for blog posts and campaigns is also useful.

Your community needs to hear from you in real-time. If you run your SME on autopilot, you risk turning off supporters and having them "unfollow" you. Use the calendar to plan ahead and to schedule some of your social media activity, but set time aside to regularly check in with fans and followers to reply to their queries, acknowledge their mentions, and engage with them.

Setting a Schedule

Social media really never stops. You can jump into any of your channels at any time of the day or night and find others there, too. You can add a tweet, a +1, a repin, or a post at any time to reach someone.

Just because you can do this, however, doesn't mean that you *should*.

Scheduling helps you establish a consistent presence online while helping you to better manage your time as you communicate and engage online. Your community wants to know when they can expect to hear from you, and you want to have regular visibility in their streams at the times that make the most sense for them — and for you.

Determining how frequently to update

People don't expect you to post around the clock, and — don't worry — they certainly aren't paying attention around the clock. Knowing when, and how often, to post requires some research and some observations as you engage.

Having an inconsistent social media presence is worse than having no presence. If your customers or prospects visit your Facebook Page or look you up on Twitter, only to find that you haven't posted anything in the past year or so, they'll likely think that you don't care much about your social media customers.

After you're using an editorial calendar and you have planned out portions of your social content, determine the best times of day for you to hop online to follow up. Plan to spend no more than 20 minutes at a time checking for replies, responding, and sending out in-the-moment messaging to drive engagement.

A fine line exists between updating too frequently and not often enough to make a blip on the busy radar of social networking.

To maintain a warm and attentive reception to your posts, share only relevant content that's useful to the followers you're trying to serve. Vet the content you post, especially if it originates from another source. Any content you publish or share should reflect your brand values. Providing value builds trust. See Chapter 4 for more on building trust so that the audience is receptive to your content.

Every social network is different in terms of how many posts per day is acceptable. Other variables in frequency include time zones and your goals. Given the many variables to posting frequency, Table 5-1 serves as a rough guideline. Modify these numbers based on your experiences over time.

Table 5-1	Posting Frequency on Popular Social Networks		
Social Network	*Minimum Frequency*	*Ideal Frequency*	*Tolerance for Multiple Posts*
Facebook	Daily	Once or twice per day	Low
LinkedIn	Daily	Once or twice per day	Moderate
Google+	Daily	Multiple times per day	Moderate
Twitter	Several times per day	Multiple times per day	High
Pinterest	Several times per day	Multiple times per day	High
YouTube	Weekly	Three or four times per week	Moderate
Instagram	A few times per week	Daily or more often	Moderate

If you're focusing more heavily on one social network over another, increase your posting frequency over time on that network to best serve your audience and your goals. Posting three to five times on Facebook isn't forbidden; however, it isn't the best use of your time either. The people who have liked your page just may unlike you if you post too often.

No one can give you a single correct answer for how often to post. All the studies in the world are only snapshots of tiny segments of the online population, and they may not reflect what you know to be true about your own audience.

Figuring out the best times to engage

Many social media experts will tell you that the greatest level of engagement on the four primary social platforms (Twitter, Facebook, LinkedIn, and Google+) occurs four times a day:

- ✔ First thing in the morning
- ✔ Lunch Time
- ✔ Mid-afternoon
- ✔ Early evening

Other experts will tell you to avoid evenings and weekends, whereas others emphasize the benefit of posting during those times and days.

Knowing your audience tells you far more about the best days and times to post to your social channels than any report or expert's opinion. If you're reaching out to parents, determine whether they're online and paying attention in the mornings while rushing to get their kids to school? On holidays when they're traveling? At dinnertime?

You can find out more about your followers' online habits over time by observing when they are more likely to respond. Shift the times on your posts until you hit the sweet spots. Ask followers what they prefer. Take a quick poll or survey specifically focused on their online habits and preferred destinations.

Depending on the time zone, it's safe to say that most of the social channels where you're trying to attract people's attention will quiet down at night. This isn't a hard-and-fast rule, but after you know the rhythms of your audience's schedule, you'll know when it's safe to assume that people you're trying to reach are asleep. We're not suggesting that you discount someone with insomnia, but chances are good that your messages won't generate the best outcomes at 3 a.m.

Base your posting timeframes more on your audience's time zones than on your own if yours don't match theirs. You might have to finagle your schedule; however, your goal is to reach the right people, not to put out well-crafted messages to the wrong audiences.

To get started, schedule your core messaging or arrange to be present in social media during "busy" times online:

- ✔ **Early morning (7 to 9 a.m.):** Many people quickly check in as they hurry themselves and their families out the door for the day.

- ✔ **Lunchtime (11 a.m. to 1 p.m.):** For people in the Midwest and on the east coast, it's nearly lunchtime; on the west coast, it's during the morning.

- ✔ **Midafternoon (1 to 3 p.m.):** An "after lunchtime" lull often occurs when people check in between tasks. Also, it's lunchtime on the west coast.

- ✔ **Early evening (7 to 9 p.m.):** As people settle down after dinner on the east coast, west coast residents are winding down their day. If your target market is on the west coast, you can skip the first timeframe and add another one even later to tap into the post-dinner social networking surge for them.

If you find your audience engaging with you during the morning and midday, but you notice responses waning in the evening, make adjustments to your schedule. If you find the opposite to be true, adjust accordingly. Continue to be present whenever and wherever your community wants to see you.

If your audience is international, you have more schedule-finessing to do. Consider hiring an assistant closer to the time zones where your core audience is located to help present a live presence in your social media channels at the most suitable times.

Deciding when to interact

How often you actively interact with followers can dictate your overall success with SME. A number of ways that you can interact are generally reactive or active. Here are some examples of reactive interaction:

- **Respond to public messages directed at you,** such as @mentions on Twitter or comments on your posts in Facebook, LinkedIn, YouTube, Google+, or other networks.

- **Respond to direct or private messages,** such as those on Facebook Page messages or direct messages (DMs) on Twitter.

- **Respond to mentions** that people make of you or your brand in social networks that you find via keyword or hashtag searches.

You can also interact more actively, by taking the initiative and reaching out to others, instead of waiting for them to mention or address you. Here are some active ways to interact:

- Share content from others such as retweets, repins, and post shares.

- Give kudos to others by linking directly to their content.

- Identify your target market or key influencers, follow them, and engage them in conversation.

Establish the best process for you by combining scheduled messaging and live responses with active engagement.

Don't post the wrong content at the wrong time. Before you start posting live — or even if you have messages scheduled — take time to review topics being discussed, including trending topics, to avoid posting cheery content at the same moment that news is breaking of a natural disaster or national tragedy.

Replying to every greeting and query on your social media channels may seem impossible. Increased opportunities to engage with customers and prospects in social channels can be a good problem to have, but it may require that you ramp up resources to connect with others where they want to connect with you.

Social media engagement should be a fulfilling aspect of your online marketing efforts. Don't plan every moment of every day. If you want to communicate and connect with someone, don't be afraid to do it simply because it isn't "on your calendar."

Chapter 6

Creating Connections

In This Chapter

▶ Defining your short- and long-term goals

▶ Pinpointing your audience and how they behave online

▶ Giving your audience the floor

▶ Motivating the exchange of ideas between you and your audience

*I*n this chapter, we tackle the importance of making contacts and connections as part of your social media engagement (SME). With each new connection, you inch closer to reaching the place where you belong in this space. You want to be a part of the online community, not merely a company that people watch from afar, and you want your connections to produce truly positive outcomes.

The book you're holding in your hands is one of many positive outcomes resulting from engaging in social media. Our own online connections and conversations on Twitter and Facebook led first to in-person meetings and then to our first joint book deal for *Mom, Incorporated: A Guide to Business + Baby*. If we weren't active in social networks — cultivating real connections and building genuine relationships — this book deal (our second) would have never happened.

With every new engagement, you find not only what most interests and satisfies your audience but also how you can work with your audience for mutual benefit. Each time you engage online, you make your brand more accessible and available for something big to happen: real connections.

Starting with Your Connection Goals

Settle in and prepare to get your hands dirty. We know that we aren't the first to preach that you should set goals and measure your progress. Establishing these goals determines not only where you're going but also how to get there and who to take along for the ride. You've identified your audience and you know where they spend most of their time online. Now you need to draw more and more people into your conversations.

The more vibrant your conversation, the more opportunities you create for yourself and your brand. We want you to set your SME goals, both short-term and long-term, so that your efforts to connect are grounded in a cohesive strategy with measurable outcomes.

Goals inspire you to shoot for the moon, to push past the limits of what you imagine you can accomplish, and to set reasonable milestones to track your progress. Plan to create at least two lists: short-term goals (the ones that you feel you can achieve more easily) and long-term goals (the ones that may seem slightly out of reach but that, with perseverance, can be reached).

Social media engagement focuses not on one-hit wonders but rather on a longer plan for interacting and connecting in order to continue the conversations and conversions. Your short-term goals should be to build toward your long-term goals.

Setting short-term goals

Align your short-term goals in social media engagement with your short-term business goals, as in these examples:

- ✔ **Increase traffic to your website.** You can achieve this goal within a few months of diligent engagement, and it can compel you to start leveraging your social media connections.

- ✔ **Accelerate word-of-mouth communication.** Though this method is a little more difficult to measure than web traffic, mentions that appear in social media — especially by social media influencers or people with larger or more loyal followings — can increase your brand exposure.

- ✔ **Make specific actions happen.** Whether you're asking people to fill out a form or to sign up for a contest or attend an event, your connections should boost actions where you can see more immediate and tangible results.

Your goals, which are often reflected in your business plan and informed by your company's mission statement, should infuse your presence online with purpose and define the way your company communicates and operates daily.

The mission of Little Pnuts (http://littlepnuts.com) — a subscription toy company with organic, ecofriendly, and natural toys designed for your "little pnuts" — is to entice kids to move off the couch to start playing and to provide families with the tools to create imaginative play. One way the company works to reach its mission is to interact with parents on its Facebook Fan Page, as shown in Figure 6-1.

Figure 6-1:
Little
Pnuts uses
Facebook
daily to
engage with
parents to
achieve a
short-term
goal.

At the end of each day, Little Pnuts founder Melissa Bossola Beese asks herself, if she was able to provide children with skillful, play-filled experiences. She analyzes and measures the engagement on Facebook and Twitter to determine if she's hitting at least one short-term goal.

Share your successes with your team to maintain morale and with your audience to highlight the milestones you're achieving with their help. When you reach 1,000 likes on Facebook, tell your audience how excited you are, as Little Pnuts does in Figure 6-2. Honor your followers and connections by saying that you appreciate them and their interaction. Your community will enjoy celebrating with you.

Figure 6-2:
An
announce-
ment and
gift for the
Little Pnuts
community
member
whose Like is
number 1,000
on Facebook.

Here are some examples of measurable and achievable short-term goals to attract, build, and strengthen connections:

- ✔ Start an editorial calendar to produce more strategic content.
- ✔ Add a subscription form to your website, and when you reach 50 subscribers, send a newsletter.
- ✔ Share your blog posts on Twitter, Facebook, and LinkedIn to attract more attention.
- ✔ Create five new boards on Pinterest.
- ✔ Generate one or two Likes on every Facebook post.
- ✔ Produce a new video to upload to YouTube every week to attract attention and build your following.

Establishing longer-term goals

Start thinking about specific goals you want to set in order to push you, your brand, or your business into the next realm, as in these examples of longer-term goals for your connections within the next six months:

- ✔ Increase traffic to your website by 50 percent.
- ✔ Receive five glowing reviews of your company in online forums.
- ✔ Double or triple the number of connections in your social media channel.
- ✔ Increase engagement in your social media channels by 10 percent.
- ✔ Increase revenue by 10 percent via direct referrals from Twitter and Facebook.

Set a specific time every quarter to assess your progress and (you hope) to celebrate wins.

If you're reaching your long-term goals easily, head back to the drawing board and push harder. You should be working for your long-term goals, not merely resting on your haunches while watching the good ship of success sail into your harbor.

Saying thank you is powerful. As you reach goals, share your successes with your team. They deserve to know what they've done well — it motivates them to continue. The same is true for your audience: Let them celebrate your success with you. Knowing that they have contributed by liking, commenting on, or sharing your content brings them back for more.

Identifying Your Audience

After you determine that you *want* to create connections, labor over goal-setting, and specify how you want your brand to evolve, you now know that you need the people — the *audience* — to make it happen. You need to find people who not only want to hear from you but also interact with your brand and share your brand messages with others.

Let's do it together.

Determining who you're trying to reach

Understanding who your audience is helps you find them online and determine the best ways to reach out to them to engage. If you sell kids' sporting equipment, for example, you likely need an audience of coaches or parents (or both) who have young children. If you're a florist wanting to specialize in weddings, your targets are likely brides and wedding planners. Recent statistics say that the average age of a bride in the United States is 25. Clearly, these audiences are unique.

Figuring out who you want to reach via your social media channels is a process that you may have already tackled while determining the target customers for your business. Use a combination of these factors to identify them:

- ✔ **Demographics:** Facts about individuals, including sex, age, education level, income level, and geographic location
- ✔ **Psychographics:** Psychological profile of people such as activities, actions, interests, behavior, attitudes, and values
- ✔ **Online presence:** Web locations where people have created platforms and are actively engaging with their own followings

Seek out the people who will be the most interested in your messages and content — the ones who are most likely to respond to you as you spend time engaging online.

Finding your audience online

Say that you sell kids' sporting equipment, such as inline hockey skates and masks, sticks, aluminum bats, and catcher's gear for baseball and also softball, football, and soccer cleats, goalie gloves — if a kid needs gear for sports, you sell it. You know you need to reach coaches and parents of young kids involved in sports. Here are some ways to find your audience, or (in marketing-speak) your *market segment:*

- ✔ **Search engines:** Be specific about keywords and even geography. Search for *kids sports in St. Louis, MO* or *coaches in St. Louis, MO* or *Parent, St. Louis.* You'll see sites and blogs to explore as well as forums, groups, and even people whose presence on social channels may be attracting your ideal audience. Coaches or even parents may have online presences that include their social media contact information listed right on their sites so that you can follow them on Twitter, for example, to establish an initial connection.

- ✔ **Social media channels:** Take advantage of search options on these channels at Twitter, Facebook, LinkedIn, YouTube, and even Pinterest. Use a variety of keywords and keyword combinations such as *sports, kids sports, sporting equipment, coach, kid coaching,* and the names of individual sports or locations, such as *St. Louis.*

   The useful tool SocialBro (www.socialbro.com) can search the bios of people on Twitter and narrow them to specific locations. If someone is identified using the word *coach* in Missouri, for example, (and there are 278 of them), the results may be people to connect with and reach out to.

- ✔ **Online conversations:** Seek out people who are talking about the topics that matter the most to you, such as kids and sports in St. Louis. Use a site such as Hashtags (www.hashtags.org) to search for people talking about St. Louis or individual sports or kids using particular hashtags.

Naturally, when you find all the "right" people, you still need to know more about them to determine whether a coach is the type you're looking for and then see whether she is active online, and *how* she's active, to identify your greatest opportunities for connecting.

Figuring out what your audience does online

Lace up your researching shoes. After you find your audience, you must determine what they're doing with their time while they're online, such as viewing images on Pinterest, quickly reading Facebook posts and clicking the Like button, or staying glued to job postings at LinkedIn. You need to know, for example, whether they would sit still to watch a 2-minute video or bolt after the first 15 seconds.

Research the activities of your audience

If your audience spends their time on Pinterest, check their Activity Feeds to see what topics catch their eye. If they're active on Facebook but mostly skim posts and click the Like button a few times, assess the topics they're liking versus the ones they take the time to share. If someone is more active on LinkedIn, a more business-oriented approach makes sense. If they watch and share videos online, YouTube may be a source of valuable connections for you.

We often mention the importance of listening, yet it bears repeating: The people you want to reach will tell you — directly in their SME channels — where they are and what they're doing. Whether they're heading to the pool, coaching a Little League game, or shopping for a birthday gift, people are using their social networks to announce their day-to-day activities — often, for the whole world to see. These announcements can give you greater insight into your target audience.

All the updating and sharing that people do online tells you something about your audience — what interests them and where you can find them. You certainly can't be everywhere, every day, but you can begin to narrow down the number of spots where they update, the times of day that they're online, and the topics that truly interest them. With this information, you can create better connections.

Connecting is about people, not about software or applications. Take the time to read people's bios and profiles and approach them to connect with no expectations or demands. Your technique — kindness, attentiveness, and interest — matters more in terms of your SME than the tools you use.

Use a personal account to research social networks where brands and companies have more limited views. Perusing only your own, personal connections can give you insights into how people who may fit your target audience are using social networks. And your personal contacts can also be some of your first connections as you spread the word about your business.

Use analytics tools

Use the free tools provided by Google Analytics as your guide to identify where your audience was online immediately before visiting your website or blog. This is a decent indicator of what they do online and which sources or platforms they trust to guide them to new content.

An alternative would be a site like Sumall.com (www.sumall.com), where all the math is done for you. You can view your daily, weekly, or monthly stats with only a few clicks — allowing you to track sales, your social media activities, and any trends. You can also have this data sent right to you. Sumall offers a free plan as well as paid versions.

Knowing that people come to your site from Facebook, Twitter, or Pinterest helps you to target your efforts to make connections. Track your analytics to see whether engaging on the appropriate networks drives even more traffic your way.

Ask questions — and listen to the answers

Ask your current followers to keep you updated on what they're doing or to gauge their interest in your products and services. Then listen to their responses to find ways to increase your connections with them by engaging in more interesting and relevant ways.

Creating a Space for Engagement

Building and cultivating a space built specifically for the purpose of engagement establishes you as a leader in your field. Your audience will grow to know your platforms are the place to go for quality dialogue, as well as a diversity of opinions.

Nurturing this type of open conversation requires your presence and your willingness to monitor the chatter for quality. In some cases, you can just ask for what you want, to encourage the interactions to happen. At other times, you must nurture the environment for the conversations to take place. Either way, be proactive and make things happen — don't build your social network profiles and expect people to connect simply because you're there.

Setting ground rules for participation

When you start conversations in any of your social media channels, especially when asking for opinions, you should also *moderate* the responses — pay attention, keep the conversations on topic, and join in whenever relevant. You should also supervise the conversations and remove any inappropriate material.

Set ground rules for people who are participating in your online community, to maintain positive and appropriate conversation topics. (See more about managing online communities apart from social networks in Chapter 8.)

Offering a forum for opinions

Knowing what your audience thinks, how they feel, and what motivates their daily activity helps you better serve them as well as convert them into customers and evangelists for your brand. Your social media channels are forums where you can interact with your audience and glean insights into their behaviors as consumers. You see what they think of your brand and help them connect with other like-minded individuals.

The easiest way to dip your toes into community engagement is to ask people for their opinions. You can always get people talking if you give them the floor. People can be quite opinionated, so soliciting their thoughts can start the conversation.

Though you want people to give specific opinions about your business, you need to build both momentum and trust so that they feel comfortable telling you what they think and feel. Explore these opinion-based topics for starters:

- ✓ **Noncontroversial current events:** If you own a jewelry store, ask people's opinions on Valentine's Day of the most romantic date for the occasion or the most romantic way to propose. Eventually, the conversation can turn to jewelry as a natural progression originating from the community rather than from you.

- ✓ **Charitable causes:** If you sell baby clothing, share a positive news article about an organization that distributes donated baby clothes to families in need. Ask people for their thoughts on this cause and what they might have in their own attics collecting dust that they would be willing to give to a similar local cause. Then your whole community can rally behind some good news and dedicated efforts in your company's name.

- ✓ **Ways to help others:** If you offer math tutoring, ask your community for their best math tips, how to multiply or work with fractions. People love to show off what they know, and they can gain useful knowledge from their peers. Contribute to the conversation yourself and demonstrate your expertise, or compile the tips in a PDF file — giving everyone credit — to share for free with your community.

Look for ways that you can start and guide conversations to encourage participation and give and receive value from those interactions. Soliciting opinions is a helpful way to start.

A quick and easy way to solicit opinions is to ask questions in a poll. You can use various applications within social networks, such as polling apps in Facebook or LinkedIn Groups or polling apps from SurveyMonkey (`http://surveymonkey.com`), Polldaddy (`http://polldaddy.com`), Wufoo (`http://wufoo.com`), and Pollcode (`http://pollcode.com`). Post poll results to keep the conversations going.

Showcasing what others know and do

You know what's amazing? Building a community where people can share ideas to make everyone better, smarter, and more informed. Doing this requires more than simply publishing your content, however.

We mention elsewhere that you need to talk about more than your company or the products and services that you're trying to sell in social networks. Your SME efforts need to be about others, not just *you*.

You can showcase others as a meaningful part of your messaging and social media publishing and interactions in many ways:

- ✔ Interview people for your website, blog, or social channels.
- ✔ Solicit guest posts from your audience and partners.
- ✔ Highlight other people's work.
- ✔ Praise and celebrate people's achievements.
- ✔ Promote other people's products or services that are compatible with yours.
- ✔ Share other people's expertise with your following, giving those experts full credit.

Cultivate an online community where you give credit where credit is due, where you promote and recognize your community members, and where you generously devote part of your online messaging and content to showcase others.

When you behave generously and kindly in social networks, you'll be rewarded with more likes, more follows, and more shares. People are more likely to gravitate toward brands that realize SME is more than a one-way street and that a person's followers and connections have a treasure trove of stories worth sharing.

Getting the Engagement Ball Rolling

Let's be honest: *Engagement* isn't exactly happening unless you create the atmosphere and then actually get the ball rolling. Initially, you're talking, tweeting, podcasting, posting on Facebook, or adding people to your circle of friends on Google+, and you may only see a whisper or an echo in response, but it is your job to encourage your audience to reply. In order to create the valuable connections that lead to opportunities and success, you need for your audience to truly respond.

And for that, you often need to begin by asking.

Asking for action

You've undoubtedly been told that you have to ask for what you want. The author and motivational speaker Shakti Gawain is quoted as saying, "You create your opportunities by asking for them." She's right.

You may think that you want more fans, more followers, more likes, more pins, more comments, or more shares. Yes, you want more engagement. But what you really want is to make connections and build relationships and then turn those relationships into mutually beneficial exchanges. You start by asking for connections.

Depending on the social network you're using, you can boost connections by asking people to take various actions on your behalf:

- ✔ **Like your Facebook Page or follow your brand:** Spell out what connecting with you provides, or offer an incentive.

- ✔ **Encourage their own connections to connect with you:** Offer an incentive for people to invite their friends to connect, but also be valuable, useful, helpful, and interesting enough that people will want to spread the word.

- ✔ **Like a post:** Craft likeable content, and every now and then, request a 'like' within your actual post. Don't overdo it.

- ✔ **Share or retweet your content so that you can make more connections:** Post content worth sharing, but also ask others to share specific content strategically when it matters most.

In Chapter 8, we talk about increasing your e-mail sign-ups and prompting your subscribers to become fans. This happens, in large part, because you're asking and encouraging them to do so. Every social network and online marketing tool can be used to build your overall social media connections. Look for ways to cross-promote your social media channels.

On Facebook, you can ask your fans to follow you on Twitter to receive more frequent updates. On Twitter, you can ask followers to also like your Fan Page in order to receive more in-depth posts and special offers. On YouTube, you can add annotations to individual videos saying "Subscribe to my channel" or asking for a thumbs-up. Figure 6-3 shows how Danielle uses annotations regularly on her videos to encourage engagement. She asks for connections or actions, such as giving a thumbs-up at a specific point.

You risk alienating your current connections if you go overboard with requests. There's a fine line between regularly asking people to follow you and asking so often that people become annoyed and start ignoring you.

Figure 6-3:
Danielle
adds anno-
tations to
her videos.

You may make a request for a connection and fail to follow through by responding when your audience reaches out. For example, if your Facebook fans follow you on Twitter and then you miss the opportunity to interact with them there, you've just blown it — you've asked them to do something without holding up your end of the deal. Don't ask if you can't follow through when people comply and connect.

Be clear about wanting people to connect with you. Show them, tell them, guide them, virtually hold their hands, walk them to your Like button and say "Click here." Be direct, but also be creative, fun, and spontaneous. Create excitement.

Offering rewards for action

The photo-printing company Shutterfly wants more people to like its Facebook Fan Page, so it blatantly offers a surprise incentive to encourage people to connect, as shown in Figure 6-4.

Everyone who likes the Shutterfly page receives a special code for a *free* (not discount) product when they use the photo service — which may have contributed to the site gaining more than a million Likes.

In addition to engaging regularly on its page to demonstrate attention and interest, Shutterfly is increasing connections with its audience by overtly telling people what they want — a Like — then thanking them for doing so with a special gift. Incentives can do wonders to increase connections.

Figure 6-4:
Shutterfly
has a spe-
cial gift for
you, but first
you have
to like its
Facebook
Fan Page.

Handling negative feedback

When you give people a platform to express themselves and share their opinions, you may not always receive in return the positive feedback you want.
Some people may be true fans, but others will see the platform as a place to
air their grievances. Be prepared.

Providing a platform where everyone can express themselves comes with
great responsibility. You must pay attention and be responsive. As we say
repeatedly, any "bad" feedback is an opportunity to turn a negative into a
positive.

Someone who has had a horrible experience at your restaurant and wants to
share their thoughts will do so with or without you, in social media channels
that you can control (ideally), such as on Facebook or in a LinkedIn Group
or in other places where you have no control, such as a Twitter feed or
Pinterest stream. We encourage you to continue asking for people's opinions,
even if you risk hearing information that's difficult to accept.

You can't solve every problem, and you can't make everyone happy. But you
can try. Make your best effort to address concerns expressed in social networks.

Seizing opportunities to do good

On Friday, December 14, 2012, the online and offline world held its collective breath as news of a tragedy in Newtown, Connecticut, trickled out. The senseless loss of 20 small children and six adults devastated a community, a nation, and the world, and many people learned of the details by way of moment-by-moment posts on social networks. The pain that everyone felt was expressed repeatedly on Twitter, Facebook, and other sites. People wanted to do something to help, but felt helpless. The weekend following the tragedy, one attentive and caring brand did something, and it all began in social networks.

Blogger Victoria Haller lost her six-year-old nephew, Noah Pozner, in the Sandy Hook school massacre. Noah's funeral was held the Monday after the tragedy, and Victoria's family wasn't able to attend. The family had hand-written letters, including some from Victoria's children — Noah's cousins — that they and Noah's parents wanted buried with the child. Victoria tweeted to JetBlue and another airline for help delivering the letters from her home in Washington state to Connecticut in time for the funeral. JetBlue responded immediately and made it happen, flying the letters from Seattle to New York and then to Connecticut.

See the exchange between Haller and JetBlue in the figure. In the same exchange, JetBlue actively and sensitively responded to Victoria as well as to feedback from other people online. This quick and thoughtful action on the part of JetBlue created a moment, initiated by the brand, that many people will remember. JetBlue didn't have to help. They didn't have to respond when Victoria sent them a tweet. And yet they did. They took their online presence and created a meaningful, lasting connection that reverberated throughout social networks and even in the press.

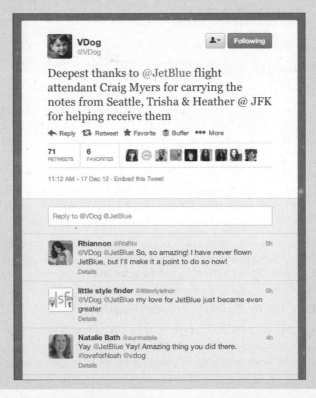

Think of ways to go "above and beyond" because it's the right thing to do, not because it will win you points in your social media engagement. Using your social networks to find opportunities to help or give back or otherwise shine, with no expectation of acknowledgement or reward, can make the difference between run-of-the-mill and superior engagement.

Remember: Avoid jumping on a tragedy in the news in an obvious, self-serving way — or be prepared for a damaging backlash. Pay attention, be sensitive, and never try to capitalize on trending topics inappropriately.

Whenever you're confronted with negative feedback, follow these steps:

1. **Review the context.**

   When you see a negative comment, dig a little deeper to make sure that you understand what's being said and why. Read conversation threads, and conduct searches on search engines to see whether you can find additional, related conversations.

2. **Acknowledge the feedback.**

   After you gain a sense of the emotion — and the facts — behind a complaint, address these issues in your response. Use acknowledgment statements such as "I understand your frustration" or "We realize that this situation is stressful." Validate the other person's feelings and perceptions whether or not they're accurate or shared by you.

3. **Address the issue promptly.**

   Timeliness is essential when you're handling and defusing negativity online. Every day, hour, or minute that you spend agonizing over your next action is valuable time wasted.

4. **Apologize.**

   When people are unhappy, a simple "I'm sorry" can do wonders to calm them. Even if you clarify the statement by saying, "I'm sorry that you feel that way — how can we help?" you're showing that you care how they feel without admitting blame when it might not be your fault. Of course, if you're at fault, admitting it is also important.

   If you're upset, nervous, worried, or shocked or you're experiencing any natural human emotions, gather your courage and express it in your response. People don't want to hear overproduced, formulaic, or canned replies to their concerns.

5. **Share the feedback with your community.**

   Explain what you're doing every step of the way so that people see progress. Keep in mind, that the person complaining or venting isn't the only one who sees what you have to say. The rest of your online community does, too.

Some people complain simply because they want to be heard. Even using the phrase "We hear you" can diffuse anger when they realize that someone from your company is listening and responding.

When confronted with negativity about your brand online, you have the chance to respond in front of everyone who is listening. Your entire online community, and the public at large, potentially have a front-row seat to observe how you listen, clarify what happened, and apologize.

Chapter 7

Driving Interaction

· ·

In This Chapter

▶ Laying the groundwork for interacting

▶ Adopting trending topics as conversation starters

▶ Advocating humor as a means of engagement

▶ Providing incentive for sharing

· ·

*I*n earlier chapters of this book, we tell you how to help your brand build trust, maintain a social presence, and create connections as the core elements of social media engagement (SME). You can use a combination of these elements to then drive interaction, which is the topic of this chapter.

On the surface, as we initially discuss in Chapter 1, SME consists of reactions, interactions, and actions. A *reaction* is a fan's quick-and-easy response to the content you share by way of social media, such as liking and favoriting. *Interaction*, which is ongoing (ideally), is the daily, back-and-forth communication between you and the members of your online community, your customers and prospects, and even the public at large, if you cast a wide net. Interaction isn't only the icing on the cake — it is the cake. An *action* — which requires the most effort on the part of your audience — is a definitive activity that takes place, such as when someone signs an online petition, fills out a survey, requests information, or buys a product.

In this chapter, we tackle the icing and the cake: the actions that your community takes daily and then how to make interaction happen, how to inspire members to continue participating, and how to inspire your community to start that level of engagement with you.

Creating the Setting to Stimulate Engagement

Social media engagement is a continuous process of being present, connecting, and sparking conversations. Everything you do at first sets the stage for meaningful interaction with your community that in turn leads them to action.

When you prepare your social media engagement strategies, and follow through on them, you're setting the stage for — and then becoming an integral part of — the action, reaction, and interaction that follows. Engaging is a give-and-take proposition: It's one part proactive and one part reactive, with a healthy dollop of heart and soul. You may be representing your company, but you're a human being, even behind the brand and logo. To want to make the choice to engage, your community must feel a level of comfort with you. For them, it's a choice — help them make the right one.

Moving past the what's-in-it-for-me? mentality

No one likes the person at the party who can't stop talking about himself. One great temptation that you may have to work to overcome is the compulsion to share your product obsessively. Avoid the hard sell. Resist the urge to talk about "me-me-me." Keep in mind that you do in fact have a product or service that you want people to buy: It's *you*. Every time you push your services or focus solely on your products (rather than on your community) or even forget about your audience entirely, you lose.

Social media is first and foremost social. Your fans on Facebook, for example, want to know that you're more than a logo. The people following you on Pinterest want to see in your pins what you like, not simply your own products. On Google+, your community shares your content because they like what you have to say, not because they want to help you sell something. (We cover these three platforms in Chapters 9, 11, and 13, respectively.)

Eighty percent of the content you share as you engage on your social media platforms should showcase your personality, share other people's contribution, or highlight content that you think your audience would find valuable. Reserve the remaining 20 percent for links to your own content.

Building a space where people feel comfortable

Consider the places you feel most at home, where you can kick your feet up, say what you mean, and mean what you say. These social media platforms or forums may help you experience a certain level of comfort knowing that you can speak your mind without judgment and feel that you're valued.

Whether you're creating a community on Facebook, responding to tweets on Twitter, or chatting with your circles on Google+, look to build a space that feels comfortable for your audience. Create a place where everyone can be

- ✔ **Heard:** Let people know that you're listening and that you hear what they have to say. An environment that encourages open dialogue, answers questions, and offers valuable information creates a certain level of comfort.

- ✔ **Human:** Knowing that the live humans who are behind the brand care about the community matters to your supporters. Whether you're chatting and answering questions, offering VIP incentives (described later in this chapter, in the section "Providing Additional Incentives for Sharing"), or responding to frustration, your audience wants to know that you have emotions as well.

- ✔ **Humble:** On any social platform that your brand manages, you have the opportunity to talk about any topic you want. Choose to make the topics of conversation more about your community than about you. Your fans will be honored that you focus on them, and they'll be pleased that you avoid hard-sell tactics.

Certainly, it's impossible to reach a level of perfection with everyone, but you should aim to create an environment that elicits enough comfort to encourage engagement.

A simple tip for getting your work shared beyond your current social media engagement platforms is this: *Ask.* Is it possible that getting people to share your message is simpler than you imagine? Engaging has always required strategy, planning, plotting, and reassessing, but sometimes, simply asking people to share, repost, retweet, or reblog prompts them to take that action.

Inspiring others to pay attention and care

The social media landscape is chock-full of people, brands, and businesses vying for attention. Everyone wants a slice of the pie. The challenge lies in attracting the level of attention you want without having to take to the sky, for example, with a message banner trailing an airborne biplane. (Even using that method, you would have to persuade people to point their noses skyward — and away from their mobile devices!)

Your next steps are to do all the little things, which we describe in this list, that encourage your audience to engage with your content because it matters to them:

- ✔ **Provide quality content.** We can't stress this point enough: Everything that you post online, on any of your platforms, must appropriately reflect your brand. If you provide thoughtful links, blog posts, and tweets, fans gravitate to you. Become known in your market as the go-to person or brand for useful and relevant information.

- ✔ **Stimulate conversation.** Ask interesting questions. Share funny stories. Inspire your community to contemplate a topic. To encourage dialogue, initiate a conversation — rather than send link after link into the wide open social media space. A compelling question or idea can motivate your community members to respond; a lonely link can turn them away from the conversation.

- ✔ **Maintain visibility.** The more present you are online, the more easily others can communicate with you regularly. If your community sees you and follows you on multiple platforms, and sees the quality content you've shared, they're more likely — and able — to engage with you.

- ✔ **Know when silence is golden.** This statement may seem to be a direct contradiction of our advice in the second paragraph in this list, but it isn't. We simply mean that you have to recognize when enough is enough. Don't clog your platforms with unnecessary ramblings. Make every post, tweet, and video count. Your audience doesn't need to be bombarded by news of every move that your brand makes or every meal that you're consuming — unless those events properly reflect your brand. Trying to keep up with too much information can overwhelm your community, and rather than pay attention, they might even tune you out.

- ✔ **Remember that kindness is king.** This is important: Share relevant material from other people whom you trust and admire. Then not only do you strengthen relationships with others by praising them but your community also appreciates hearing this information from you — and you build your following in the process.

✔ **Emphasize your brand.** If your brand has a unique characteristic, embrace it. If your brand contributes to a particular cause, talk about it. If a popular celebrity wears your brand's clothes, for example, show that person in a video. As shown in Figure 7-1, the soccer superstar David Beckham was featured in a video that the clothing store H&M released on Google+ (to much approval from the brand's fans). Whether you create makeup tutorials, answer tax questions in early April, or specialize in dog training, embrace what you do well — and in your own way.

Figure 7-1:
The soccer superstar David Beckham helps showcase a clothing store.

Starting Conversations

With the goal of inspiring dialogue as a starting point, consider the ways that you might strike up a conversation with a stranger at a party. You certainly wouldn't walk up with your business card in your outstretched hand. You wouldn't shout, begin the conversation with a monologue about your achievements in business, or say hello and then walk away — not if you hoped that the person would ever respond to you and interact with you.

Conversations about you happen online whether you're there or not. Your goal is to be a part of them, by listening, starting related conversations, joining others, and doing so appropriately. Knowing what to talk about can be half the battle.

Tapping in to trending topics

Finding universal themes that resonate with your audience can start the conversation. Current events and trending topics make for interesting fodder for dialogue with your community and fans. Be thoughtful in the way you discuss major world or national events when you engage online, and look for common ground with your audience to strengthen your connections.

Don't talk about current events gratuitously, expect publicity, or turn your expressions of concern or support into sales pitches. Be sincere and use good taste when you start speaking about sensitive topics online. Keep the sales pitches separate lest you become considered both insensitive and opportunistic.

During the October 2012 disaster of Hurricane Sandy — a topic that was on everyone's minds and trending on every social network — many brands punctuated their traditional platform messaging with thoughts and prayers and offers of assistance for people on the East Coast who were struggling. Delta Airlines, for example, offered condolences by way of its Twitter account to those affected by the storm, and it continued to respond to its community members who had questions about flights in the wake of the storm, as shown in Figure 7-2.

Trending topics can inspire creativity as you carry on conversations in your social media platforms. For example, February 22 is National Margarita Day. Who knew? But National Margarita Day was then a trending topic for two days in a row in 2013. For many businesses — restaurants, in particular — using the word *margarita* in their messaging helped make their message more visible.

Ask yourself: What are people talking about right now? Then join the conversation — but only if it's a fit for your brand. If it happens to be a particularly slow news day or you determine that the trending topics are too controversial or not reflective of your brand, head to Google Trends (www.google.com/trends) to see what other topics are trending online.

Lighting a fire with hot-button issues

If you want to light a communication spark, tackle the truly hot-button issues of any given day. But be prepared for potential backlash, and above all, make sure that these topics align with the image of your brand.

If you decide to wade into the waters of politics, religion, or culture, you will most certainly see some responses. Not everyone will agree with you, and some may even be negative and unkind. If your brand wants to side with a political candidate, express an opinion about the resignation of a church or government official, or take a stand on gun control, women's rights, or same-sex marriage, you will see a divide in your community. Some will staunchly support you, and others will fall away, unfollow, unsubscribe, or unlike.

Figure 7-2:
The Delta
Twitter
feed, during
Hurricane
Sandy.

After you initiate a controversial conversation, follow these guidelines as you continue to engage:

✔ **Stick to clearly worded statements.** For example, rather than post an editorial opinion about a politician's platform and stance on individual issues, you can make a positive, supportive statement that leaves no room for interpretation, like this: "Starwood Groceries is proud to support Gina Wonders for state senator, and we look forward to a bright future."

✔ **Avoid insults.** Insulting someone is never good form, especially in a public arena like social media. Doing so on hot topics invites a reverse attack. Yes, you want to start a conversation, but you don't want to bring in the wolves.

✔ **Refuse to argue.** By engaging on a hot-button issue, some people will view your statements not as the beginning of a dialogue, but rather as an opportunity to start an argument. It's you versus them. You may find yourself on the receiving end of an attack. Especially in social media, an argument can easily escalate rapidly. Walk away instead. The potential for damage to your reputation isn't worth it.

✔ **Accept differences of opinion.** Recognize that not everyone will agree with you — that's just fine. By opening the door to engage on a touchy subject, you're inviting people to have an opinion *about* your opinion. Some will love you more for it, and others will decide that it isn't their style. There's no right or wrong. It's perfectly acceptable for you and your audience to occasionally stand on different sides of the aisle.

You and the individuals who represent your brand should be careful to avoid sharing personal opinions about hot-button issues on company time. Be especially careful not to express personal opinions while using company accounts. Every tweet or post that's shared from a company account is a direct reflection of your overall brand, and missteps can negatively affect your business.

Turning to humor

You like to laugh, and so do your fans. In an oversaturated social media world, humor stands out. The videos that make you laugh are almost always the ones with millions of views. The beautiful thing about making your customers smile and laugh is that you grab their attention without spending a penny.

On December 12, 2012, Facebook, Google+, and Twitter feeds alike were inundated with posts about the uniqueness of the day December 12, 2012 (12-12-12). The monotony of the "12 posts" on every social network was broken by the good people at *Sesame Street,* with humor and a flashback to childhood, as shown in Figure 7-3. Well played, *Sesame Street,* well played.

In an example of the beauty of one brand responding to another brand with a solid sense of humor (rather than with snark), AMC Theatres commented on a tweet from Oreo about sneaking its version of the perfect snack into a movie theater. The response from AMC, shown in Figure 7-4, was nothing short of perfection.

You can't help but smile as you read AMC's response tweet to Oreo. That's what humor does: It makes the brand — both of them, in fact — relatable.

Figure 7-3: Whoever was running the *Sesame Street* Twitter account on 12-12-12 was on their toes.

When choosing humor as a means of sparking conversation, follow these suggestions:

- ✔ **Be consistent with your brand.** Ensure that your sense of humor matches the perception of your brand. Whether you're trying to elicit a loud guffaw or a quiet giggle, it needs to match who you are as a company. If slapstick humor isn't your forté, aim for a milder effect.

- ✔ **Keep it clean.** Witty humor is priceless. Tacky humor is worthless. You know which category you would rather be in.

- ✔ **Avoid highly sensitive topics.** Take race, gender, politics, and other possibly inflammatory topics off the table. Entertain your community and make them laugh rather than offend them. Running the risk of causing outrage with risky humor isn't worth your time or trouble. (For details on broaching hot-button topics safely, refer to "Lighting a fire with hot-button issues," earlier in this chapter.)

✔ **Use humor sparingly.** Funny is wonderful, in fact, it's brilliant, but you don't need to be funny all the time. Well-placed humor that happens occasionally is enough to stimulate successful engagement with your community. Attempting humor daily can fall flat if you don't have the talent to sustain it.

Figure 7-4: AMC Theatres used humor to respond to another brand's tweet.

Building engagement by way of inspiration

To help your community to move from their initial reactions of liking, pinning, and favoriting your content to a greater commitment, motivate them to engage with you on a deeper level by commenting, sharing, acting, or purchasing. To make this happen, you need to reach them via an emotional connection by tapping into trending topics or hot-button issues or turning to humor.

Excitement, surprise, gratitude, laughter, and heartfelt sympathy can all move your community to act. Every time they share a post on Google+,

LinkedIn, or Facebook, comment on your blog, or retweet a tweet on Twitter, they're giving their own, personal stamp of approval to you and your brand. That's your goal.

In February 2013, Blood: Water Mission, a nonprofit organization with the goal of overcoming the HIV/AIDS and water crisis in Africa, began the 40 Day Water project, looking to inspire people online to drink only water between February 13 and March 30. The idea behind the project was to donate to the project the money saved by forgoing coffee, soda, wine, beer, and other drink options to help build wells in Uganda. The group made use of blogs, Facebook, and Twitter to share its goals and thank participants, as shown in Figure 7-5. By sharing an inspiring message, it aimed to involve more and more people in its campaign, tapping into people's desire to do good deeds.

Figure 7-5: Thanking contributors publicly for supporting the 40 Day Water campaign on Twitter.

Providing Additional Incentives for Sharing

Staying in touch with the human side of social media engagement keeps you grounded in providing value to other people and helps you determine the incentives you should offer to motivate your community to share. We're not here to dictate to you what's valuable, though we urge you to create and share content that you believe is of value.

Knowing what's valuable to your audience starts with knowing your audience. We say it often: "Know your business goals, and know your audience." What's valuable to one community won't necessarily be valuable to another, and vice versa.

To determine value, consider these factors:

- **What your target market does online:** Observe the people that you're trying to reach — to see what they talk about and what they share — to understand their behavior and preferences. Do they prefer humor or human-interest stories that tug at the heartstrings? Do they publish content themselves or report it from other sources? Observation is a first step toward understanding.

- **Reactions from your community:** If you already have a following, ask questions not simply to get a reaction but to truly learn more about them. Gauging how you're doing regularly helps you determine your next step.

- **What best conveys your brand image:** No doubt about it, you want your brand to be known for giving 100 percent effort, for listening carefully, and for providing quality customer service. Consider the qualities that are important to you and your brand — make sure that they're front and center with every interaction in the online space. Allow these qualities to guide you in incentivizing your audience to engage with you.

- **The actions you're trying to make happen:** For example, is your ultimate goal to increase your fan base, to get people to start talking, to send traffic to your blog, to sell a service, or to encourage your community to purchase a product? Knowing your goal helps you decide what your incentive should be.

Watch how your target market acts on your competitor's Facebook page or on Twitter or any other social network when they aren't interacting with you. See what your competitors do well to stimulate interaction. Always stay true to your own brand, mission, vision, and goals; however, don't engage online in a vacuum. Adopt and adapt best practices that you observe when they're relevant to your brand.

Offering freebies and discounts

Every social media engagement platform is a place where you can offer something special to each and every one of your fans: VIP status. By choosing to engage with you on Pinterest, Google+, Facebook, Twitter, YouTube, or even Instagram, your audience raises a hand to say, "I like you, and I want to know more about you."

By connecting with you and following you in social networks, people are hoping for the inside scoop, for news that the average person doesn't see, and for discounts or coupons like the one you see on the Sephora Google+ page, as shown in Figure 7-6.

Figure 7-6:
Sephora offers tips and links to discounts and freebies on Google+.

Holding contests and sweepstakes

According to a recent online survey, a whopping 79 percent of Facebook fans are more likely to purchase from a brand they have already liked. So it's no wonder that brands are making a concentrated effort to hold on to their audience.

One of the best ways is to entice people to your page is by offering this type of discount or even to run a contest or sweepstakes to keep them engaged and coming back. Though contests or sweepstakes can be run on any social network, they do especially well on Facebook, Instagram, and Pinterest. Before you set about holding one, ask questions to determine your goals: Are you looking to increase engagement with your current fans, grow your community, showcase a new product, or simply deepen brand awareness?

Following the laws and guidelines

This list describes a few legal and technical aspects to consider as you plan a contest or sweepstakes:

- ✔ **Know the law.** Know the difference between contests and sweepstakes. Every state has different laws specifying the types of contests you can run, even on the Internet, and these laws are handled by the attorney general's office in each state. For example, if you hold a sweepstakes, you cannot ask contestants to do anything else, such as submit a photograph as a critical part of entering to win — you submit a photograph to be judged in a contest.

   Be very careful about mixing random drawings with judged contests and vice versa. We aren't lawyers, so we encourage you to check with yours before holding contests or sweepstakes online.

- ✔ **Remember the rules.** Whatever platform you choose, you *must* know the rules specifically about running contests. Are you allowed to hold them on the network? Can you announce your winner on your page when the contest ends? The Facebook terms of service, for example, state that you cannot hold contests on your page and that you must use a third-party application to house your contest elements. Do *not* jeopardize your brand or your standing on any social network by breaking its rules.

- ✔ **Choose an appropriate prize.** As appealing as it may seem to offer a Kindle Fire or a brand-new iPad, giving one away will probably do nothing to showcase you or your brand. The device that you choose as a prize should give your fans a feel for who you are and what you have to offer. The prize should give winners a taste of your company.

- ✔ **Spread the word.** Remember to share news about the contest on other platforms. If you're asking people to "pin to win," for example, you can still tweet about it and mention it on Instagram. The same advice holds true for Google+, YouTube, and Facebook.

For Facebook contests, the rules are quite specific about holding contests using a third-party app. Some popular apps for contests and sweepstakes include Wildfire (`www.wildfireapp.com`) and Strutta (`www.strutta.com`).

Setting the rules

For every contest or sweepstakes you run online, you should publish official contest rules. Usually, they're composed by lawyers; however, you can use your favorite search engine to find templates online. These rules specify how the contest is run, its duration, who's running it, the dollar value of prizes, who can enter and who cannot, including states where the contest cannot be held, and many other details that you should disclose.

On Pinterest, contests are visual and typically invite users to pin pictures, highlighting either the brand's product or one that the user loves — or both. Girls Crochet Headbands ran a contest in January 2013; they posted photos of entrants and asked their fans to create a Pinterest board titled Girls Crochet Headbands Dream Football Outfit Contest, pin an entire outfit from the GCH site, and include at least one football-themed item. The sponsors of the contest listed official rules on the site and offered to answer questions on Facebook. A winner was chosen by the entire GCH staff.

Aligning your company with a cause

Nine out of ten consumers want brands to tell them the ways they're supporting causes, according to the Cone Cause Evolution Study. (`http://ppqty.com/2010_Cone_Study.pdf`) Why do they want to know? Because they often prefer to match their dollars with the brands that are "doing good" in the world on an ongoing basis. Your audience wants to know which causes are close to your company's heart.

The Con Agra Foods Foundation has been a longtime advocate in the fight against child hunger. The cause is so important to the company that it has started its own campaign, Child Hunger Ends Here, which renews a few times annually with the support of its family of brands. The campaign has its own website, shown in Figure 7-7, as well as a Facebook page and YouTube and Twitter accounts.

In choosing to align with a particular cause, be sure to find one that fits authentically with your brand or business. Picking a cause just to sound good feels fake to you and to your community. Connecting with a cause isn't a fad — it's a commitment.

Figure 7-7:
This founda-
tion offers
consumers
information
about its
campaign
to end child
hunger by
linking to
social
networks.

Part III
Examining the Basic Engagement Tools

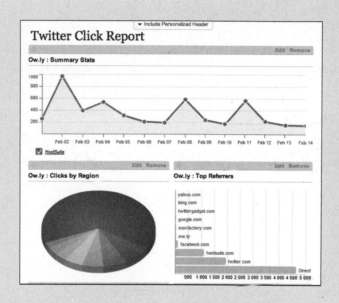

In this part . . .

- ✔ Reexamine traditional online communications tools to enhance your social media engagement efforts.

- ✔ Attract and interact with more customers via Facebook.

- ✔ Find your audience and drive them to take action through Twitter.

Chapter 8

E-mail, Forums, Blogs, and Websites

In This Chapter

▶ Enhancing your e-mail newsletter

▶ Managing your online community

▶ Forming groups in social networks

▶ Engaging on your blog or website

*I*n some cases, you can be more effective by replacing some of your traditional online marketing tools with social networks. In other cases, you can serve your customers and prospects more effectively by sticking with the traditional or combining traditional with newer tools.

This chapter covers several traditional forms of online communications and marketing: e-mail newsletters, online groups, websites, and blogs. We detail how to incorporate these tools with social media features so you can make them a part of your social media engagement tool kit.

We also cover how to integrate traditional tools into your social networks wherever possible. We don't want you to ignore what still works for you or what serves a very specific purpose because we know not everything needs straight social media alone.

Creating Social-Powered E-mail Newsletters

Gone are the days of plain vanilla text e-mails — or plain vanilla text *anything* online. Multimedia and social media features abound and can add oomph and interactivity to any message you send and share. Depending on your budget and your needs, you can choose from an array of e-mail marketing tools that can help you publish e-mail messaging to your subscribers.

At a minimum, professional e-mail marketing tools track e-mail opens and clicks. More and more, they also provide ways to entice your readers and social media followers to interact with you and share your e-mails with their connections on social networks. Though you can easily become enamored of social networks, none of them can provide the direct-push messaging that e-mail still provides.

Choosing an e-mail marketing tool

E-mail marketing is no longer about broadcasting. E-mail marketing services offer a wide and growing array of features to garner your business. You have choices — sometimes too many choices.

Deciding which features you need

Although social media engagement features aren't the only criteria for choosing your e-mail marketing tool, using a solution that's social media–ready makes it easier for you to merge your e-mail activities with your more conversational social ones. Here are some basic features to look for:

- **Social distribution:** You need tools that let you easily share links to your e-mails to your social networks. The distribution tools should be built in with an option to announce each newsletter as it goes out or to easily post a link to your social networks.

- **Social sharing:** You should have one-click simplicity so your e-mail subscribers can seamlessly share your e-mail content onto their social networks.

- **Social network integration:** You need to be able to embed subscription forms for your e-mail newsletter into your Facebook Fan Page as an app. If the marketing tool you're looking at doesn't have this option, make sure the other features it offers are important enough to your business to have to deal with a work-around.

Evaluating candidates

Table 8-1 breaks down the social media features of some of the most popular e-mail marketing tools.

Table 8-1	E-mail Marketing Tools and Their Features				
Service	*Social Distribution*	*Social Sharing*	*Facebook App*	*Mobile-Friendly*	*Poll/ Survey*
MailChimp	x	x	x	x	x
Emma	x	x	x	x	x

Service	Social Distribution	Social Sharing	Facebook App	Mobile-Friendly	Poll/Survey
Mad Mimi	x	x	x	x	x
iContact	x	x	x	x	x
Constant Contact	x	x	x	x	-
AWeber	x	-	x	x	-
Infusionsoft	x	x	-	-	-

Some tools support additional features such as Flickr integration (Emma) and Pinterest integration (Mad Mimi). Look for the e-mail marketing tool that gives you the features that best suit your business needs.

E-mail marketing services are adding increasingly more social media features to remain competitive. Facebook integration, for example, is offered by both Constant Contact (`http://constantcontact.com`) and MailChimp (`http://mailchimp.com`), shown in Figure 8-1.

Figure 8-1: Aliza integrates her MailChimp e-mail subscription form into her Facebook Fan Page.

Other e-mail marketing solutions include Campaigner (`http://campaigner.com`), Campaign Monitor (`http://campaignmonitor.com`), Contactology (`http://contactology.com`), VerticalResponse (`http://verticalresponse.com`), and Infusionsoft (`http://infusionsoft.com`).

Some of the larger and more robust e-mail marketing systems, such as Infusionsoft, do not have a Facebook app, so you're forced to use a third-party iFrame app-generator to host the form code. Try Woobox (`www.woobox.com`)

or ShortStack (`www.shortstack.com`) for custom iFrame apps. Then copy the e-mail subscription form code generated by your e-mail marketing tool and paste it into the app generator in HTML mode.

Putting out the word

Let people in your social networks know about your e-mail newsletter in several ways, including these:

- ✔ **Provide social content.** Use excerpts from your newsletters such as tips or facts that provide valuable content that your following will appreciate and pass along. Include a link to your e-mail newsletter subscription form to draw a clear line between the content and your e-mails. Example: "You can add an e-mail subscription form to your Facebook Fan Page using MailChimp's app." Include link here.

- ✔ **Post conversation starters.** Reference your e-mail in a post but don't make it your main point. For example, you can say "Mobile apps are becoming increasingly popular as I mention in my upcoming weekly e-newsletter. What are your favorite apps?" Include a link to your e-mail subscription page.

- ✔ **Publish promotional messages.** Craft messages that clearly and succinctly promote your e-mail newsletter. Your followers won't mind promotional messages in your streams as long as the messages are clear and don't dominate the conversation. You can couple it with a conversation starter (see the preceding item). Example: "In my last e-mail newsletter, I talked about how to get more followers. How do you do this?"

- ✔ **Offer calls to action.** Sweeten the pot with a call to action that includes an offer. Example: "Subscribe to my e-mail newsletter this month and get my free handbook on QR code marketing." Include link here.

- ✔ **Encourage sharing.** A simple message at the top or bottom of an e-mail that states "Feel free to pass this e-mail along" can be effective, but your message has to be worth sharing.

As you engage with others through social media, your immediate goals will change and adapt based on what is happening or being talked about at any given time. Your underlying goals should remain constant. So, although you may want more subscriptions to your e-mail newsletter in the future, you always want strong connections to continue the conversations with and better serve your customers and prospects.

Prompting subscribers to become fans

If people are subscribed to your e-mails but not following you in social networks, you want to drive them to connect with you in a social setting as well.

Getting more of your friends, fans, and followers to subscribe to your e-mails requires a bit of finesse, however. In this new age of quick, fast, and easy, as well as information overload and overwhelm, convincing someone that she needs one more e-mail in her inbox can be a hard sell. The following sections present a few techniques that can help.

E-mail marketing and social media marketing should be complementary, not competitive. Don't stop sending out a regular e-mail simply because you now communicate in social networks. Each communications and marketing tool has its strengths and weaknesses so using both well gives you a stronger set of tools.

Increase your visibility

Chances are you're only sending out your e-mails on a weekly, bi-weekly, or monthly basis, so there are many days between messages when you aren't in touch with your customers and prospects. To get more of your subscribers to follow you in social networks where you can connect with them daily or almost daily, make it easy for them to do so from your e-mails. Simply Stacie provides blogging tips in her e-mail, as shown in Figure 8-2, and provides ways for subscribers to connect with her on a variety of social networks.

Figure 8-2:
Facebook, Google+, Instagram, Pinterest, Stumble-Upon, and Twitter icons in an e-mail newsletter.

Increase your reach

Make it worth someone's while to be a subscriber as well as a fan or follower so you have multiple opportunities to reach him. You also need to give him a good reason to connect with you in other places such as

- Valuable content published more frequently
- Special offers reserved for Facebook fans or Twitter followers, for example
- A relevant community to participate in

Offer extra value

Everyone is motivated to connect with brands for different reasons. Providing additional value through social media and talking about it in your e-mails gives your subscribers incentive to connect with you more frequently in social networks.

Position your e-mails as a way to get exclusive content that your followers can't get anywhere else. Just as you provide special offers exclusively for your social networks, assign some specifically for your e-mail subscribers. One way to make your e-mails more enticing is to provide your e-mail subscribers with first notifications of offers and events such as early-bird specials or first sneak peeks of new products.

Find out what subscribers want

Survey your subscribers to find out more about them, their interests, and what they expect from you and your e-mails. Check the last column in Table 8-1 to see which e-mail marketing services offer survey tools.

Driving more than clicks

You want to increase your clicks within your e-mail to drive actions, and there are many tips and tricks for getting more clicks. The e-mail marketing tool you use should provide reporting and analysis of how people are interacting with your e-mails.

You can increase clicks from your newsletter using some of the following techniques:

- **Position of links:** Links get more clicks when you place them toward the top and *toward* the bottom, but not *at* the bottom. Figure 8-3 shows the MailChimp click map displaying statistics for each link in an e-mail.

- **Repetition of links:** Important calls to action bear repeating toward the top and bottom of your e-mail.

- **Visual links:** Changing the font color or size or adding a clickable graphic can attract the eye and encourage a click.

- **Contextual links:** Adding links within useful information could invite a click.

- **Conversational links:** Although some people may argue with the use of the words *Click Here* to prompt someone to click a link, sometimes stating the obvious works.

- **Social sharing links:** Include easy ways to share your e-mail to social networks. (Refer to the icons shown in Figure 8-2.)

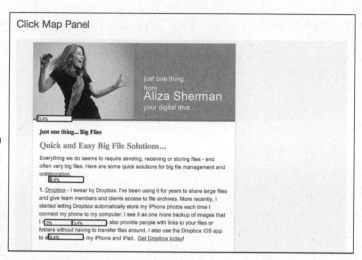

Figure 8-3:
An example
of click
analysis
within an
e-mail.

People click links or share content when they feel the content is valuable. Valuable content is in the eye of the beholder. What's important to you may not be to someone else. Getting to know your audience can get you closer to providing the type of content they want.

Review your e-mail newsletter stats in the weeks after you send it to gauge how people respond. Especially note which links get the most clicks and examine where links are positioned in an e-mail and the surrounding content. Find the sweet spots in terms of content and layout to make your e-mail more effective.

If you provide too much content or too many links in an e-mail, recipients won't know where to click and might miss the links leading to the actions most important to you. Use links sparingly and repeat some of the most important ones so you get the results you want.

Participating in Online Communities

Social networks seem to be the dominant destinations for most people who are looking to connect and communicate with others, including brands, online. Believe it or not, engagement still takes place in online communities hosted on a variety of platforms besides social networks.

Entering the conversations in these communities is a form of online outreach and can be effective when done appropriately. Over time, however, these more closed or contained communities are more challenging to infiltrate, particularly with a commercial message. Forming your own online communities gives you the ability to interact freely.

Forming and growing an online community

Online communities are made up of people brought together by common interests. People participating in them express their opinions, interact with one another, and expect you to be present to respond to them as well. Communities tend to run through several common stages as they form and grow, as we discuss in this section.

Formation: First impressions

You've built an online presence in a social network, you've populated it with quality content, and you have an ongoing plan for publishing more content. You've invited people to your network, and you're trying to gain traction by eliciting responses from followers. At the moment, however, the numbers are small. Don't panic: This situation is normal.

Infancy: Just watching

Your following is growing very slowly. People are only lurking, not contributing. Your analytics reports may show that people are consuming the content you're publishing, but nobody is responding. (Crickets.) Don't worry: Silence at this stage is common. Often, no one wants to be the first person to comment. Seeding a few comments can break the ice.

Courtship: First interactions

You've seeded a few comments and likes (don't overdo it), and you've received a few from community members. Recognize them. Thank them. Acknowledge their efforts. People like to be noticed. Pay attention to what catches their attention and what gets them to respond. Do more of it.

Participation: Superficial interactions

Clicking the Like or Favorite button or the thumbs-up icon or the heart is easy. You're thrilled that people in your community are doing it, but keep in mind that it's a fleeting action. Sure, the numbers look good when you advance from single digits to Like tallies in the double, triple, and quadruple digits, but at this stage these fast actions probably aren't translating into tangible results. Look for ways to push engagement further.

Engagement: Deeper interactions

Hurray — you've received your first tangible and meaningful action! Someone has subscribed to your e-newsletter, responded to your question in detail, requested more information, provided his mailing address, or bought something. Whatever you've determined are positive and measurable results, you're getting them now. People have moved beyond the easy click to meatier interactions and transactions.

Sample community guidelines for engagement

Your community guidelines should reflect your corporate culture and values. Here's some language that can be used in your community guidelines. (We recommend that you have your lawyer review any rules or guidelines that you post online.)

We appreciate your participation in our online community; however, we reserve the right to remove inappropriate comments or posts. By *inappropriate,* we mean overly commercial, obscene, libelous, or rude or a personal attack.

Here are some more of our community rules:

✔ **Be kind.** When in doubt, follow the golden rule: "Do unto others as you would have them do unto you."

✔ **Be discriminating.** Share only appropriate content or links to appropriate content.

✔ **Be honest.** We cannot verify the truthfulness of every post, but we will not tolerate blatant deception.

✔ **Don't spam.** We like to promote what you do, but please do not use our forum and community to post blatantly commercial messages.

✔ **Add value.** Look for ways to contribute in a positive way to the conversations that take place in our community.

Evangelism: Organic ambassadors

Your community is growing, and your community members are actively helping you spread the word. They're sharing with their own networks the content that you're putting out there. They're consuming your content and then choosing to help you spread it. They're inviting their friends to join your network, to pay attention to you, to like your page or follow you or connect with you. Congratulations! You're in the zone of social media engagement.

See *Online Community Management For Dummies,* by Deborah Ng (published by John Wiley & Sons, Inc.), for extensive details and examples of how to harness the power of online communities for your business.

Identifying the people you want to reach

As with all marketing, targeting your online marketing is essential. To avoid a scattershot approach to online outreach that inevitably yields few results and is difficult to track, follow these strategies:

✔ **Know your market.** Identify whom you're trying to reach, including demographics and psychographics so you have a profile of the ideal prospect and customer.

✔ **Find your audience.** Learn what your targets do online, including the social networks they use. Also find out on what other sites and in what other forums they spend their time.

✔ **Target your audience.** Craft messaging particular to your target or segments of your audience and reach out to them where they gather.

With a clear picture of the people you're trying to reach, you can engage with them beyond social networks. Although it may seem counterintuitive to talk about traditional online forums and social media engagement, engagement online doesn't stop everywhere else on the web because social networks are on the scene. Sometimes you have to dig a little deeper and be a little more creative to find your target audience and engage them.

You can browse group listings on web-based group-hosting sites based on category, or search each of these sites for specific topics and keywords to find related groups and conversations.

Depending on whom you're trying to reach or the conversation topics you're seeking, you may have an easier time finding related groups by doing a wider search on Google first, then drilling down into specific groups where they're hosted.

Even though many people are using social networks daily, that also means that many brands are clamoring to reach them in those busy, noisy spaces. Sometimes reaching out to people in other forums helps your messages stand out to attract their attention.

Crafting appropriate messages

To anyone familiar with communicating on social networks, web-based forums and groups may seem quaint and simplistic. For those who continue to use them, they are rich, vibrant, engaging, and valuable online communities. Reaching out to people, your audience specifically, where they are most comfortable consuming information and connecting is smart marketing.

Many of the web-based forums and groups lack all the bells and whistles of social networks. They also tend to feel a lot more cohesive and contained than faster-moving messaging streams that often don't emphasize threaded messaging.

In crafting your messages, consider the following:

✔ **Your business goals:** These are the tangible and measurable results you hope to gain from engaging online.

✔ **Your target audience:** This means your target market consisting of prospects and customers.

✔ **Actions you want others to take:** Messaging can be combined with calls to action and embedded tools, or links to tools, that facilitate those actions.

✔ **The forum you're using:** No amount of internal planning can compensate for the different technical tools and dynamics inherent to each web-based forum or social network.

Knowing the way people communicate on each network helps guide your messaging. The messages you compose for social networks vary from network to network. Some of the aspects of your messaging that may need to change include

- *Content:* The words and tone of the message for both your audience and the tool you're using

- *Length:* The number of words or characters dictated by the forum

- *Frequency:* How often you post or repeat messages based on the rhythm of how people tend to communicate within any given forum

- *Presentation:* How you're able to present your message, including text-only, using links and, where possible, embedding images and multimedia

We detail in Chapter 5 how to develop a messaging map that guides the content you craft and post to Facebook, Twitter, and other social networks. Even without the social media tools, a messaging map can help you craft more targeted and appropriate messages.

Use a signature file with a few links to your website or key social networks so others can connect with you further. Most web-based forums and groups let you add a signature file in your account settings. Otherwise, include one or two links under your name each time you contribute to the conversation.

Entering conversations effectively

Whether you're engaging with people within more contained web-based forums and groups or through their messaging streams on social networks, knowing how to properly step into a conversation without offending anyone is a skill.

Jumping into someone else's conversation can be akin to interrupting. In the online world, it can also come off as creepy and invasive. Other than a few variables among forums, you can enter conversations that are already taking place online in better ways. Take these steps to avoid common mistakes:

1. **Search for keywords to find relevant conversations.**

You can find conversations either by using the search tools provided by some of the web-based forums or through a Google search that can pull up conversations in public groups. If you're an accountant, you could search for *taxes, tax time,* and *small business tax* to find appropriate threads.

2. **Listen to what's being said.**

When you find questions and comments around the topics you've pinpointed, read the threaded messages related to those topics. Gauge the sentiment. If people are ranting, you're better off looking for a less volatile dialog. If people are asking questions, this could be your in.

3. **Consider how you can contribute.**

Answering questions is a tried-and-true way to insert yourself into someone else's conversation in a meaningful and valuable way. If you have concrete and useful information to share that can help others, look for the places you can share your knowledge.

4. **Post an appropriate message.**

"Appropriate" is in the eye of the beholder, but if you've done your homework and take steps to make sure your message is on-topic, useful, and courteous, chances are you can engage with others in a web-based forum without a negative incident.

After you post a message with the intention of entering an existing conversation, be attentive to any reactions or responses. Despite your careful consideration and good intentions, your message may fall on deaf ears or ruffle some feathers. Be prepared to apologize if someone takes offense or to bow out politely if your message is not welcome.

Turning contacts into connections

Over time, you need to turn contacts you make in web-based forums into longer-lasting connections. Many web-based forums and groups let you "friend" or otherwise connect with other members. Keeping connections going in these forums can be time-intensive. Encouraging others to "follow" or "like" you can be helpful to manage your resources, but realize that you could weaken those connections by trying to move them over to Facebook or Twitter.

Who you're trying to reach and where you're able to reach them can help you determine if you should seek them out in web-based forums versus — or in addition to — social networks. Although it may seem easier to use social networks with all their interconnected messaging tools, discounting more traditional online forums could leave out a key segment of your target market. In some cases, web-based forums may be the only place you can effectively reach your target.

If you have or can hire the expertise to position your brand as the go-to source of useful and reliable information on a topic relevant to what you do, look to establish a presence and engage in online forums based around Q&As such as Quora (`http://quora.com`).

You'll risk getting banned from web-based forums and groups if you seek out prospects and blast them with commercial messages. Read the group guidelines if they've published them. Listen to what others are saying, and contribute meaningfully to the conversations with relevant questions and responses.

Forming Your Own Groups and Forums

We'll be the first to tell you that maintaining an online community for your business is hard work and very time-consuming. Cultivating online communities across your various social channels can be a full-time job, a real challenge for any business owner.

We'd be remiss if we didn't at least acknowledge that you can use online groups and forums separate from social networks to form and nurture an online community for your business. Keep in mind that the main difference between an online community on a site that lets you host groups versus groups within a social network is the technical features they provide.

Social networks can provide group features with more interconnected ways to reach larger pools of people — friends of friends and other users of their network — while custom groups tend to exist more as islands with limited reach to a bigger user-base. If you're looking for big growth, go the social network route. If you're looking for smaller and more contained, custom groups could fit the bill.

Evaluating the benefits of a custom group

Setting up your own custom group is a big undertaking, as is any kind of online community building. Having your own community can happen organically on your blog or in your social networks, although it more often requires a lot of time and attention on your part to stimulate the conversations to the point of growing into a cohesive community.

Having your own custom group online creates a more defined space where you can engage with others. The way you engage in groups online is in a much more direct way than engaging with others through social networks where the majority of people are passive followers who may or may not engage with you.

A custom group can benefit your company in many ways including

- ✔ Reaching a more captive audience for ongoing conversations
- ✔ Getting greater visibility for your posts
- ✔ Engaging in more in-depth dialog with others
- ✔ Strengthening relationships with your customers and prospects
- ✔ Being able to manage who is part of your online community
- ✔ Having a greater ability to guide and moderate conversations
- ✔ Delivering unique content to segmented groups

Even if you establish a group, you still need to promote your group to attract members. Use the online and offline marketing and promotional tools that you'd use to promote anything you do online, including mentions in your newsletter, e-mails, website, social networks, and even online ads.

Choosing a group management tool

The tools you might use to build an online community outside of a social network usually lack the interconnected features that provide exposure to your brand and help speed up growth of your following. For example, there are no "retweets" or "shares" within most of these web-based forums to a much wider audience.

Some of the sites that host groups and provide tools to manage your groups include

- ✔ Yahoo! Groups (http://groups.yahoo.com)
- ✔ Google Groups (http://groups.google.com)
- ✔ GroupSpaces (http://groupspaces.com)
- ✔ Ning (http://ning.com)
- ✔ BigTent (http://bigtent.com)
- ✔ Meetup (http://meetup.com)

Both Yahoo! Groups and Google Groups are offshoots of old-style e-mail lists and still provide an e-mail component as well as archived threaded messaging boards on the web. GroupSpaces is one of the services specifically developed for building groups online, and Ning offers even more bells and whistles, giving you features that let you create your own custom social network. Both BigTent and Meetup offer online forums for offline groups and organizations.

Although most web-based forum and group-hosting services operate separately from social networks, Table 8-2 breaks down which of the popular forums and groups provide social media integration as well as which are free versus fee-based.

Table 8-2	Forum and Group-Hosting Services	
Service	*Cost*	*Social Integration*
E-mail lists with web forums		
Yahoo! Groups	Free	Users can sign in with Facebook or Google but no other integration
Google Groups	Free	Google +1 button
Web forums		
GroupSpaces	6 pricing plans from $14.99 to $99 per month	Log in with Facebook, import your Facebook Timeline, sync group events with Facebook, Facebook Like button, and Like Box
Ning	Starts at $24.95 per month	Extensive social network integrations
Online/offline hybrids		
BigTent	Free (fees for support)	Facebook login
Meetup	$19 per month, discounts for three and six month plans	Facebook and Twitter share buttons, more extensive Facebook and Twitter integration

Now's the time to pick up *Online Community Management For Dummies*, by Deborah Ng (John Wiley & Sons, Inc.), for the nuts and bolts of building and running your online community regardless of where it's hosted.

Building groups in social networks

Going old-school with your online community building tools can be beneficial to reach very specific audiences. If you want to cast a much wider net, you need platforms that offer more ways to reach more people. This is where social networks come in.

To get the cohesive and more intimate feeling of a group combined with social networking features, consider a few platform options. Facebook Groups and LinkedIn Groups are two top social networks that specifically have group-building options. Twitter doesn't have a group feature. Technically, Google+ has Circles that group together individuals and messages but do not provide a fully-defined "place" to congregate. Pinterest offers group boards and secret boards (see Chapter 11), but these aren't fully fleshed out community-building platforms. We discuss all these services in more detail in Chapters 9 through 13.

Enhancing Blogs and Websites for Engagement

When you think social media engagement, your static website probably isn't the first thing that comes to mind. Of course, there's always your blog. You might think the comments feature on your existing blog offers the possibility of engagement, especially if you get comments and then reply to those comments.

You may even start to recognize people who leave comments on your blog posts because they keep coming back. Some conversations may take place in the comment sections of your blog, giving you the feeling that you're building an online community. With all the options for connecting with others, your blog's standard comments section is no longer enough to truly engage with your audience.

Facilitating sharing with social network widgets

Bridge the gap between your existing website or blog with your social networks using widgets. Widgets typically sit on your sidebar showcasing content from another location: Twitter, video from another site, even the weather.

Widgets are lines of code such as JavaScript that can be added to the HTML code of your website or blog to pull content in from other sites. When the content on those other sites is updated, the widget dynamically updates with that same content on your site.

For better social media integration, you can embed widgets in two main ways on your website or blog:

- ✔ Add social sharing features so your site visitors can easily share your content to their social networks.
- ✔ Pull in social network content onto your website or blog.

Each major social network provides free widgets for your site or blog, some of which can be easily customized in terms of size, shape, color, and features.

Table 8-3 lists common social media widgets offered by the top social networks for sharing and pulling in dynamic content.

Table 8-3	Common Social Network Widgets	
Social Network	*Widgets for Sharing*	*Widgets for Content*
Facebook	Like button	Like Box with or without fan photos and update streams
Twitter	Tweet button	Twitter badge with number of tweets and Follow button options
LinkedIn	Share on LinkedIn, Follow company, Recommend	Member profile, Company profile, Job listing
Pinterest	Pin It button	Pinterest feed
Google+	+1 button, Add to Circles	profile badge, page badge

Expanding commenting with apps

You can add new life to your website or blog by adding social-powered tools so your sites and social channels are more interconnected. Social commenting tools such as Facebook's Comments Box and third-party software add-ons such as Disqus (www.disqus.com) and Livefyre (www.livefyre.com) let people log in to your website to comment using their social media accounts or identities. Each social plugin offers some similar functionality, including integrating your website or blog comments with your social network conversations.

Facebook's Comments Box can sync comments to your Facebook Fan Page and can spread the conversations to your site visitors' Facebook friends. When commenting on your site, your visitors can opt to post their comments to their Facebook Timelines. Comments show Facebook users the most relevant comments from their friends, friends of friends, and most active discussions.

You can add Disqus to your WordPress, Blogger, and Tumblr blogs or one built on Drupal to increase engagement. The Disqus add-on works with HTML5 and also using a JavaScript plugin. Using Disqus, you can add real-time conversations to your site or blog instead of only the asynchronous messaging of standard comments. When a Disqus user is logged in, she can see when other Disqus users are also on your website and even watch in real-time as others are typing comments. Disqus also has ratings and sharing features; moderation tools and analytics; and Disqus Discovery so Disqus users can discover your content when they're visiting other sites and blogs.

Livefyre also provides a social comments feature for your blog or website. Like Disqus, it provides live, real-time commenting and an administrative tool to moderate comments and control spam. Livefyre users can have profiles so you can get to know your site visitors and community members. They can tag their friends in comments to bring more people to the conversation. Livefyre's SocialSync works similarly to Facebook's Comments Box to tie together conversations happening on your site with related conversations happening on other sites.

All the social plugins in the world cannot stand in for your active participation in your online communities. Your attention, presence, and responsiveness can mean the difference between random chatter and guided, relevant conversations that lead to specific, measurable actions.

Chapter 9

Facebook

In This Chapter

▶ Seeing the benefits of using Facebook for business

▶ Attracting and keeping community members

▶ Making your page more prominent in News Feeds

▶ Benefitting from advanced features

*F*acebook may be one of the first sites you think of when you consider deepening your digital experience as either an individual or a business. According to statistics on AllFacebook – the 'Unofficial Facebook Blog' (`http://allfacebook.com/morrison-foerster-time-spent-face book_b105616`) an average user spends just less than seven hours a month on the site, updating their status, connecting with friends and family members, liking pictures, and skimming for news from their favorite brands and businesses. This is more than any other platform. Facebook is the first online site that many users visit to start their day and the last one they click to in the evening before shutting everything down. What this means to you is that Facebook offers a huge, active potential audience — and huge rewards for any business that knows how to engage this audience.

In this chapter, we walk you through the best ways to deepen your relationships with your community on Facebook, post quality content in your News Feed that draws the attention it deserves, and master the many specialized features in Facebook.

Every time we say *Facebook Timeline,* we're talking about a personal or individual page, and every time we say *Facebook Page,* we're talking about a brand, company, or business page. Also, though the term fan is no longer used by Facebook to refer to someone who likes your business page, we still refer to fans rather than "Likers" for simplicity's sake. Got it?

Building Deeper Relationships on Facebook

As of September 2012, Facebook had more than 1 billion active users. (To put this figure in perspective, consider this fact: If Facebook was a country, it would be the third-largest in the world, after China and India.) Those 1 billion users include 11 million businesses with Facebook pages, all of which, like you, are striving to strengthen relationships with their communities.

Businesses use their pages primarily to

- **Engage with customers:** Generate conversation and become more than the logo. Ask your customers questions, and respond to customers whenever they ask a question or reply to yours.

- **Share pictures and videos:** Show and tell. Highlight events that are happening around you, with your company, or with your products. Give your audience a sneak peek behind the scenes of your company, and make them feel like a part of your tribe. In Figure 9-1, Lisa Lehmann, of Studio Jewel, regularly uploads photos of her jewelry — pieces that she's working on now and the ones she has available for immediate shipping (especially around holidays).

- **Provide news and updates:** Use Facebook as an opportunity to keep your community "in the know." Share your newest product launches, company updates, and related industry or topical news that would be of interest to your fans and followers.

- **Sell products:** In addition to sharing news about your products, you can take the extra step to create an e-commerce option for your Facebook fans and followers and sell directly to them from your Facebook page. The National Retail Foundation found that more than 25 percent of Facebook users have purchased directly from a business page, and that number continues to grow with the introduction of Facebook Gifts (http://www.facebook.com/about/gifts), a feature that lets Facebook members buy products for each other by way of the Facebook site.

eBay Stores (http://stores.ebay.com), Etsy (www.etsy.com), Shopify (www.shopify.com), and a variety of other sites offer apps that can be linked directly to your Facebook page to offer a sales option. These apps plug directly into your business page so that the shopping experience for your fans is seamless and they don't have to leave Facebook to buy from you.

- **Make community members feel special:** Treat your Facebook community as members of a special club. Make them the first to know about company news and product updates. Make them eligible for special contests, giveaways, and discounts.

✔ **Provide customer support and care:** It's your chance to turn every customer into a raving fan by responding to queries and concerns directly and honestly.

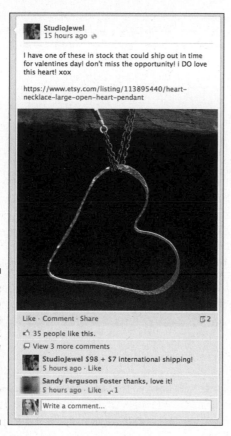

Figure 9-1: Studio Jewel lets its Facebook fans know when pieces are available for shipping.

Growing Your Page Community

Someone from your community who likes or comments on your Facebook business page obviously wants a connection with you. That person wants to feel special and to be acknowledged and to know that you're paying attention. Clicking the Like button is an investment of their time and attention. They're publicly endorsing your brand. Your fans are the people who want to know more about you and who are interested in connecting with the community you build — a community of people with shared interests whether it's healthy, prepared food that's delivered to your home or cowboy boots or photography.

Increasing follower loyalty

A recent study by www.socialmediaexaminer.com found that 51 percent of Facebook users said they're more likely to buy from brands they follow. A person initially follows your brand on Facebook because he genuinely likes you or wants to learn more about you. If your brand is engaging, you can establish a connection with those prospects and help them feel that they belong. With increased engagement and responsiveness, you move from someone liking your brand with a click to increased brand recognition and loyalty.

Here are some of the best ways to create a loyal following from the community at your page:

✔ **Craft a plan.** Determine your target market. Is your ideal audience made up of families who want to have their healthy food delivered? Or are you looking to reach moms with little girls? After you pinpoint who you want to reach, finding and attracting an audience to your page isn't a short-term process. Put in place a plan to help grow your page.

✔ **Provide quality engagement.** Everything you put on your page — every picture, every video, every status update — is a reflection of you and your brand. Aim for quality. Know that every post can be shared, so don't slack off on paying attention to the information you publish. If your audience likes what you have to say, they'll pass it on, and when they do, your name — your brand — will be attached. The more people share what you publish, the more exposure you receive to continue building your community.

✔ **Establish trust.** Your community consists of your people. Talk to them as though you respect them. Ask their opinions. Answer questions when they ask them of you. Every time you do something right, and every time you share, they not only return the good word about you but also spread it around.

✔ **Be real.** If you're an authentic brand who is staying true to your values and vision, your community will notice. gDiapers, the "earth-friendly hybrid of diapers," uses the Australian expression *fair dinkum* to describe its overall company culture and philosophy. Its employees aim, as part of their company mission, to be genuine and real with everyone they encounter, so it comes as no surprise to the company's nearly 47,000 Facebook fans when the brand chooses to support a specific charity with the sale of one of its products, as shown in Figure 9-2. gDiapers is sticking to its mission, and its fans take notice.

✔ **Stick to a schedule.** Consistency is vital to the success of your page. As with other SME platforms, it's worse to establish a presence and stop posting than to never have a presence in the first place. Decide whether to post daily, twice a day, or more. Later in this chapter, we offer suggestions for optimum posting.

✔ **Listen and respond.** One major benefit of having a business page is that it gives you the opportunity to connect with your audience, to let them know that they've been heard. The Kraft brand Lunchables has a policy of responding to every comment on its page (whether the comment is a compliment, question, or complaint) within four hours, but someone often manages to reply much sooner. See an example of this responsiveness in Figure 9-3.

✔ **Track progress.** Be diligent about whatever it is that excites your community. Do they share your pictures like crazy? Do they love to be asked their opinions? Or do you hear crickets (silence!) the more you add standard status updates? To better engage with your fans on their terms, do more of what they love.

Figure 9-2: gDiapers announces charitable donations tied to the sale of a product.

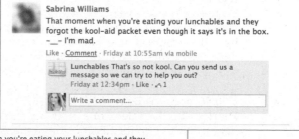

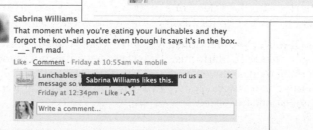

Figure 9-3: The Lunchables response to a customer, which the customer liked.

✔ **Take your time.** You're in this for the long haul. Building a community that you can be proud of requires a time commitment and a willingness to continually improve what you're doing as you go.

Managing your community on Facebook is obviously a big job — for more information on best practices to create connections within your community, refer to Chapter 6.

When your audience and fans feel connected to you, they like the content you put on your page. When they enjoy the communication you have together, they like your page, and they like your pictures, your links, and your videos. When they trust you, when they feel heard, when they know that you're listening — in essence, when they truly feel engaged — they go even a step further and share your brand with others.

Your goal is likely to attract more comments and more likes on your page, but what you *really* want are more shares — because they lead to more likes and comments. It's one big circle of engagement.

Consider these tips for increasing your post likeability:

✔ **Ask a question.** Though it may seem to be a good idea to ask it at the beginning of a post, we recommend that you ask it at the end of a short post. Ask the question after a link or accompanying a picture. One study by Buddy Media aimed at determining the keys to effective posts estimates that interaction increases by 15 percent when you add a question at the end of a post — and you may even see twice the number of comments.

```
http://michaellorinfriedman.com/wp-content/
        uploads/2013/01/Strategies-for-
        EffectiveWallpost_2012_Final.pdf
```

✔ **Ask for what you want.** If you want someone to comment, to caption a picture, to share your post, to like your page, or to respond in another way, simply ask. The maker of the KitKat candy bar told its fans to share — and share they did, as shown in Figure 9-4. Be direct and ask for what you want your fans to do. They were already visiting, already 'liking' what they were reading or watching — you are simply asking them to say it out loud.

✔ **Ask your community to fill in the blank.** Would you believe that you're four times more likely to draw a response to your post by creating a fill-in-the-blank scenario? An example is a chocolatier asking fans to complete a sentence such as this one:

```
If I were a chocolate, ___ would be my flavor.
```

Filling in the blank would be fun for fans and an activity that they might like to share. Pair it with a mouth-watering photo of chocolates, and the company could have a viral post on its hands. Facebook users like to play games on Facebook — so let them do it on your page.

✔ **Run a contest.** Get your fans involved by inviting them to participate in a giveaway, sweepstakes, or contest. See Figure 9-5 for a look at the Got Milk tablet giveaway in the Sack the Soda contest on its Facebook page.

Figure 9-4:
Kit Kat's request for shares of a simple picture was carried out more than 250 times.

Be careful about running contests on Facebook or you risk violating its terms of service. Facebook states that you must carry out contests on your page using a third-party solution. Popular tools include Wildfire (www.wildfire app.com) for promotions and Rafflecopter (www.rafflecopter.com) for giveaways.

Figure 9-5:
Fans followed the directions on the Got Milk page to enter a contest to win a tablet computer.

Promoting your business page with your personal Timeline

Naturally, your personal Timeline is a completely different animal from your Facebook page. Though your page is all-business-all-the-time, the Timeline has all your personal connections to friends, family, and interests. Some crossover likely occurs between the professional you and the personal you, but you need to decide how to handle that blurring line — and how often.

Determine whether and how you want to use your personal Timeline to promote your business page. Your personal Timeline can be an additional place to provide greater visibility to your business and potentially place your brand in front of a larger audience who may not have made the leap to like your business page.

Make the connection obvious between your personal Timeline and your business page by linking your personal Timeline to your professional page:

1. **Click Update Info.**

2. **Click Edit Work and Education.**

3. **Type the name of your Facebook page.**

    The page name should show up along with other, similar ones.

4. **Select the correct page name.**

5. **Click Done Editing.**

6. **Return to your personal Timeline page to confirm that the link has connected.**

Use your personal Timeline to thoughtfully promote your page. Tag your page by using the @ sign and typing the name of your page, and then select your page so that the name becomes clickable (similar to the way you tag your friends).

From your Timeline, your friends can head over to your business page, if they're interested, or even like the page without ever leaving your Timeline, because the Like button appears as soon as you hover the mouse over the link, as shown in Figure 9-6.

Figure 9-6:
When you tag a business page, your friends can easily navigate to it.

Standing Out in the News Feed

In the grand field of Facebook content, it can feel like you've undertaken Mission Impossible to try to stand out in the crowd. The latest estimate from Facebook (late 2012) says that 2.5 billion pieces of content — pictures, status updates, and videos — are being shared every single day.

```
http://gigaom.com/2012/08/22/facebook-is-collecting-your-
                data-500-terabytes-a-day/
```

And, Facebook has adjusted its Pages algorithm so that businesses need to make even more of an effort to strive for visibility. (Talk about making messages multi-colored in a world of black-and-white!)

As we mention earlier in this chapter, you must consider your efforts on Facebook to be part of a long-term journey. A single post or a single status update doesn't have the viral capability that a YouTube video might. In fact, more than 90 percent of the people who like your page initially don't return to your page. It's up to you to attract their attention in their News Feeds. It's a combination of understanding Facebook's EdgeRank, crafting the right kinds of posts, and playing all the right games to increase your noticeability.

Navigating EdgeRank

Quite simply, *EdgeRank* is the algorithm that determines what information appears in your Facebook News Feed. EdgeRank, naturally, ranks "the edge" that each piece of content — a picture, a video, a link, or a status update — has as it floats through the river of significant subject matter you may or may not want to see each and every day. The higher the EdgeRank, the more prominently placed your updates and content are in your fans' daily feeds.

Three measurements make up the complex formula of EdgeRank: *affinity* which, in essence, is how often your content is liked, commented on, or shared; *weight,* which measures the quality of the engagement you receive — for example, 'weighing' comments as more important than likes; and *time decay,* which factors in how long your content has been online.

Your goal is to make Edge Rank work for you. You want Facebook to weigh your content as important enough to keep it regularly visible to your audience. This means you need to monitor if what you share is engaging enough to receive comments and likes.

The combination of affinity, weight, and time decay determines the EdgeRank of a Facebook brand or business page. The higher the EdgeRank, the greater the page's visibility in fans' news feeds.

Crafting engaging posts

To master EdgeRank, find a way to attract attention to your brand page and posts. Work your way into the hearts and heads of your community to secure a greater edge. Surprise them, inspire them, delight them, make them laugh, teach them something new — you can even shock them, if it's appropriate. Find different ways to convince people that what you have to say is worth liking, commenting on, and (especially) sharing.

According to PageLever.com, your page posts reach, on any given day, only 3 percent to 7.5 percent of your fans. Though this number seems incredibly low, your priority is to increase the engagement from the fans who are seeing your content.

Think about how often you post. Too much engagement is the number-one reason that the people who have liked you decide to hide you from their News Feeds or, in some cases, to unlike your page. If your community or your fans hide your content, as shown in Figure 9-7, that action decreases your EdgeRank, making it even more challenging for you to continue to appear in the News Feeds of your remaining fans. On the flip side, if you post too infrequently, you'll quickly be forgotten.

Figure 9-7:
Click the arrow to the right of any post to hide that content from your feed.

Start slowly, posting from one to three times a day, and change the frequency depending on how much engagement you receive as you post. Consider people's emotions when you craft posts each day. Keep in mind that pictures and text updates are the posts that garner the most engagement.

The best way to create an engaging post is to opt for emotion, but be brief. Inspire your community. Don't be afraid to throw in elements of surprise (to keep them intrigued). Most important of all, write posts from your heart. You aren't making a sales pitch or requesting your fans' opinions. A simple statement describing how you feel at that moment humanizes your brand. When the fitness bar Zone Perfect did this at the end of 2012, it received positive fan reactions, as shown in Figure 9-8.

Sharing personal news and scenes from the real lives of the people behind your brand can often generate authentic reactions from your community. People love to know the names and faces of your brand representatives because it confirms that the reps are real people who are living real lives. Your brand becomes more relatable to your fans. The children's clothing company Matilda Jane shared news of an employee's new baby, as shown in Figure 9-9, and quickly received love and affection from the community on its Facebook page.

Figure 9-8:
A simple congratula-tions from ZonePerfect was shared, commented on, and liked.

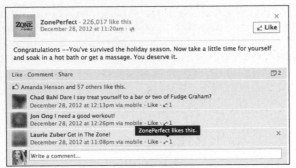

Figure 9-9:
When baby Alys joined the Matilda Jane family, the com-pany's page received more than 500 likes and comments.

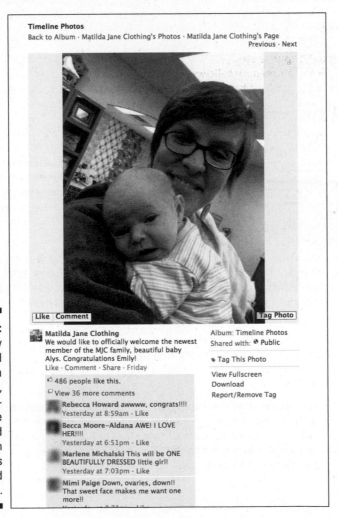

In addition to photo posts and video posts, you can post links and text-only status updates. Though the Facebook EdgeRank has placed a priority on the most visual posts, experiment to determine what your audience notices. Mixing the types of posts you publish can be effective in attracting attention.

Adding visual elements to draw instant attention

As we often say, if you want your posts to be seen in someone's News Feed, use a visual of some kind. In some instances, Facebook and EdgeRank have crowned the photo post as the king of engagement, at least as far as pages are concerned.

According to the same study mentioned previously by Buddy Media (in the earlier section, "Increasing follower loyalty"), photo posts are 39 percent more likely to receive some level of interaction. Plain-text status updates come in second, followed (distantly) by video and links.

In essence, use a picture! Here are some ways to leverage the photo post:

- **Make basic photo posts.** The basic photo post is the easiest to make and to recommend. Visually share highlights of what's happening in your company's world — whether a new product is launching soon, the people in your office are hard at work, or you're showing scenes from a conference that you're attending or the view outside your office door.

- **Run caption contests.** Share any basic photos and ask your community to caption the photo for you. If possible, share the pictures that have the most personality. Now your photo has dual purposes: It has higher EdgeRank because it's a photo, and your engagement should jump *even more* if people approve of the idea of offering the caption.

- **Ask for community pictures.** Ask your community to send you pictures — preferably based on a theme that relates to your business. You can then share the pictures and tag the fans who submit them. (We talk more about tagging later in this chapter, in the section "Tagging photos and posts.")

- **Create and share your own images.** Create your own funny or inspirational photo to share. Use a personal photo combined with an inspirational quote, for example, or head to a site such as www.someecards.com for humor that's being shared. To avoid copyright issues, however, create your own brand of funny.

If you have a picture to share, use your favorite search engine to find a quote to accompany it — whether it's funny or inspirational. Then use a photo editing website such as PicMonkey (www.picmonkey.com) to add the text easily to the image without having to use an expensive photo editing program on your computer. Save the picture and post it on your Facebook page.

Reaching out to other pages

The last thing you want to do is spam someone, let alone other business pages; however, commenting thoughtfully on pages with similar interests can increase your own page engagement. The key is to find businesses that are complementary to (not competitive with) your own business and then like their pages while you're using your business page (and not your personal account).

Interacting from your page on Facebook can be an effective and subtle way of gaining greater visibility and exposure to a new audience. When you're using your Facebook business Page, regularly monitor your News Feed for the business pages you've liked for relevant content that you can like, share, or comment on. Your brand name then appears on the other business' pages, so be intentional and thoughtful when you comment.

You don't need to engage on other pages every single day, but add this task to your weekly rotation of engagement activities. If you have a team of people working on your brand, assign one person the responsibility of page-to-page engagement. The more visibility your page has, the more opportunities you create for liking and sharing.

Don't do anything on someone else's business page that you wouldn't want them to do on yours, and don't use a commercial tone to tell people to visit your page. Interact like a true fan, and be a good community member in their communities to gain exposure without offending anyone.

Determining post timing and frequency

Naturally, your head spins as you imagine all the factors you must consider as you craft your posts. You want them to be engaging. (Remember that visual posts are the key.) A bit of Goldilocks is hidden in this theory — not too much, not too little, but *just right*. Post too often and your community will run screaming from your content, unable to find the Hide Posts button quickly enough. Post once every few days and you will all but disappear from the News Feed.

Begin by posting once daily and work up to posting three or four times a day, depending, of course, on the amount of engagement you're seeing from your fans. Additionally, monitor your analytics to track your engaged users. (We tell you more about analytics later in this chapter, in the section "Analyzing Facebook interactions").

In order to maximize your time and keep up with the appropriate frequency for posting on Facebook, be succinct, post both during the week and on weekends to reach all of your fans, don't rely on third-party apps alone to post your content as Facebook's algorithm prioritizes manual posts, and do use full links when you post so your audience can see where they are heading.

Driving traffic to your page with cross-posting

Consider the importance of driving traffic to Facebook from other locations. For example, cross-post from Facebook to Twitter to let your Twitter audience know about your Facebook page. Follow these steps to find the specific URL for an individual Facebook post in order to post it in other locations.

1. **Pick an individual post that you've already shared on Facebook.**

2. **Click the time stamp on that post.**

    You can find the stamp immediately under the name of your page, at the top of an individual post.

3. **Find the URL.**

    When you click the time stamp, you can see the permanent link (every post has one) for that specific post.

4. **Copy and paste that URL to Twitter.**

5. **Add some text to promote the post.**

6. **Click send.**

Congratulations — you've promoted a specific post from your Facebook page on Twitter.

Leveraging the Advanced Features of Facebook

Simply hearing the word *feature* can make a person think *extra*. Using the extras that Facebook has made available to boost your business page is bound to make you and your brand stand up and stand out — assuming that you know how to make the best use of them. Fortunately, that's why we're here.

With new features continually being introduced (Graph Search and Facebook Gifts are the latest that come to mind), you have many opportunities to increase engagement: You can add apps to your Timeline or business Page, use your mobile device, embed social widgets for greater visibility, and even pay for advertising.

Tagging photos and posts

Epiphanie Bags created its Facebook business Page back in 2009. Now more than 42,000 likes strong, the page is decorated with photos of the brand's key products — a line of camera photo bags. The kicker is that most of the pictures appearing on Epiphanie's business Page aren't ones shot by the brand but, rather, by customers and fans.

Inspire your customers to take their own pictures of your product and post them to your Facebook page, by way of a contest or simply by word of mouth. This is yet another way to encourage loyalty and engagement.

Typically, when a fan posts a picture and tags the brand by using the @ symbol (as is the case with Epiphanie), the photos appear not on the brand's main page but rather on the right side of the page, under the Recent Posts by Others on Epiphanie. However, Epiphanie doubles up on engagement, showing off to their entire audience the pictures their fans have taken, by reposting the pictures in their main News Feed and tagging the fan, as shown in Figure 9-10. Fans are rewarded for posting great-looking photos on their Timelines, and more people then engage in this activity to get the same recognition.

Epiphanie also shares posts from other blogs that talk about their bags. By doing this, they show extra appreciation to their fans, they share the kind of content (photos) that the Facebook EdgeRank algorithm focuses on, and they showcase their own product. It's a win-win situation for everyone.

Scheduling posts for the greatest impact

We recommend that you're as present and as engaged with your audience as possible — you must therefore be diligent about any decisions to schedule posts on your Facebook page.

Scheduling can be a good option to relieve the extra pressure of posting frequently, and it can encourage you to post consistently. Using the built-in scheduling option in Facebook can help ensure that your EdgeRank isn't negatively affected by using third-party apps to schedule your posts.

Figure 9-10:
By call-
ing out
customer
photos,
Epiphanie
carries them
to the main
page and to
the News
Feed.

Here's how to schedule a post using the Facebook scheduler:

1. **Fill in your post as you normally do, including text, links, photos, or videos.**

2. **In the lower-left corner of the Update field, click on the tiny gray clock.**

   The clock feature lets you schedule, or even backdate, your post starting with the year.

3. **Enter the year, month, day, hour, and minutes — in 10-minute intervals — when you want the update to post.**

   See Figure 9-11 for an example.

Figure 9-11:
Adjusting
the time that
you want a
scheduled
post to
appear.

4. **Click Schedule.**

    Your post is added to the *activity log* — which shows you all activity
    that has happened or is set to happen on your page. To check your
    scheduled posts, choose Edit Page at the very top of your page and then
    Activity Log — you'll see scheduled posts and the dates and times that
    they'll be posted.

Your post appears seamlessly on your page at the scheduled time. If you need
to edit the post after it has been scheduled, you can go to the activity log by
clicking on Edit Page at the very top of your page. The only setting you can
adjust is the time that your post is set to "go live." You can change the time
by clicking on the arrow in the top-right corner of your scheduled post. If you
suddenly notice a misspelling, for example, you have to delete the post and
start the process over again.

Optimizing your page for search engines

When you're trying to draw people to your Facebook page by creating amazing and engaging content, remember that a large percentage of the basic
traffic you see on your site is based on good, old-fashioned search — that is,
people find you based on what they type into a search engine. Your Facebook
page should be optimized so that search engines can easily find you, a process called *search engine optimization*. In case you've neglected a few basic
principles while getting your page up and running, go back now and edit the
following items to get more search bang for your buck:

✔ **Choose a strong name.** It's basic advice, yet you can easily choose the
   wrong name. Picking a name that's too generic makes it difficult to be
   found, just as choosing one that's too wordy (such as Tom's Sporting
   Goods — Football, Hockey, Baseball, Golf, and More!) can make your
   fans less likely to share your posts because it feels "too spammy."

Google assigns the greatest importance to the first word in the title of your Facebook business page, so choose wisely.

✔ **Create a customized vanity URL.** After you have attracted at least 25 likes on your page, Facebook lets you choose your own, custom URL. As when you choose your brand name, choose wisely. If your business name has been taken, pick a name that indicates what your business is about. Go to `http://facebook.com/username` to select your page name, and carefully select your business page versus your personal Timeline.

✔ **Use keywords carefully.** Use keywords throughout your page, especially in permanent areas such as About Page, Company Overview, and Mission. All three of these content areas are indexed for search, meaning that Google *crawls* or searches these pages for a way to identify you and allow your audience to find you.

✔ **Link liberally.** Link to your Facebook page from as many of your online social media platforms as possible, such as your website and blogs. Google places more importance on pages that have a greater number of inbound links.

✔ **Add local information.** It may seem silly to list your address and phone number when many of your sales may originate from online traffic, but it's still wise to make yourself available for local search results.

Addresses and phone numbers can increase the overall SEO of a site because Google indexes sites with specific information at a higher priority. Google refers to this information as NAP (Name, Address, and Phone) data.

If you have restricted your page access in any way (such as a liquor company restricting access by age or a company restricting geographical access, to visitors only from the United States), your page won't be seen by members of the general public on the web who aren't logged in to their Facebook accounts.

If Facebook cannot verify the age or location or other restriction criteria, a person not logged in to Facebook always arrives at the Facebook home page and is prompted to log in. Your page isn't visible to them until they're logged in — and only if they meet the criteria based on the restrictions you set.

Graph Search

As of this writing, Graph Search isn't available to all users or in languages other than English, but it does have the potential to change the game for small businesses. With its ability to hyper-search users based on interests, locations, and pages 'liked', businesses will be able to assess the fans of their competition: Who loves Nike in Dallas? Are they female or male? In their 30's or 40's? Avid runners or new to the sport? Additionally, Graph Search enables businesses to develop deeper connections with those fans who have liked their brands because they are true fans as compared to having a momentary interest.

Graph Search allows you to search by friends, photos, games, or restaurants, and narrow your hunt very specifically. Figure 9-12 shows how Graph Search's algorithm instantly populated sample searches for Danielle based on her interests and where she lives.

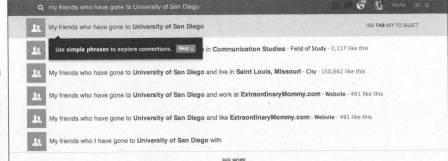

Figure 9-12:
An instantly
populated
sample
search.

Advertising on Facebook

You may want to see more interaction with your fan base — and see it *now*. One quick and efficient way to make it happen is to explore the Facebook advertising options. You've likely been wringing your hands and working tirelessly to build your community in a completely organic fashion. If it's working beautifully, by all means, keep it up; if you're looking for a boost, however, the ad choices that Facebook presents just might be the route to take.

If you have 100 or more fans, you can pay to promote your posts or create specialized offers or discounts on products and services for your audience. The barrier for entry used to be 400 likes, but that number changed in January 2013.

A promoted post is more visible in the News Feed, making it easier for your audience to see. You can easily promote a post by clicking the Promote button underneath your status update. Facebook offers you a budget — usually beginning at $5 — and tells you, based on that amount, how many people you can expect to reach. You can choose to increase the budget, if you want.

Let's take a look at the more advanced ad options:

1. **Head to** www.facebook.com/advertising.

2. **Assuming that you already have a Facebook page in place, click Create an Ad.**

At this point, Facebook asks what you want to advertise. You can see whether it will populate any pages you might have, so you can easily click on those — or enter a specific URL if you're choosing to advertise an event, a website, or a destination outside of your Facebook pages.

3. **Choose your goal.**

   You may be looking to grow your audience by increasing the number of people who like your page, to ensure that your community sees the content you're sharing, to promote a specific post, or to explore additional advanced options.

4. **Create the ad.**

   Fill in the headline and text for the ad, and choose a picture or an avatar to accompany it.

5. **Target your audience.**

   You can choose who you want to see your ad by state, age, or interest or by broad categories such as family status, DIY/crafting, or gaming.

6. **Set your price.**

   Ah, yes — the final step concerns how much it costs. The beauty of this step is that you get to decide how much you're willing to invest or budget. Facebook makes recommendations, but, ultimately, *you decide*. The amount that's set is based on the cost per mille (CPM), or cost per million impressions. If you switch to the Advanced Pricing option, you can choose to be charged instead on cost per click. In this case, you can also set the budget.

   The lowest bid available for cost per click (CPC) is one cent (.01); however, Facebook warns that choosing an amount this low isn't likely enough for your ad or sponsored story to be seen. Choose an amount in the suggested range.

Jen Estes owns Manestream Studio, a full-service hair salon in St. Charles, Missouri, a suburb of St. Louis. In making an effort to increase engagement on their Facebook page, Manestream changed the way they communicate with their fan base, by increasing the number of posts, offering incentives, and setting an advertising budget.

In one of Manstream's first advertisements, they doubled up on their engagement by offering a discount within the ad. In Figure 9-13, you can see the spike in their visibility and engagement in their statistics from the beginning of January 2013. In the first series of sponsored posts, the number of likes they received increased by 12 percent, the number of people under the People Talking about This link increased by more than 400 percent, and their total weekly reach (the biggest jump) was more than 1300 percent.

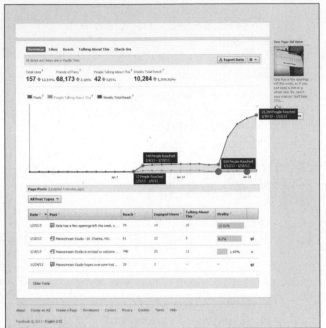

Figure 9-13:
Use
Facebook's
analytics to
monitor your
engagement.

When you purchase ads on Facebook, you have the option to select mobile-only options to make your ad show up only when someone accesses Facebook from a mobile device.

Embedding social widgets

Knowledge is power. Your goal is to make your business page known to others so that they find it, like it, and engage with you there or by way of your posts. As surprising as it may seem, some people don't automatically assume that you have a Facebook presence, and still others may assume that you do but not take the time to look for you.

By integrating Facebook directly into your website, you drive traffic to your page. If you make this process easy by embedding a Facebook social widget (as Amy Porterfield did, as shown in Figure 9-14), people who already know and like you (they're visiting your website and other social platforms, after all) are more likely to click the Like button to show your updates in their News Feeds or to scoot over to your page to explore how you engage with your audience.

Figure 9-14:
This page
has a wid-
get that
tallies the
number of
times some-
one has
clicked the
Like button.

For a simpler option, you can choose to simply add the Facebook Like button, as Diet Pepsi has done, which encourages fans to like the page, as shown in Figure 9-15. The Diet Pepsi Facebook Like button tells potential visitors how many other fans have liked the page (more than 700,000), and the widget is grouped with other SME options, such as Twitter and Pinterest.

Figure 9-15:
A social
widget
encour-
ages fans to
follow the
brand.

To embed a widget in Facebook, follow these steps:

1. **Go to the Facebook Developers page (**`https://developers.face book.com`**).**

   You can select widget options that work well for you and your website.

2. **From the site, choose Web (on the right side) to integrate Facebook with your website.**

3. **Click the first option: Integrate with your website.**

4. **On the left side, click the Core Concepts link.**

5. **Click Social Plug-ins to see your options.**

6. **Choose the social plug-in that makes the most sense for your website.**

   See Figure 9-16 for some options.

Figure 9-16: Choose a social plug-in.

7. **Fill in the specific URL, adjust the sizing (if necessary) to fit in the sidebar, and click Get Code.**

   See Figure 9-17 for some sample code. For the Like button, you populate the fields to see a sample of the widget before placing the code on your site.

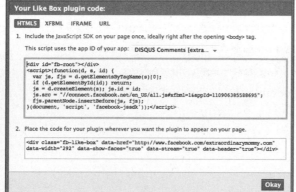

Figure 9-17: Some sample code.

8. **Place the HTML code wherever you want to place the widget, such as on your website's sidebar.**

Analyzing Facebook interactions

You may have invested hours, days, or even weeks planning your Facebook page strategy, and then implementing it and (you hope) watching your community begin to grow. The key is to pay attention to the correct metrics, to ensure that you're doing more of the activities that help you progress and cut back on any activities that might stunt your social media growth.

Facebook keeps track of in-depth analytics for you — in a comprehensive way — and makes them available to anyone who is an administrator of your Facebook page. The public cannot see these details — only administrators have access to Facebook Insights. Your analytics include not only how many people are engaging with your content but who they are, where they live, how old they are, and what content grabbed their attention the most.

You can access Facebook Insights from the top-center of your page, in the Admin panel. Facebook curates — and displays in Facebook Insights — valuable data about your audience and your content, and how the two engage together. The three primary measurement categories are

- ✔ **Reach:** The number of fans who see your posts
- ✔ **Engaged Users:** The number of fans who engage with your content by clicking on it
- ✔ **Talking About This:** The number of fans who engage with you or your content by commenting on it or liking or sharing it

To become more efficient with your time and energy, you need to understand where your platform is succeeding and which areas of it might still need work. Facebook Insights can help you do that.

Set aside time weekly or biweekly to understand what is working for your Facebook page and to determine which parts need adjustments from day to day. Conduct a monthly analysis of your progress based on your Facebook Insights to see the big-picture view of what's working and what isn't.

Chapter 10

Twitter

. . . .

In This Chapter

▶ Listening to your Twitter community for maximum engagement

▶ Establishing credibility by maintaining authenticity

▶ Mastering the art of winning tweets

▶ Measuring your Twitter footprint to achieve your goals

▶ Evaluating the newest ways to increase your Twitter following

. . . .

*W*e love Twitter. Is that a fair way to start this chapter? Sure, we're slightly biased because we both can draw a direct link between our enthusiastic and regular use of this platform to a boost in our personal brands and a strengthening of relationships that have been invaluable to our careers and businesses. And Danielle has Twitter to thank for launching her career in this space as it was through conversations on this platform that she developed in-person relationships that led to some of her first correspondent work — including being sent to the Vancouver Olympics on behalf of P&G's Thank You, Mom campaign in 2010. Thank you, Twitter.

On Twitter, you can engage with the people you need in order to move forward in your business — and it happens in real time, 24 hours a day, seven days a week. You *tweet* via 140 character messages — sharing thoughts, quotes, inspiration, links and general conversation. This platform doesn't break for Christmas or Hanukah, and it doesn't stop when you get sick or experience a natural disaster.

In this chapter, we walk you through the best ways to maximize your time on Twitter and ensure that your community embraces — and interacts with — you and your brand. By knowing the best ways to engage, you measure your time in quality engagements, in actual conversations that members of your community find relatable. Whether you're discussing the topics that matter the most to members of your community, offering incentives for them to visit your site, or simply proving that you're more than a brand, they want to come to you as you ditch quantity for quality.

Engaging in Real-Time via Twitter

"I don't care what a stranger had for lunch!" stresses Danielle's father, through gritted teeth, summing up what seems to be an entire generation's take on Twitter. Rather than deliberate the number of people who do, in fact, share what they ate for lunch (and the many more who do, in fact, appreciate it), we do our best to explain to you why *you* might care what a random stranger had for lunch.

In social media engagement (SME), the people sharing their lunch plans, news of their children's lost teeth, descriptions of their favorite wines, breathtaking pictures of storms rolling in, or quotes from a favorite poet are giving you a front-row seat to who they are, to what interests them, and to how you might engage them if you're interested.

And any of these people just might be the connection you need, the customer you're seeking, or the follower who will pay attention to what you have to say as well.

By far, one of the greatest benefits of Twitter is its real-time reach. If an earthquake strikes California, an uprising begins in the Middle East, the supply of the iPhone begins to run short, a beloved celebrity passes away, or your favorite restaurant runs a special, Twitter is the place to find the news first, as shown in Figure 10-1. The people who use Twitter are creating a space where they're reporting what they see, acting as citizen journalists, engaging with each other, and creating business connections like never before.

Figure 10-1: The Breaking News update shows how real-time Twitter can get.

Understanding how individuals, brands, and small businesses use Twitter

According to Dictionary.com, *engage* means "to attract and hold fast." Certainly this definition specifies how all of us would love for people in our digital spaces to respond to us and to the content we share.

We're sure it doesn't surprise you to read that you have a variety of ways to use Twitter successfully — and unsuccessfully — for social media engagement. We want to highlight the most effective Twitter use strategies, all of which start with choosing to care about the people on the other end of your tweets: those you want to respond to you.

As people can do in traditional conversation, people who follow you on Twitter can sense when you're being disingenuous. A quick look at your Twitter stream indicates whether you're having conversations: Do you have any @replies (pronounced "at replies")? In other words, are you having a conversation by using the @ and someone's name? Or are you simply repeating your sales messages — *broadcasting* — and not using an @ in the hope that someone will "buy" whatever you're selling?

Consider Twitter as an opportunity for you to find the people who share your interests and who will want to evangelize your message, and for whom you will want to do the same. Twitter is a give-and-take concept: For every message you put out there, seek out the nuggets in other people's content that you can to pass on to your community.

Sharing what you like to do

When you share good content, people want to follow you and connect with you. It's human nature: People simply can't help being drawn to others who capture their attention. Sharing can be as simple as letting people know your business-related interests — technology, the latest iPhone news, stocks, real estate tips, or how-to fashion tips.

Or you can use Twitter in a more personal way, by tweeting a song, movie, or wine recommendation, by sharing a recipe, or by letting people see photos from a recent vacation. The more conversational you are, the more you invite people to connect with you and to respond. The information you share should be in line with the image you want to project. Even a business can benefit from conveying a personal touch.

Beware of *broadcasters* who only spew forth links (typically, only to their own content) in the hope that someone will click. Their Twitter streams contain only promotional tweets and little to no conversation with individuals (and therefore no @ signs). To address an individual, you direct tweet by adding the @ sign before the person's Twitter handle. For example, Danielle would tweet to Aliza like this:

> Writing Social Media Engagement for Dummies with you @AlizaSherman has been just as much fun as I imagined.

However, if Danielle was only broadcasting about this book repeatedly, she would use different versions of this tweet:

> Writing Social Media Engagement For Dummies has been a tough but rewarding process (`www.amazon.com/Engagement-Dummies-Business-Personal-Finance/dp/1118530195/ref=sr_1_1?ie=UTF8&qid=1365029805&sr=8-1&keywords=social+media+engagement+for+dummies`)

Listening to determine who's talking about you and your industry

Identifying who is mentioning you in the Twitter stream is an important task to address every day. Use Twitter search tools to locate customers who already have something to say about you, and make an effort to respond promptly. If someone praises you on Twitter, you have an excellent opportunity to express gratitude, to humanize your brand and to keep customers coming back. If someone tweets a critique, on the other hand, it's also an opportunity: Let them know that you hear their concern and care enough to respond and that they matter to you and your business. In this day and age, consumers expect these interactions from brands.

Seeking and finding specific topics

Is your business selling wine? Graphical design work? Yoga classes? Leverage the myriad ways you can search on Twitter for the people who are already talking about these topics to find new people to follow, to join conversations with people who share your personal and business interests, and to connect to the people who are the ideal targets for your message.

For example, try searching for *family vacation Florida* if you're a travel agent or a business owner who wants to target families as they arrive in your state. When you find a related conversation, join in — but avoid the hard sell. Rather than send a canned response with a pitch and a link to your site, seize the opportunity to create a relationship by asking questions: When is the family thinking about traveling? Where in Florida do they want to go? Have they been there before? Let them know that you're happy to help them make decisions if they need it.

Promoting your message

You have a business message that you want people to see. Eighty percent of the content you "promote" should be useful, informative, and engaging but not necessarily promotional, and the remaining 20 percent should consist of your marketing and sales messages. This way, your audience relies on you as a trusted voice in your field without feeling the push of a hard sell every time they hear from you.

Ideally, your followers rely on you as someone who curates and publishes worthwhile content. Aim to become a valuable resource for others, to be known as an expert in your business field.

If you're posting five times a day, make one or two tweets promotional, or link to your own resources. Though it's certainly acceptable to share good news, don't overwhelm your audience with too much "me-me-me."

To avoid the appearance of insincerity, avoid the *humble brag:* Though it's certainly good for a laugh, it's a tweeter's way of boasting while feigning humility. One Twitter account exclusively retweets — a *retweet* occurs whenever a tweet is repeated by someone else — the tweets of people who head down this patchy road. In Figure 10-2, you can see what to avoid — and how not to appear insincere.

Figure 10-2:
The humble brag monopolizes a tweet.

Adding a visual hook

Adding visual elements is an effective way to humanize you and your brand. Don't simply tell the audience that you make to-die-for cinnamon rolls — show them. (Or in the case of homemade cinnamon rolls from Cedar Creek Center, make their mouths water, as shown in Figure 10-3.) Similarly, don't tell your community that you're planning three brand-new photo shoots this weekend — *show* them the highlights.

Figure 10-3: Can you see why these homemade cinnamon rolls from Cedar Creek Center in Missouri create an effective tweet?

Add a see-what-I-mean image to your tweet! Telling everyone that a brand-new restaurant was packed on opening weekend sounds great. Showing them the line snaking out the door makes them wonder what they're missing. Never underestimate the power of show-and-tell.

You can use any number of applications to upload photos to Twitter. The tools described in this list integrate with Twitter to help you enhance your tweets with images:

✔ **Instagram:** (http://instagram.com) Offers a popular image-sharing network with a highly engaged community. With Instagram, you can share pictures not only on Twitter but also on other social networks.

✔ **Twitgoo:** (http://twitgoo.com) Gives you another opportunity to share pictures easily. You can upload from your computer or directly from another app.

✔ **Twitpic:** (www.twitpic.com) Helps you easily share photos and videos on Twitter by giving you the option to upload directly from your phone or via an e-mail address.

✔ **yFrog:** (www.yfrog.com) Provides tools for sharing photos and videos on Twitter. Simply take pictures and send them.

Asking a question

When you ask a question, you raise a digital sign telling your community that you value their input. Questions also give you perfect opportunities to engage immediately in conversations to show that you're listening and that you care.

Ask questions that encourage your community to talk about themselves, to give their opinions, or to show off their knowledge. Depending on the number of responses you receive, responding to each one may seem to be a daunting task, but don't miss out on any opportunity to connect for fear of responding too much or too little. You'll acquire the skills over time — and incorporate the tools — to help you manage responses from a growing community. See the later sections "Measuring Twitter engagement" and "Being 'present' even when you're not" for information on specific tools that can help manage your Twitter communications.

Keep these concepts in mind when you tweet questions:

✔ **Relevance matters.** If you typically tweet about business, for example, stay on topic. Your community will know what to expect from you and be more willing to respond.

✔ **Responsiveness reigns.** If seven people respond to you, make it your mission to reply to all seven. If the size of your following and your typical engagement level mean that 75 people respond, you still need to be present and responsive. To manage the load, choose a handful of people to receive an individual response, reply to a group at once, retweet a few answers that resonate, and even send out the more general message "Thank you for all of your responses." Your community needs to know that you're listening and that you appreciate their feedback.

✔ **Retweeting should be simple.** If you limit questions to 120 characters, your followers can more easily retweet them the old-fashioned way — by adding the letters *RT* in front. Some may still opt to click the Retweet link; however, people will always choose the simplest method. See the upcoming step list for an easy, old-style retweeting option.

✔ **Flexibility can expand your reach.** Repeat a question at different times and intervals, for example, so that you can reach more members of your community. People use Twitter at varying times, so repeating questions increases your exposure and your opportunity to engage. You may even learn an important piece of information — the time of day that your community is most active — so that you can more strategically post messages.

You have several choices for retweeting directly from Twitter or from applications such as TweetDeck and HootSuite — two applications that connect to Twitter, allowing you to streamline your activity and follow multiple conversations at one time. We discuss TweetDeck and HootSuite in more detail later in this chapter, in the sections "Being 'present' even when you're not" and "Building connections via lists and columns."

Follow these steps to make an old-style retweet (Aliza's personal preference) from Twitter:

1. **Open the tweet you want to repeat.**

2. **Copy the tweet by highlighting the text and pressing Ctrl+C.**

3. **Paste it in the message area by pressing Ctrl+P.**

4. **Move the cursor to the beginning of the text and type the letters** RT **(to indicate that this is a retweet).**

5. **(Optional) To share your opinion, add quotation marks around the tweet or type a note or thought in front of the letters** *RT*.

6. **Click Enter or Send.**

   This tweet (a *repeat* of someone else's original tweet) will now originate from your account, with the other person's Twitter username or handle, and will be visible to all your followers. Alternatively, you can click the Retweet button to send the tweet as a standard retweet (without comment or opinion), as shown in Figure 10-4.

Check out *Twitter For Dummies* (written by Laura Fitton, Michael Gruen, and Leslie Poston and published by John Wiley & Sons, Inc.) for more details on retweets and retweeting.

Conveying who you are on Twitter

When spending time engaging on Twitter, give your followers and potential followers a clear idea of your personality and intentions — who you are, what you do, and how and why you do it. Are you funny, serious, or silly? Do you intend to inspire, educate, or motivate? Are you in-the-know, the first of your friends or business associates to break news, or a thought leader with valuable information to share? Being clear about who you are helps the digital community connect with you and your message.

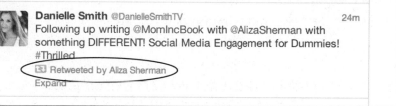

Figure 10-4:
Retweeting
a tweet.

Being your authentic self

Authentic has become a bit of a buzzword in social media marketing. The term is used to describe many "wants" in life, such as an "authentic relationship" or "authenticity" from businesses. Consumers want the real deal. The same is true of their digital presence in social networks.

These tips can help you "keep it real:"

- ✔ **Allow your personality to drive your content.** If you're a no-nonsense, just-the-facts kind of person, your content should match that persona. A misplaced joke would confuse your followers.

- ✔ **Maintain consistency.** Suddenly tweeting 45 times a day when your followers are used to 5 or choosing to tweet about politics when you traditionally stick to business may catch your community off guard. We aren't saying not to be yourself, but consider how your audience might respond to sudden deviations from the "you" they've come to know.

- ✔ **Avoid the hard sell.** Moving from a typical engaging conversation into a blatant sales pitch can be uncomfortable for your community. They will recognize a friendly "Hello!" that turns into this pushy question: "You know what you need?" And most won't like it.

✔ **Focus on your passion.** Let your interests and the passion you feel for your mission or cause be the driving force behind the information you share. Speaking from the heart makes you attractive to followers. The sincerity of your conversation moves them to respond and to act on your tweets — and to share what you have to say with others.

Knowing your boundaries

Letting your personality and passion be your guide for tweeting doesn't mean that you should forget how to behave in public. You're sharing some of your interests, and you may have included personal information about your family, but some topics should be considered off limits, especially if you represent a business.

Avoid tweeting about these topics:

✔ **Intensely personal situations:** Examples are divorces, criminal proceedings, and financial issues.

✔ **Politics or religion:** Avoid these classic argument-starters unless you're already known for engaging in these areas.

✔ **Libel:** Defaming someone in a tweet can come back to haunt you.

✔ **Hate speech of any kind:** Just don't do it.

If you represent a business, keep it in mind while you're tweeting. As an employee, your tweets can be mistaken or interpreted as the opinions of your employers, so watch what you say. Overall, we recommend steering away from negative tweets unless it's part of your brand to be snarky or snide or anything less than positive.

If you employ others, establish guidelines for your employees and contractors to determine what they should and shouldn't tweet. Put the guidelines in writing, and ask staff to sign off on them. Clearly state the repercussions of violating the guidelines for Twitter or any other social network or public space online.

Don't drink and tweet. Don't party hard, take a picture, and tweet it. Twitter has no Do Over or Take Back button. Even if you press Delete seconds after you've mistweeted, someone *somewhere* may have taken a screen shot. What happens during your off-hours is best left untweeted. Put your phone away until the morning after. You'll be grateful that you did.

Devising a plan to keep up with fast-moving conversations

Twitter moves fast, and keeping up with it can be difficult. We would be lying if we told you anything else. We would also be lying if we told you it's possible to keep up with 500 or 5,000 followers without dedicating time and paying attention. Quite simply, there's no substitute for paying attention. Listening on Twitter is important. Listening attentively is as important as thoughtfully crafting the tweets you publish. Unless you know what is being said and who is saying it, it's impossible to determine what to do next. That requires a plan.

Like any social media engagement you employ, Twitter requires planning, to keep up with the flow of conversation. If you've ever watched a Twitter stream flow past your eyeballs in real time, you know that your brain can barely register a single tweet before another batch of tweets has taken its place.

To create a master plan, follow these guidelines:

- ✔ **Know who is in charge of your account.** Decide whether one person or multiple people will keep up with your company's account. Then a designated person or team can familiarize themselves with the flow of conversation and develop a rapport with the people who engage with you the most. Your most frequent and interactive Twitter followers deserve the most attention, and someone who is familiar with your account comes to know these favorites.

- ✔ **Schedule regular, uninterrupted "Twitter-time."** Set specific times during the day to engage and, if necessary, specific days during the week when interaction is at its peak. Avoid jumping online for five minutes, asking a single question, and then disappearing for the next six hours. Plan out specific time slots for Twitter engagement, and check back frequently enough to respond when someone communicates with you.

- ✔ **Prioritize responses.** If you have only a certain amount of time on any given day, give top priority to people in your community who actively listen and engage with you. Reply to everyone who has tweeted to you, and take the time to reach out to a few new people who share your interests so that they know you're paying attention. People like to be recognized and feel that they matter. Outreach on Twitter can help you make that kind of connection.

To ensure that your account remains relevant and useful, "sweep" it periodically to uncover — and unfollow — dormant accounts and spammers. You can use Twit Cleaner (http://thetwitcleaner.com) or ManageFlitter (www.manageflitter.com) to find out which of the people you follow haven't tweeted in the past six months or more or who might be using Twitter as a spamming forum.

Measuring Twitter engagement

At the end of the day, yelling into an empty canyon ensures that the only response you receive is the echo of your own voice. And that, friend, means that you're doing it wrong — stop and assess how you're using Twitter. On the other hand, if you're seeing an uptick in the number of people who follow you or the number of times your content is shared, responded to, or favorited, or if your bottom line is moving in the right direction, continue doing more of what you're doing. Measuring your engagement on Twitter helps you assess how this platform is affecting your success in this space.

This list describes several popular Twitter measurement tools:

- **bitly:** (`https://bitly.com`) Shortens links to allow for maximum reach — because your tweets can be easily shared. Each URL you shorten is specific to you and can be tracked for statistics. You can use bit.ly metrics to see how many people clicked a particular link and how often it was shared.

- **Buffer:** (`http://bufferapp.com`) Analyzes every tweet you send, telling you whether someone favorited it, retweeted it, or clicked the link. As a multipurpose app, it also schedules your tweets at optimal tweeting times.

- **Tweet grader:** (`http://tweet.grader.com`) Ranks the power of your Twitter profile against millions of others in your city and in specific categories. It's particularly helpful in determining how you measure up against other tweeters in your local area.

- **TweetReach:** (`http://tweetreach.com`) Measures the number of accounts your tweets reach over a certain period and the tweets that received the most attention, and showcases the people who are most often sharing your content.

- **Twitter Counter:** (`http://twittercounter.com`) Allows you to closely track followers. You can see how many followers you've gained or lost on any given day. Noting the peaks and valleys of your following gives you insight into what may or may not have worked when you were tweeting. You can also use the search function to find and follow people in a specific category.

You may be tempted to try to use all these tools to measure engagement, but *you will drown* in data and numbers. Spend a little time exploring the benefits and limitations of each one as it applies to you and your business, and then choose the one or two that make the most sense for your specific needs.

Making an Impact in the Twitter Stream

What you say in social networks matters to your business, and you hope it matters to the people who are following you. To fully engage with your community on Twitter and to capture your followers' attention and keep them coming back for more, use wisely the 140 characters per tweet that you're allotted.

Now we want to share ways to maximize your impact with each tweet: Gain more shares for your content, engage more deeply with followers, and grow a community that meets your expectations and helps you achieve tangible business goals.

Avoid "text speak" in your tweets, and use proper grammar and spelling to avoid sounding either careless or uneducated (or both). For starters, resist the temptation to replace the word *you* with the letter *u* (the extra time that you believe you're gaining by not typing the other two letters won't counteract the bad impression you're creating) and, for the love of all things, remember the difference between *your* and *you're*. (The former indicates possession, the latter is a contraction of *you are*.)

Crafting attention-grabbing tweets

After you know how to measure the rate at which your tweets are being shared and how to see on which days you gained more followers than normal (find out how to keep track in Chapter 2), consider the following principles to maximize your Twitter social media engagement — and to maintain your authenticity:

- ✔ **Know the numbers.** You may already know that a tweet consists of 140 characters or fewer. Deduct 20 characters from that total. Consider 120 characters the new "magic number" for tweets. In addition to providing stellar content, make it easy for others to retweet you, by requiring little or no editing. Those 20 extra characters make room for the retweet (RT), such as when someone else "reshares" the tweet you have sent, your follower's Twitter name, and maybe even a short comment. If someone uses the retweet link, the shorter tweets don't matter — but you're catering to those who might not.

- ✔ **Shorten your links.** Shortening links allows you to have more room within the 120-character limit and to track your tweets if you use a service such as bit.ly.

✔ **Add attention-grabbing headings.** Extra! Extra! Think about the words that grab attention and use them in your tweets. Be concise and compelling. Assume that you have one shot to grab someone's attention — and that shot should lead to a click on your content.

✔ **Play to people's emotions.** Consider the positive energy you can generate when you decide to include good news in your stream every week. Create a Twitter account that people want to follow for the good feeling it brings into their day. Understand the power of people's feelings. Humor makes us human and makes us laugh and feel connected. Share a picture of a baby panda, and people will probably fall all over themselves to pass it along. A good quote can evoke emotions, and many are frequently retweeted on Twitter.

✔ **Use hashtags.** Adding the *hashtag* (#) in a tweet includes it in the conversation or search results related to that keyword. The hashtags you use identify you within a given community and make you visible to anyone following that topic. When you watch the #Emmys or the #WorldSeries or talk about #MS (multiple sclerosis) or #leukemia, you raise your virtual hand to say, "I'm here" and "I want to be part of this conversation." However, be careful not to use hashtags indiscriminately or to spam others.

A *hashtag* is a keyword that starts with the hash mark or pound sign (#) to identify and group a conversation or a group of related tweets on Twitter. For more about hashtags, refer to *Twitter For Dummies,* written by Laura Fitton, Michael Gruen, and Leslie Poston (John Wiley & Sons, Inc.).

✔ **Promote others.** Include other people's content in your tweets, and give them credit to let them know that you're listening and that you care enough about what they say to share it with your following. Giving kudos increases your own profile as well as those you retweet and reference. You become an authority based on the content you curate and recommend. Be someone on Twitter who provides quality content and who is willing to champion others.

Getting noticed is one thing — inspiring a reaction is your goal. Ideally, your followers monitor your progress online, but more than that, they share your wisdom with others. On Twitter, the holy grail of sharing is the retweet because it shows that a follower likes what you have to say enough to share it with *their* followers. A retweet says, *I read this, loved it, and think you should too!*

Leveraging links to get results

Engaging with your community on Twitter consists of equal parts showcasing the "real you" and building trust to work toward a goal by driving awareness of, and interactions with, your business. The interactions may be customers who purchase from you, but more often they're word-of-mouth results as your followers spread the word about you or your company, brand, products, or services.

Boosting your retweet potential

If your goal is engagement, it makes sense to reach as many people as possible with your message, thoughts, and conversation. The more engaging your initial tweet, the greater potential for your content to be passed along.

Follow these tips to inspire followers to retweet more of your tweets:

- **Limit tweets to 120 characters.** Sure, Twitter gives you 140 characters at a time to express your thoughts, but limiting the length of a tweet slightly makes it easier to retweet.

- **Tweet important tweets more than once.** You can even tweet *critical* messages several times a day. Your followers who miss them the first time around will appreciate the extra opportunity to see your latest content.

- **Tweet breaking news.** If you're one of the first people to share about the latest earth-quake in California, a politician's gaffe, or a celebrity's most recent escapade, your content is sure to be shared. The news should originate from a reliable source, however, before you pass it along — you don't want to be caught sharing a rumor. Also, the news that you share should align with your image and be relevant to your audience.

- **Express gratitude.** When people retweet your content, say "Thank you" to encourage them to come back for more. People love to be seen and heard on Twitter and on any other social network.

- **Schedule tweets during peak hours.** Yes, at certain times during the day, more people are tweeting. Fewer people are on Twitter in the wee hours of the night — unless they're in another time zone and you're targeting an international crowd. People tweet differently during the workday versus the evening and weekend. According to research done by bitly, the peak hours for tweeting range between 1 p.m. and 3 p.m. Monday through Thursday. When scheduling tweets, consider the time zones of the people you're trying to reach.

- **Tweet amazing content.** Easy enough, right? You recognize good content when you see it and especially when you see the results: This content constitutes your most frequently retweeted messages (as we explain in the earlier section "Crafting attention-grabbing tweets"). Take note of the tweets you see most frequently shared. Do more of it.

One outstanding way to inspire people to click the links you tweet is to feature content that educates, motivates, or inspires. Share the content you create, such as blog posts or articles, and link to that content. Find and share content from others that is relevant to your business and that may be of interest to your followers.

When you share memorable and moving information, your community becomes a willing evangelist for you — spreading your message and carrying your content beyond your initial boundaries. They do this not only because they like what you have to say but also because they appreciate how you operate.

As your followers become accustomed to you sharing their content and the content of others in addition to your own, they begin to trust that what they see from you is quality content. When someone trusts your content, they pass those same links along to their own communities, amplifying your message.

Retweeting and @mentioning others

We agree that the overall goal on Twitter and on any social network is engagement. We also acknowledge that the "end goal" should be a tangible outcome that helps your business thrive, such as building a larger customer base or increasing your revenue. Though it may seem counterintuitive, you can build a stronger and better following by retweeting and mentioning others on Twitter, not by talking only about yourself.

The results of retweeting and @mentioning others regularly is that you

- ✔ **Build trust:** By retweeting relevant content, you build trust with followers. If they click a link and find it interesting, they're more likely to click again the next time they see you sharing.

- ✔ **Meet potential new followers:** Retweeting content from someone who interests you is a way to let that person know that you're online and paying attention. If they don't respond to your retweet initially, you can begin a conversation with them based on that (or another) topic you shared.

- ✔ **Convey gratitude:** Clicking a link in a tweet is a passive way to say, "I find this information interesting" or "I appreciate this story." It's a way to thank the author of the link for sharing information that you find valuable or for being an online presence who enriches your digital space.

- ✔ **Contribute to the success of others:** Retweeting is a helpful way to say, "I think you're doing something well." Passing the link on to your own community adds your own, personal stamp of approval on it and allows you the privilege of adding (you hope) to another's success.

- ✔ **Recognize the value of conversation:** It's pretty darn difficult to have a conversation on Twitter if you never use the @ sign to talk to anyone. You should be using this symbol to reply to the people who have sent you tweets, to communicate with the people who are on your "must follow" lists, and to start conversations with people you find interesting.

If you send a message that starts with the @ sign, the only people who will see that message are the people who are following *both* you and the person you're tweeting. To make that message visible to all your followers to include them in the conversation, place a word in front of the @ sign and the name — for example, "Thank you @AlizaSherman, for keeping me on track while writing our book." If I remove the text *thank you,* a large percentage of my followers won't see the tweet. Some people place a period (.) in front of the @ sign to achieve the same result, but that method is awkward and less personal.

Being "present" even when you're not

One key to successful social media engagement is, of course, *engaging* with others. We want to be realistic as well and make sure that you can manage your Twitter account. Making an impact on Twitter usually requires far more content than on most other social networks. What we're about to tell you may seem to fly directly in the face of engagement, but we want you to know how to automate your tweets — *some* of your tweets, that is. Take everything in moderation, and automation is no exception. Don't let the tips and tools described in this section replace the time you spend interacting; instead, they can help you share more — and more often.

Schedule tweets that contain the strategic messages you want to be sure to post, but that you may not remember to post. Make 80 percent of your tweets nonpromotional, and put automation to good use to schedule the remaining 20 percent.

It's impossible to be on Twitter all day. Yet sometimes in a 24-hour period, you would love for your content to reach the people who might be most interested, even though you're busy with work and life. Even though you aren't sitting in front of your computer or tweeting from your phone at any given time, your community may still be online and be receptive to your messages.

Scheduling tweets can come in handy and accomplish a number of goals:

- **Maximize your exposure.** Planning tweets to hit at different times during the day allows you to reach a wider audience. If you're able to be online only at 8 a.m., your messages may not reach someone jumping on Twitter in the afternoon or evening. By scheduling a few messages to hit at various times of the day, you can get more exposure for your content.

- **Maintain a consistent message.** Scheduling tweets requires you to plan ahead. Planning ahead helps you stay on track with your messaging. Don't hop online at odd hours and wonder, "What should I say now?" Scheduling tweets puts in place a system for you to be more thoughtful about your tweets.

- **Remain visible.** You've heard the saying "Out of sight, out of mind," right? As clichéd as it sounds, you want to remain "top of mind" to your audience. The more you're seen online with a consistent, relevant message, the more likely people will notice your tweets and remember you. Even if they don't engage with you immediately, you're building your brand recognition.

- **Save time.** Automating some of your tweets should prevent you from jumping online 27 times throughout the day. You can focus instead on being productive and ensure that time-sensitive tweets are strategically placed to highlight events and activities without having to watch the clock. In theory, you can better manage your time knowing that a bit of the burden of frequent tweeting is lifted from you.

Scheduling tweets doesn't let you walk away from Twitter and never have to engage. Even after you have set tweets in motion, you *must* set aside time to check in on your Twitter community. If people have referenced you in conversation or shared your content, you can't acknowledge them or respond if you're never there. You'll lose followers, or at least lose their interest and attention.

These popular apps can help you schedule tweets:

- **TweetDeck:** (www.tweetdeck.com) Schedule days in advance, at any point throughout the day, and maintain columns and categories of lists of people you don't want to miss.

- **HootSuite:** (http://hootsuite.com) In addition to setting tweets in advance, save even more time with this bulk scheduler. It's also integrated with Facebook, LinkedIn, and Google+ (see more in Chapters 9, 12, and 13, respectively).

- **Buffer:** (http://bufferapp.com) Run analytics to determine the best times of day for your tweets to post, and then schedule them accordingly. This app offers free and upgraded (paid) versions.

- **IFTTT:** (https://ifttt.com) We call this app a miracle automation tool. Use If This Then That to send out tweets triggered by specific actions. For example, "If I share a new item in my Google Reader, post it to Twitter" or "If this person I follow tweets a link, retweet it." The combinations of actions triggering tweets are seemingly endless.

Increasing Engagement via Twitter Features

Conversation is both a goal and a reward of being active on Twitter. When you tweet and someone else responds, you know that you're being heard, that your message is relevant, and that the people who are following you are interested and attentive.

Of course, you want to keep those interactions alive and turn them into actions such as clicking your links and sharing your content. In addition to dedicating time and energy, you must be willing to try new strategies to continually improve how you use Twitter.

Giving kudos using Favorites

The Favorite link on Twitter serves several purposes. It's a way for you to let someone you're following know that you value her content. That person receives a notice every time you favorite one of her tweets. It's a helpful way to make a connection. Similar to retweeting, favoriting carries your personal stamp of approval. However, unlike a retweet, which eventually drops off your Twitter stream, a favorited tweet remains on your Favorites list on your main Twitter page for all to see.

Many people use Twitter favorites as sort of a bookmarking function to save information that they want to read or access later. Though it's handy, keep in mind that you're saving those tweets in a publicly accessible archive that's attached to your Twitter account.

If you favorite a tweet to save it for later reading and then decide that you don't want it archived or displayed on your account, simply click the Favorited link (next to the star) to "unfavorite" it and remove it from the Favorites list.

If you haven't used the favoriting feature in a while, look through the tweets you have saved to ensure that they're an appropriate fit for you and your brand. If not, unfavorite them.

Building connections via lists and columns

Lists and columns on Twitter come in handy for not only the purpose of keeping track of the people you're already following but also to create connections and nurture new relationships. Start your Twitter list-making by aggregating (collecting) the names of people you must follow — whether this list consists of the people who engage with you the most, who are the best advocates for you and your business, or who simply share the content that you don't want to miss.

Twitter lists can be public (by default) or private. Public lists should be based on topics or categories that make sense for you to share with others. Private lists are useful for helping you keep track without publicizing your intention to the world.

Creating lists and columns

No matter how many people you're following, you cannot keep up with all of them. In your business, your goal is to create meaningful connections with potential customers, make contact with people who are influential in your field, and strengthen relationships with the people who already love you and your brand. Though it sounds like a lot of people, it still won't be everyone who is following you.

One effective way to keep up with the people who matter the most to you and your business is to create lists and columns. You can create a *list* in Twitter to follow people whom you group based on a specific topic. Lists can be created on any platform, including traditional Twitter (www.twitter.com). A list is typically a way to group individual people by category: fitness, breaking news, parenting, social media, or real estate, for example. A list lets you follow a specific conversation and can help you access tweets from others based on a topic area. You don't have to follow someone in order to place the person on a Twitter list, so lists also help you clear the clutter in your Twitter stream.

A *column,* on the other hand, is the traditional way to group followers on specific applications, such as TweetDeck and HootSuite. These two apps let you add individuals to columns, or delete them, to make it easier to keep up with conversations. Again, a column may be based on a category, or it can be dedicated to an individual. For example, Danielle might have a column on TweetDeck dedicated entirely to Aliza so that she never misses a tweet that Aliza sends out. But Danielle may also have a separate column that includes brilliant minds that she likes to follow — and Aliza would be one of them.

Both applications let you create lists based on whatever categories are relevant to you, and they can help you hone in on specific conversations.

Create a category or list with a search for your company name, your Twitter username, and any common variation of your brand name in case people mention you without including your username or abbreviate or misspell your business name. Having these additional columns ensures that you see what is being said about you on Twitter and provides you with the opportunity to interact with the people who are talking about you.

Helpful uses for the Favorites feature

The Favorites list on your Twitter page is more than an archive of tweets and articles you hope to read someday. It is a tool that allows your followers to learn more about you — what interests you, what you find worth starring, and, if used correctly, it can highlight what tweets of yours have been found noteworthy by your followers.

✔ **Endorsements:** If someone tweets something kind about you, writes an article about you, or quotes you in a media piece, favorite it. Use your Favorites list as a testimonial page for you and your company. When you favorite these types of tweets, your Favorites list becomes a supplement to your Twitter Bio.

✔ **Backgrounder:** Keep track of the links and tweets that help tell your story and convey your message. This list is an additional guide for potential new followers to let them know more about you by the tweets you favorite.

✔ **Market Research:** Pay attention to which of your tweets is a favorite of your followers. Every time your tweets are favorited, you strike gold. You're being told, "I like what you've said," and it's your cue to do more of what resonates with your followers. Keep track of your tweets that others have favorited over time to determine what common denominators, if any, are making those messages more popular than the rest.

To set up a column on TweetDeck, follow these steps (you can download it from www.tweetdeck.com to get started):

1. **Click the Add Column button at the upper-left corner of the TweetDeck application.**

2. **Click the Search Icon (represented by a magnifying glass) in the top row.**

3. **Enter a #hashtag or keyword in the open field for whatever you want to find on Twitter, and press Enter.**

   The term you searched for populates on the right side of the screen.

4. **Click the Add Column button to add the new column to the TweetDeck application.**

5. **To add another column, repeat Steps 1 through 4.**

To set up a column on HootSuite (www.hootsuite.com), log in to HootSuite and follow these steps:

1. **Click the Add Stream button in the upper left portion of the HootSuite dashboard.**

2. **Choose the type of column to add by clicking the small, horizontal tab on the Add Stream screen. You can choose**

   a. *Stream:* Select an account to access from the drop-down menu and the type of stream you want to see, such as Feed, Mentions, or Direct Messages.

   b. *Search:* In the open field, type a search query, such as *"wine + cabernet."*

   c. *Keyword:* In the open field, enter a word or phrase (up to three words), including a hashtag.

   d. *List:* Select an account to access from the drop-down menu, add a name for the list in the Create A New List section, add a description (optional) in the next field, and choose to make the list public or private.

3. **Click the Add Stream button at the bottom of any of the Add Stream screens detailed in Step 2 to insert a new stream to the dashboard.**

   Note that you can add only ten streams per tab. You can group streams under different tabs. To add another tab, follow these steps:

   a. *Click the + sign to the right of the default tabs across the top portion of the dashboard.*

   b. *Give the new tab a title, such as Brand Searches or Important Lists.*

   c. *Press Enter to see the Add a Stream option. Click that button and start at Step 1 again to add a stream.*

   You now have a new column and, if you need it, a new tab.

Creating additional lists outside your obvious circles lets you discover people and form new connections. The thought leaders in your industry, for example, may be people with whom you want to connect. Follow them, add them to a public list to get on their radar, and then check the list to pay closer attention to what they're sharing. Share their content or @mention them to get noticed and spark conversations.

Creating lists using third-party tools

Increase your online visibility by adding yourself to Twitter lists via third-party applications. Many of these tools are organized by topic or location. The beauty of this strategy is that people who share your interests and search by proximity can discover you as easily as you can find them.

Here are a few of our favorite Twitter list tools:

- **JustTweetIt:** (`http://justtweetit.com`) Find Twitter users like you with a series of labeled categories. You can search yourself *and* list yourself.

- **Listorious:** (`http://listorious.com`) Search for people on Twitter by the topics they specify or by their cities or professions. Add yourself where relevant.

- **Twellow:** (`www.twellow.com`) By letting you click a map to locate people in nearby towns, this app connects you to people locally and by category. Like the others, you can list yourself and seek out people who you believe would be good connections.

- **WeFollow:** (`http://wefollow.com`) This Twitter directory is organized by tags and categories. Users list themselves in individual categories and are then displayed by their number of followers. An increase in followers can mean a moving up the list.

Getting personal with a direct message (DM)

Your followers have, presumably, some interest in engaging with you, so sending one of them a direct message — no links allowed — with a compliment about a post or with a customized thank-you message for a retweet or another form of praise can help you begin a more personal conversation.

You can send direct messages only to your followers. Use that trust wisely.

Do not use direct messages to send links to personal promotional pages, résumés, or bios, such as your Facebook page or sales pitch. You most certainly wouldn't attach your business card to the outside of your coat and begin talking about yourself with every stranger you meet, so don't do it online.

The direct message has come under attack from an influx of spam. Hackers can worm their way into your account by using deceptive direct messages (DMs), like the one shown in Figure 10-5, and make everyone more wary of receiving them. For example, you receive what appears to be an inflammatory DM suggesting that you've been spotted in some compromising pictures or that your site is under attack or an equally nerve-wracking circumstance, so you click the link and give the spammer access to your password and account. It's the domino effect: The same message you received is then sent to many of *your* followers from *your* account. You can easily see how any DM with a link in it can become suspect. If you aren't 100 percent sure, always reply to the sender first to verify that the link was sent to you intentionally. Your only defense is a strong offense: *Do not* open the link.

Figure 10-5:
A spam
tweet like
this one
is almost
certainly
hacker
spam.

 Never send an automatic direct message when someone begins following you. Even though you might be sending what you perceive to be a stab at initial engagement, a generic "Thank you for following me" message can come across as fake and spammy. People often unfollow the senders.

Attracting more followers with widgets and buttons

Adding followers can initially feel like Christmas morning. You eagerly explore information about each individual, assessing their compatibility with you by examining their avatars, their bios, the number of followers they have, and the number of people they're following. When you start out on Twitter, you may even take the time to look at the nitty-gritty details — what have they had to say for the past week and *who* are they following.

Now you want more of what you already have: people who are engaged with you and with the messages you're sharing. One way to encourage others to follow you on Twitter is to present them with the opportunity where they're already finding your content: on your website, blog, and other social networks.

You can easily add any of these options on Twitter to increase your following and increase shares of your content by others:

- ✔ Follow button on your blog: Reminds your community to find and follow you on Twitter

- ✔ Sharing button on posts at your blog or website: Lets readers easily pass along your content to their communities, as shown in Figure 10-6

- ✔ Widget (Recently Tweeted) on your blog sidebar: Showcases your most recent tweets to engage your community in the latest conversations

This.... this is the answer I seek.

Get Shareaholic for Google Chrome

Related posts:

1. The CMA Awards – Life List Item Checked (6.4) It almost felt like I could reach out and touch...
2. The True Rules of Soccer (and Life) (5.5) Rule Number One. Have Fun. The First Grade Boys Soccer...
3. Lessons From Oprah's Life Class in St. Louis: Stop The Pain (5.3) I had a date last night. With Oprah. Now,...

Related posts brought to you by Yet Another Related Posts Plugin.

Figure 10-6:
The Twitter sharing button lets community members easily pass along content.

Twitter now offers not only embeddable tweets but also fully customizable and interactive timelines. According to Twitter, your community can now follow and reply to you (or — gasp — unfollow you), and can even favorite and retweet your tweets, without leaving your website. When customizing an embeddable Twitter stream, you can specify the content you pull in as well as the size of the widget.

You can embed a custom Twitter stream based entirely on your company's name or #hashtag or a conversation to showcase a specific campaign. In fact, with a widget like this one, you can customize the content and size of the widget. We can almost see the wheels turning as you think about the possibilities for leveraging Twitter's interactive timelines.

Adding Twitter to Facebook (and vice versa)

Here's a social media topic of great debate: should your Twitter and Facebook accounts be linked? It's certainly possible to do so. If you link Twitter to Facebook, every time you tweet, the exact same message shows up on Facebook. Linking Facebook to Twitter makes every status update you post on Facebook automatically appear in your Twitter stream, truncated (shortened) to 140 characters.

Setting up these links can save you time, but not every short cut is necessarily worth it. We don't recommend linking Twitter to Facebook. Twitter moves so much more quickly than Facebook with far more messaging, and your Facebook followers will likely be turned off by the onslaught of messaging. Also your tweets often contain symbols that aren't found on Facebook so your updates on Facebook will look cluttered with the @ and # characters.

After you link Facebook to Twitter, you can't switch it on and off per update. Be careful not to be repetitive by duplicating messages in both places in the same or similar timeframe. Linking Twitter and Facebook can be confusing so if you choose to do it, manage the process with care.

Consider that some people will follow you on both Twitter and Facebook. On one hand, if they see the same verbiage appear in both locations, you won't look organized or "on the ball." On the other hand, the chances of a person who follows you in both places seeing you cross post are slim. It isn't likely that they'll be on both Facebook and Twitter and paying attention to your messages on both at the same time. If they see your cross-posts on rare occasion, they're unlikely to hold it against you if they like you and your content in general.

For the most part, people who connect with you in multiple places aren't connecting with you in all those places at the same time. And though you will definitely have some crossover in your Twitter followers and Facebook friends or fans, not everyone will connect with you actively in multiple places.

If you're sure that you want to link your Twitter account to post to Facebook, use Selective Tweets (`https://facebook.com/selectivetwitter/`). With this app, not all of your tweets post to Facebook — only the ones you tag with #fb.

Accessing Twitter on the go

With the constant go-go-go flow of tweets on Twitter, it shouldn't surprise you that a large percentage of the platform's users access the site from mobile devices. In September of 2011, Twitter announced that 55 percent of its traffic originated from mobile devices. However, according to Twitter CEO Dick Costolo (http://marketingland.com/twitter-400-million-tweets-daily-improving-content-discovery-13581) the number jumped to a full 60 percent of its 140 million users during the summer of 2012.

The official Twitter mobile app is easy to navigate, and it's a fairly reliable option for tweeting from your device. Though it lacks the special options that power users desire, it's functional. Feel free to experiment with other mobile apps for tweeting. Table 10-1 lists options for Twitter mobile apps depending on the platform you're using — Android or iOS.

Table 10-1	Twitter Mobile Apps by Platform
For Android OS	*For iOS (iPhone, iPad, iPod)*
Buffer	Buffer
Plume	Echophone
Seismic	Tweetbot
Twitterific	Tweetcaster
UberSocial	Twitterific

Conversation is the key. Followers have no interest in engaging with a *bot* (an account masquerading as a real person) that gathers @ replies like trophies. This isn't a game that everyone wins. When you genuinely engage with your community, they respond in kind.

Part IV
Engaging Through Additional Social Channels

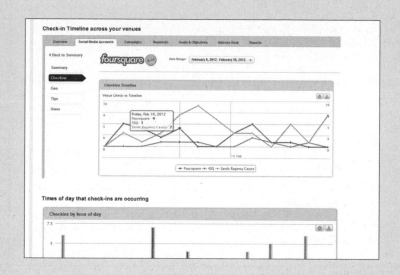

To find out how to use Google Hangouts for video-based engagement, go to www.dummies.com/extras/socialmediaengagement.

In this part . . .

- ✔ Leverage visual elements to attract and engage your customers in new ways through Pinterest.

- ✔ Build a connected professional presence and community on LinkedIn.

- ✔ Attract more of the right audience and expand your reach by using Google+.

- ✔ Tie physical locations to your online activities and promotions by using location-based services.

Chapter 11

Pinterest

In This Chapter

▶ Using your Pinterest account to create connections

▶ Harnessing the power of Pinterest to attract followers

▶ Leveraging Pinterest to engage your audience

▶ Measuring the benefits of Pinterest

*P*interest is the fastest-growing social network and boasts a higher percentage of female users than the other popular social networks in the United States. Even if your target market is not predominantly female, you can still benefit from using Pinterest to build your brand and to drive traffic to your other sites and social networks.

We both use Pinterest to build our personal brands as well as to enhance what we share on the other social networks we use. We have a Social Media Engagement board on our Pinterest profiles that we both contribute to. On this board, you can find images that link to articles and additional resources on the topic of social media engagement for ongoing learning and inspiration. Find our shared Pinterest board by going to `http://bit.ly/engage board`. We also have a Pinterest account for our previous book, *Mom, Incorporated* (Sellers Publishing, Inc.), that we use as another means for connecting with our specific target audience, in this case, moms.

In this chapter, you find out how to tap into the power of Pinterest to build on the ways you engage with your following and boost your efforts to attract an even larger following. For example, we show you how to pin, repin, like, and comment on other people's pins to create connections and reach out to your target audience. You also find out how Pinterest users engage versus Facebook or Twitter users. (We cover Facebook and Twitter in Chapters 9 and 10, respectively.)

Creating Connections by Incorporating Visual Elements

If a picture is worth 1,000 words, Pinterest is a valuable asset to your online marketing efforts. Pinterest's main features are pins and boards. *Pins* are individual posts of images or video, and *boards* are the organized collections of pins based on categories or themes. The main ways to interact with others on Pinterest are to like, repin, or comment on their pins. Pinterest taps into the power of images and how they attract our eye or how they make us think of or feel something in an instant.

Knowing how to create the right mix of pins and boards can be the key to maximizing the benefit of your Pinterest account.

Preparing your business account

Pinterest offers companies and brands the option to set up a business account instead of a personal Pinterest account. In the business section of its site (http://business.pinterest.com), it provides a number of case studies to get you started. As you set up a profile for your business account, Pinterest prompts you to verify your website, a feature also available on personal accounts. To verify your website, follow the instructions provided by Pinterest including placing a unique line of code Pinterest provides onto a page on your web server.

Although the features of business and personal profiles are virtually the same, the move toward business accounts makes way for new features that will benefit brands looking to use Pinterest for marketing and sales. As of early 2013, metrics are now a feature offered through business accounts. Other anticipated features include promoted pins and boards.

Expect Pinterest to add new features as it matures. To remain competitive and to grow, the company has to serve other businesses looking for more marketing and sales-oriented features to justify using the network.

If you're already using Pinterest with a personal account, you can convert it to a business page by logging into your current account and going to http://business.pinterest.com. Click the large red button to "Join as a Business," and your personal account information will populate the form. Select a business type from the drop-down menu at the top of the page, add a Contact Name, double-check the rest of the information, agree to the Terms of Service, and then click the Convert button at the bottom.

Setting up the right boards for your brand

If you set up your Pinterest account while the site was still in beta, Pinterest gave you a number of default options for your boards' themes such as Books I'm Reading and For the Home. Pinterest no longer prompts you with board ideas, so it's up to you to determine your board-naming strategy to attract attention and get followers.

Start with your goals, your audience, and the actions you want them to take; then craft board names tied directly to achieving your goals and communicating a clear message. The think-through process for naming your boards should go something like this:

1. **What are my business goals?**

   Suppose you run a consulting business and want to build your profile so people hire you. Outline business goals that are measurable and get more people to notice you such as "increase traffic to my website" and "get people to share my content."

2. **Is my target audience on Pinterest, and if so, how are they using it?**

   You should already be connected to your target audience through other popular social networks such as Twitter, Facebook, and LinkedIn. Survey them to see who is on Pinterest. Follow them and observe what they pin and how else they leverage Pinterest, such as on their websites.

3. **How can Pinterest help me reach my target audience?**

   If you've located some of your target audience on Pinterest, interact with them to get noticed. Specify how you'll use Pinterest to attract their attention, including leveraging Pinterest on your website and other social networks.

4. **How can Pinterest help me achieve my business goals?**

   If your goals are to increase traffic to your website and to get people to share your content, for example, identify the Pinterest activities and features directly related to those goals. You can pin images and video from your website or link back to your website in pins you upload. Make sure your images are compelling so that people repin them and lead others back to your content.

5. **What topics or keywords are relevant to my business?**

   Identify the topics that are most relevant to you based on who you are, what you do, and how others might find you. If you're a social media consultant, for example, your keywords should include *consultant* as well as your areas of expertise such as *mobile, social media,* and *social networks.* Don't forget broader topics, in this case *technology, marketing,* and *business.*

Use clear and related keywords when you name your boards to help attract more attention and ensure your Pinterest account shows up in relevant search results. Be creative but not too off-the-wall so your boards are easy to find.

6. **What board names best convey the topics that represent who I am, what I do, and what I want to communicate to others?**

   When coming up with board names, be creative but also remember your keywords. The keyword *mobile* can be a Make Me Mobile board, *social networks* becomes a Love Social Networks board, and *marketing* becomes a Marketing Tips for Your Business board. Let your personality shine through.

Choosing board types

After you come up with great board names, think about the types of boards you want to build. We have both made it a priority to include boards that highlight our brand messages as well as our personalities. On our Pinterest boards, you're likely to see images that inspire the work we do as well as the items that interest us personally: wine, the beach, travel, the landscape of rural Alaska, technology, fashion, and our children.

You have various choices for the types of boards you can create on Pinterest:

✔ **Content-themed:** One common type of board represents a content theme such as travel, food, or home. Content-themed boards can be highly targeted or cover niche topics such as Travel with Kids, Gluten-free Desserts, and Japanese Gardens. The pins on content-themed boards are visually related to a specific topic or theme and should lead to relevant source articles, blog posts, or sites. Figure 11-1 shows an example of a content-themed board: a wine-related crafts board curated by the Wine Sisterhood.

Figure 11-1: This board features wine-related crafts curated by the Wine Sisterhood.

Think of the various ways you can directly and indirectly convey your message through your boards. The Wine Sisterhood's parent company develops and markets new brands of wine. The crafts it pins to its Wine Crafty board are not its own designs, but they are complementary to the company's overall business and appealing to its target market.

✔ **Event-related:** Create an event-related board before an event to promote it and use the board during the event as a repository for images from the event to drum up awareness and engagement. After the event, add even more images and turn the board into a permanent visual archive of the event. Use links to the board and pins in posts on other social networks to bring people back to the archive.

Figure 11-2 shows a board that documents a film festival where the documentary film *Day in Our Bay* was screened. The film's producers pinned photographs live from the film festival that lead back to their website.

Figure 11-2:
Documenting
a film
festival.

✔ **Visual-themed:** This type of board is a little less straightforward, but really creative. With visual-themed boards, the way an image looks tends to be more important than what is represented in the image. Think of these boards as eye-candy focused on a common visual aspect in each image, such as shape (all triangular things) or color (chartreuse objects).

Figure 11-3 shows a visually themed board with images of the unusual icosahedron shape. In this case, designer Sean Dougall devotes a Pinterest board to the very unusual icosahedron. The objects in the images are of different colors, textures, and sizes, but all contain the same complex shape. A visual-themed color board features objects and scenes having little more in common than that all are dominated by a particular color, such as the board shown in Figure 11-4. Monochromatic boards attract the eye and stand out from other boards.

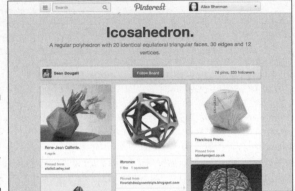

Figure 11-3:
A board
focused on
a particular
shape.

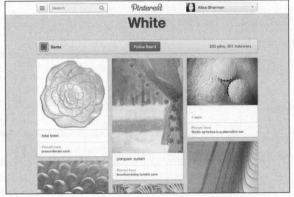

Figure 11-4:
A color-
themed
board in
which white
is the domi-
nant color in
each image.

Arranging boards for effect

The way you position your boards on your Pinterest account page can give others an immediate impression of not only your interests but also your brand image and personality. Rearrange your boards so that the ones you want to emphasize are toward the top. The upper boards tend to get the most attention and interactions. However, don't neglect to put content onto the boards toward the bottom of your Pinterest page.

Consider building boards purely for their visual impact, such as putting together rows or columns of boards to represent frames, borders, or separators. The pins on these types of boards are deliberately chosen to create specific colors or patterns.

Put thought into all the types of boards you build. Highly targeted and focused boards help you better attract and reach your target audience as well as compel that audience to interact with you.

Pinning to clearly convey your messages

Knowing a picture can convey meaning, inspire action, or generate emotion, what words and thoughts are the images you pin conjuring up in people's minds? When interacting on Pinterest, most users are going on instinct and gut reaction, responding to an instantaneous visceral feeling they get from an image. Although some pinners are more strategic, the majority of everyday Pinterest users are more emotional and less analytical about their pinning and repinning habits.

Given the limitations of how people use and interact with pins — and given that only a small percentage of users comment on pins — your chances of engagement start with clear, distinct images that communicate a message. Not everyone will interpret the message you put on Pinterest through a pinned image in the same way. Your pin description therefore plays an important role in clarifying your message. The destination of your pin, or board, should also reinforce your message.

When you pin images and their corresponding content, think about what you want others to know about you or your brand. Your boards act as archives for your pins, but your pins are the active and current messages you post to the Pinterest stream, or *pin feed*, on a regular basis. You can pin videos — your own or other people's — as well as images to your board. Look for ways to incorporate video into your Pinterest stream for increased interactivity.

When you upload your own pins, watermark them with a digital watermark or type a photo credit or your website URL directly onto each image. Don't rely on the image description to provide your copyright or branding because these can be altered or deleted over time.

Move beyond the obvious content and image choices for your boards and think about where you want your boards to lead before you start pinning. You can modify the link on anything you pin to your boards. If you upload your own pins, where you link each image can lead people to the sites and social networks where you can further engage with them. Consider sending them not only to your blog or website, but to your Facebook or Twitter page for increased engagement.

Connecting using pins, repins, likes, and comments

According to stats reported regularly by Repinly, a company that provides a directory of popular content on Pinterest, Pinterest users are more likely to like or repin than they are to comment. The bulk of Pinterest activity is focused on pinning, repinning, and liking, so understand that most pinners may not be looking to enter conversations on Pinterest. Someone who is paying close attention to who is repinning her pins may be more likely to respond if you comment on her pin than someone focused on the pinning process.

To increase interactions on Pinterest, start with great images. Pinning and repinning build your boards and fill your Pinterest page with content. Pinning and repinning may also help you communicate with other Pinterest users; this is your way of inviting them to connect and interact with you.

You reach out and cast a wide net when you pin. The quality of your pins may attract attention as they appear in the pin feed or add value to your boards. But repinning is a much more direct action to stimulate engagement on Pinterest. Through repinning you can

- ✔ **Give kudos to another pinner.** Pinterest users are notified of repins, so the act of repinning lets them know you liked what they pinned enough to share it on your own boards.

- ✔ **Get the attention of your target market.** When you identify Pinterest users who are your target market, a repin lets them know you exist, and they have the option to follow you.

- ✔ **Build relationships with other Pinterest users.** After you follow someone on Pinterest and he follows you back, repinning shows you're paying attention and reminds him you're there.

- ✔ **Leverage other people's images to communicate your message.** When someone else has similar interests, tastes, or messages, repinning her images is an easy, effective way of displaying relevant content to your own following.

Liking someone's pin requires less commitment than placing her pin onto one of your boards. Instead, the action of liking a pin shows up in your activity stream as well as in the stream of the person whose pin you've liked. Similar to other social networks, liking something someone else has posted is a way to get on her radar.

Clicking the Like button on someone else's pin can be an impulsive act. Pause for a moment before liking someone else's pin to consider how that pin reflects on your own brand image. Don't agonize over the process of liking pins, but don't like indiscriminately either. This is not a game of he or she with the most pins, wins. The effort you make reflects the "you" that you want your community to see.

You can comment on someone else's pin, but also consider the content of that pin, where it leads, and the message in the description. All of these factors could reflect on your brand. Even though it's visually driven, Pinterest is still considered a social network. Make the effort to reach out to your target market by actively liking and commenting.

Don't get discouraged if nobody responds to your comments. Focus your energy on finding and pinning compelling and relevant images and strive to constantly increase repins of your pins.

Quantifying the value of Pinterest

As with any newer social network or online marketing tool, the longer and more frequently people and brands use Pinterest, the more case studies and data are published to quantify the power of pinning.

As of this writing, Pinterest hasn't yet opened its *Application Programming Interface (API)* widely to other programmers. A site's API is the code that runs the functions of that site. When a site has an open API, other programmers can create their own tools that mesh with the main site.

Until Pinterest added its own analytics for business accounts, getting precise analysis of Pinterest stats was challenging. If you are still using a personal account, you can look at your website statistics and note new surges in traffic or interactions that you can then trace back to Pinterest.

Some of the initial numbers you can examine on Pinterest to get a sense of its impact on your social media engagement include

- ✔ **Number of followers:** You can view your followers on your Pinterest account page.

- ✔ **Number of repins:** As you receive e-mail notices from Pinterest regarding actions taken on your account, keep a tally. Eventually, Pinterest will provide tools that calculate this number for you.

- ✔ **Number of likes:** Again, tallying from Pinterest e-mail notices is the first way to arrive at this number. In the future, look for third-party services that calculate this for you in a more thorough report.

- ✔ **Number of comments:** Pinterest notifies you of comments on your pins in the same way it does repins and likes (through e-mail), which means more tallying for you to do until a tool is available.

You can see who has recently followed you as well as which pins they've repinned or liked by viewing your Pinterest Recent Activity stream that appears on the left side of your Pinterest Home page (your main view at Pinterest.com when you are logged in). Note which of your pins generate attention.

With a Pinterest business account, you can track more specific metrics including the following:

- ✔ **Number of people pinning from your website.** Make sure you have verified your website as instructed by Pinterest.

✔ **Number of people seeing your pins or "Impressions."** Watch for activity trends on your account based on your own activities.

✔ **Most repinned and most clicked pins.** Gauge what is most popular amongst your followers and other pinners and optimize your pinning.

Pinterest sends regular notices to Pinterest users about recent account activity as well as a weekly summary e-mail that provides some cursory stats and trends, including how many people followed you the previous week. Look more closely at your followers to determine not only how many followers you're gaining, but also what percentage of them are your target market. Figure 11-5 shows a notification of activity by other people on a Pinterest account. Figure 11-6 shows part of a weekly summary by e-mail from Pinterest that includes the number of people who followed you in the previous week.

Figure 11-5:
Notices of actions taken by other people on your Pinterest account.

In addition to Pinterest analytics, you can track the performance of your pins by running a Pinterest pin campaign using a site such as Reachli (`www.reachli.com`), a tool that adds metrics to your pins. You can measure your Pinterest influence and effectiveness with a tool such as Pinpuff (`www.pinpuff.com`).

Track other numbers on your social networks that can help demonstrate how Pinterest is driving interactions. Keep an eye on referrers listed in your website traffic logs. If you're not yet using it, set up Google Analytics on your website to better measure Pinterest traffic. Check your stats culled by third-party sites like the free Repinly (`www.repinly.com`) and the fee-based Piqora (`www.piqora.com`) to glean more data. Figure 11-7 shows a stats page from Repinly, which indicates Pinterest stats and a score calculating your popularity, activity, and influence on Pinterest. The top score is 100.

Figure 11-6:
A weekly summary from Pinterest.

Figure 11-7:
Repinly gives Pinterest stats and a score.

Pinpuff measures your popularity, influence, and reach on Pinterest, as shown in Figure 11-8. Every site that calculates scores for any other site uses its own formula for calculation, so comparing scores is similar to comparing apples to oranges. You can use these stats however, to get a sense of how you're doing on Pinterest in a more general sense. But don't get too caught up in the numbers.

Take note when Pinterest shows up in the top 20 referrers of traffic to your site. After you begin to see Pinterest listed as a referrer, continue to monitor how much traffic you receive on your website from Pinterest to see how your Pinterest efforts translate into actions and engagement.

Figure 11-8:
Some
Pinpuff
stats.

Don't get so caught up in the numbers that you overlook the overall value of the engagement you do get. You are strengthening relationships with customers and potential customers who are also avid Pinterest users and meeting them in a place where they are comfortable and content. Sometimes it's difficult to measure relationships, and numbers don't always reflect the power of those connections.

The statistics you can access about your Pinterest account are more valuable to you combined than looked at individually. Knowing who your followers are and how they interact gives you better insights into your Pinterest community and level of social media engagement.

Getting Noticed In People's Pin Feeds

The opening of Pinterest's floodgates caused a rush of new users, translating to many more pins. The more popular Pinterest becomes, the harder it is for your pins to stand out.

Develop your own style and pick eye-catching images to start, then look for ways to modify what, how, and even when you pin to have more impact on engagement. You also want to keep your pinning frequent and consistent. We're not saying become a Pinterest addict, but don't pin as an afterthought. Really find a way to integrate Pinterest into your online activities.

Don't limit pins to photographs — use graphics, too. You can generate a lot of successful interactions through Pinterest by pinning *infographics* — visual interpretations of information on any topic that's made into a graphic for the web, as shown in Figure 11-9 — as well as images with quotes on them. Graphics with quotes like the one shown in Figure 11-10 are quite popular in social networks and can boost your Pinterest interactions by generating repins. Use infographics and quote images that are relevant to your brand messages.

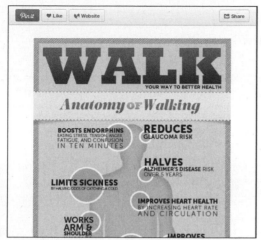

Figure 11-9: An infographic.

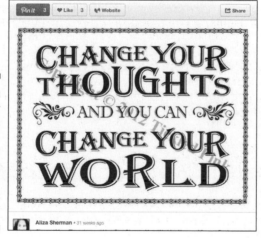

Figure 11-10: Some of our favorite (and most popular) quote images are inspirational or motivational.

Seeking and pinning winning images

Where do you find good pins? You may be tempted to start with or stick with your own images on Pinterest. In some cases, this may be a company guideline and limitation you have to work within. If it's not company policy to pin only your own copyrighted images, your pin-able selection greatly increases. Start rubbing your hands together in eager anticipation.

Use the images in Pinterest's Popular category as a gauge to see what's gaining traction with other pinners. Then search for similar types of images on the web to pin directly from their sources. Access the Popular page — or any other category page — using the drop-down menu in the upper-left corner of any Pinterest page (to the left of the Search field).

Some of the initial places you can go for pin inspiration include

- **Your Pinterest Home page:** When you're on Pinterest.com, the stream of pins you see by default are of the pinners you follow.

- **The Popular category:** See what's getting the most repins and likes at any moment on the Popular category page, accessed from the drop-down menu of categories on the upper-left side of your screen.

- **Everything feed:** Access the Everything category page to see pins from all Pinterest members as they are pinned.

- **Trending on Pinterest:** Access this information in your weekly Pinterest e-mails or through sites such as Repinly.

- **Popular boards:** Pinterest and Repinly both provide a list of popular boards each week via e-mail.

Pay attention to trending pins and popular boards through Pinterest business analytics or Pinterest's weekly e-mails coming straight from the most reliable source of data. Each e-mail contains a trending pin at the top, half a dozen popular boards from all Pinterest users, followed by Pins You'll Love, highlighting nine popular pins from people you follow. The most popular pin of all time (so far), according to Repinly, is the Hasselback Garlic Cheesy Bread, from LaurensLatest.com, shown in Figure 11-11.

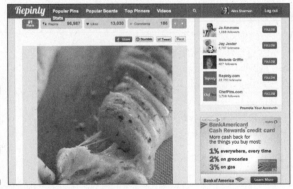

Figure 11-11:
A pin with more than 90,000 repins.

Use an RSS feed reader such as Feedly (www.feedly.com) to keep a close eye on popular pinners or some of your favorite or most relevant pinners. Use each pinner's unique RSS feed URL. A user account feed is `pinterest.com/username/feed.rss` and a specific board feed is `pinterest.com/username/board/rss`. Replace *username* with the pinner's actual username and *board* with your specific board name.

The idea behind picking effective pins is to attract attention, convey a message, and compel others to interact with you and your Pinterest boards and pins. Keep going back to your goals and the image you want to project as you choose pins.

Honing your repinning strategy

As with any social network, with Pinterest you're combining publishing with individual interactions along with community management. Consider what your target audience is pinning and repinning as well as what is trending on Pinterest to find the sweet spot of what you should be pinning and repinning. Interacting on Pinterest should not happen in a vacuum.

Don't forget your online manners. If you pin someone else's images or repin someone else's pins, be careful to follow these pointers:

✔ **Maintain the integrity of the links of the source material.** Click each pin before repinning it to make sure it leads to the source website. Also check the credit in the pin's description before you repin it. Add a source credit if it's missing. Checking sources of repins takes more time, but also ensures you pin and repin quality, credited work. The extra effort saves you from repinning things that lead to error messages or Pinterest warning messages, or images that don't clearly represent or lead to the source of the image.

✔ **Don't deliberately change the destination link on someone else's image or pin to your own URL.** When pinning or repinning, switching destination URLs could be interpreted as a copyright violation. As long as you check to verify a pin leads to the appropriate source, leave the destination as-is when you pin or repin something.

By repinning other people's pins, you move beyond publishing, which is a one-way action akin to broadcasting. Repinning can help start interactions with not only the people you follow on Pinterest, but also other pinners you identify on the network with whom you want to connect.

De-clutter your Pinterest stream by following only the boards that are relevant to you and your audience. Go to the board you want to follow and click the Follow button instead of clicking Follow All when you first arrive on someone's Pinterest profile. You might find that you want to keep an eye on her Women in Technology board, but could pass on her Cats and Dogs board. Be selective about the boards that fill your Pinterest stream.

Repinning someone you're following or who is following you can keep you top-of-mind with him. We tend to pay attention to what is familiar and who we know. You can strengthen relationships with your Pinterest community by repinning their pins. You can also expand your Pinterest network by repinning others not in your immediate community.

You can find new people to pin in many ways, including

- ✔ **The Popular Pinterest page:** If someone has popular pins and pins relevant to your interests, chances are you'll want to follow them. Access the Popular page via the drop-down menu to the left of the Search field on the upper-left side of any Pinterest page.

- ✔ **Your followers:** People who are interested enough in you to follow you may be people you want to follow back. Click the Followers link at the top of your Pinterest account page to peruse your followers. Click and follow their boards that interest you or Follow All.

- ✔ **The people who you follow are following:** Click the Following link toward the upper-right side of your Pinterest profile page to see the list of who you're following; then click the Following link on their profile to see who they follow. Chances are good that if you like them, you'll like whoever they like.

- ✔ **Who repins you:** Because anyone can repin anyone else's pins without having to follow them first, you can find new people to follow based on who is repinning you but not yet following you.

- ✔ **Summaries of popular pins:** Whether from Pinterest, Repinly, or other sources, listings or directories of popular pins, boards, and pinners can lead you to new people to follow.

Look for tools that can help you analyze the connections you make — or not make — through Pinterest. An iOS app from Innovatty called Followers on Pinterest for iPad, iPhone, and iPod Touch shows you who is not following you back and who unfollowed you. You can also track new followers, find mutual friends, and view fans.

Knowing how often and how much to pin

True social engagement is not an exact science. Human interactions ebb and flow. Although studies can show some patterns in online behavior and response, the days, times, and frequency of your pinning are unique to you and your audience.

To determine the pinning frequency for you or your team, start with these suggestions:

- ✔ **Put a clear strategy and plan in place.** Having a road map and guidelines for pinning make your efforts more effective.

- ✔ **Assess your resources.** Figure out how much time you have to implement pinning.

- ✔ **Integrate Pinterest activities.** The more you connect Pinterest with other networks, the more efficient your efforts become.

- ✔ **Allot the time.** Find the pinning rhythm that works for both you or your team as well as your audience. Identify the times when responses seem to be the highest.

- ✔ **Adjust your attitude.** Don't think of pinning as yet another work task to tackle. Leverage the visual aspect of pinning to enhance your sites and social networks and increase engagement in new ways.

The key to effective pinning is to get to know your followers and serve them at the times they seem to be most active. You also want to get to know those who are in your target market but not already following you to determine when they're active on Pinterest. You want to be visible to them so they can interact with you.

Until Pinterest opens its API, you can't schedule your pins. The moment it does, tools such as Repinly may offer this function. Then other social media dashboard tools such as HootSuite will add Pinterest scheduling to their features to remain competitive.

Pinning regularly keeps your pins in the pin feed and top of mind for your followers looking to find new content. Because the pin feed moves so quickly, pinning daily is a good practice. At any given time, pinning a handful of images or videos will cluster your pins for the greatest visibility.

Pinning several times a day increases your ability to reach people who pin at different times. Again, by clustering your pins anytime you set to the task of pinning, you are more likely to attract attention than pinning a single image. On Pinterest, frequent pinning will prove beneficial far more than occasional pinning.

Avoid *pinbombing* your followers by pinning continuously over a long stretch of time. Although it's tempting to go on a pinning jag when you have time or are in the mood, think of your pins flooding someone else's pin feed as spam. Nobody wants to see only pins from the same person taking up their entire stream. If they are overwhelmed or turned off by your glut of pins, they'll most likely unfollow you.

Leveraging Pinterest Features to Increase Engagement

Pinterest engagement methods are pretty straightforward and simple — pins, repins, likes, and comments. Pinterest also offers a few other features you can leverage to increase the interaction with your followers and other pinners.

Adding hashtags to attract attention

Even though Pinterest users don't comment on pins as much as they repin or like pins, one way to get your comments and pins noticed is to use Pinterest hashtags. *Hashtags* are keywords that group together similar information and consist of words with a hash mark or pound sign in front of them such as #social or #wine.

Pinterest uses hashtags a little differently than Twitter. When you add hashtags to a pin's description, the hashtags become clickable live links that lead to search results similar to Twitter. Unlike Twitter, clicking a hashtag on Pinterest generates search results of pins related to the keyword after the hashtag and not the results of the hashtag itself. There is no limit to how many hashtags you can use but avoid overdoing it or it could be a turnoff. Figure 11-12 shows an example of hashtag use on Pinterest.

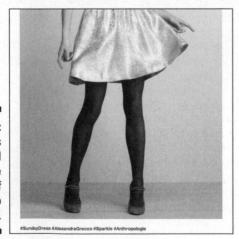

Figure 11-12: Hashtags should relate to the content of the pin or to your brand.

#SundayDress #AlexandraGrecco #Sparkle #Anthropologie

When you click a hashtag, the Pinterest search results URL contains %23 in front of a keyword. This is called a *URL Encoded Character* and it represents the # sign. When you search for a keyword without the hashtag, the search results contain some of the same pins but also some different ones. By using hashtags strategically, you can

✔ **Group together similar pins.** Hashtags bring together content you publish, making it easier for people to find more of your pins based on the same keyword.

✔ **Add your pins to a stream of similar pins.** When someone clicks a hashtag someone else has used that you've also used, your pins show up with her pins and other related pins.

✔ **Increase your pins' searchability.** Your pins are more likely to show up when someone searches Pinterest for a hashtag or keyword you've used.

Getting noticed by tagging others

One way to draw people's attention to your comment is to mention them in the comment in a way that triggers a notification to that person. Tag another Pinterest user by adding the @ symbol and that person's username — similar to using the @ symbol in front of a username on Twitter.

Type the @ symbol in your pin's description or a comment you make on a pin followed by the first letters of the name of the person you're tagging. A drop-down menu of Pinterest users you follow appears based on the letters you type; you can then easily and accurately add his username.

Mentioning others in your pin descriptions should be a genuine gesture and not a way to spam the people you follow on Pinterest. Be thoughtful about when and how you mention others in pins.

When you mention another Pinterest user you follow in a comment or pin description, her name with the @ symbol in front of it appears as a live link similar to Facebook tagging. The link is clickable directly to her Pinterest profile page. All the more reason to be thoughtful about who you tag in a pin because you're aligning yourself with them and potentially driving traffic to them when others read your comment. In Figure 11-13, you can see that a tag of someone's name on a pin becomes a live link that leads to her profile.

Figure 11-13:
Mentioning
others in a
Pinterest
description
or comment.

A Pinterest user you've mentioned in a pin receives a notification by e-mail that she's been mentioned. Likewise, if someone else mentions you, you are notified. When that happens, it's an open invitation to engage further, continue the conversation, and further strengthen your relationships with others in your growing Pinterest community.

Running a contest to increase interactions

One way to attract attention and boost participation through Pinterest is to run a contest or special promotion. Contests on Pinterest can vary widely, but most incorporate the pinning function.

Judged contest: Threadless Valentine's Day challenge

The t-shirt community Threadless held a Valentine's Day–themed Pinterest contest that challenged people to build boards based on specific rules. The company asked users to create a Threadless Valentine's Day Challenge board and fill it with gift ideas for a person they love.

Part of the contest criteria was to pin ten images, five from Threadless.com and the other five from anywhere else on the web. The grand prize was $100 in Threadless cash, the site's online currency, and a $100 Amazon gift card. The company picked a winner, as shown in Figure 11-14, from more than 350 submissions and not only received website traffic, branded pins, and interactions with its Pinterest account but also garnered positive comments on its blog and in social networks.

Figure 11-14:
The win-
ning board
for the
Threadless
Pinterest
contest
with a
Valentine's
Day theme.

Don't run a contest online without posting official contest rules. You can find templates for contest rules on the web. At a minimum, state your privacy and security policies, how you'll use the information given to you by entrants to the contest, and spell out each step of how the contest works.

Sweepstakes: Wine Sisterhood Pin-to-Win

Wine branding company Canopy Management ran a contest over a number of months that required an offline component. Pinterest users and members of the Wine Sisterhood online community were encouraged to seek out the company's new wine, aptly named Wine Sisterhood Wine. Only one nation-wide retailer carried the wine at that time, so the Wine Sisterhood commu-nity manager gave several clues about the retailer without specifically stating where the wine was carried.

Women were encouraged to seek out the wines, take a photograph of the wine bottles on the store shelves with their mobile phones, and pin the image to Pinterest using the #winesister hashtag. To ensure all entries were found, rules included e-mailing the Wine Sisterhood with a link to the pin. The com-pany repinned the pinned entries to a Pin-to-Win contest board, as shown in Figure 11-15.

Each month, the company's social media manager randomly drew a winner from the submissions for a gift bag of Wine Sisterhood merchandise. The grand prize winner won a trip for two to Napa, California for the 2nd Annual Wine Sisterhood Gathering. The contest drove website traffic, Pinterest inter-actions, and even foot traffic and branding for the retailer that carried the wine.

Figure 11-15:
Wine
Sisterhood
pinned or
repinned
the photos
pinned by
contestants
to a contest
board.

Inviting participants to group boards

Pinterest provides a way for pinners to add to group boards together for collaboration. You can add contributors to your boards at any time to start collaborating. Others can also invite you to their boards, and you can choose to accept their invitations to participate or ignore them. If you invite others to your boards, make sure they are people you trust or monitor the boards to ensure quality pins.

Creating or participating in a group board on Pinterest can be beneficial in a number of ways. Collaboration is a productive way to engage with others as you work together to build a shared resource. Creative collaboration can be a team-building exercise and a way to bring different perspectives into a project.

Pinterest e-mails all board contributors for every pin added to collaborative boards, which increases visibility and interactions. Collaborative boards can identify shared interests, reveal personalities, and foster stronger relationships. More than 70 people from all over the world participate in this collaborative board, as shown in Figure 11-16.

You can also create a secret board on Pinterest and invite up to three other people to it. The immediate benefit of a secret board is to collaborate privately with others such as your clients, vendors, or team members. You can also use secret boards on your own. Although you cannot turn an existing public board into a secret board, you can decide to make your secret board public at any time.

To invite others to a group board on Pinterest, you must follow at least one board from the person you invite. You can add names when you first create a new board to invite contributors or edit an existing board then invite others later while in Board edit mode to turn it into a group board.

Figure 11-16:
A group
board.

If you're looking to build a niche community of fans or customers, a group Pinterest board provides a visual creative space to interact. However, a challenge of a group board is that the more contributors you invite, the harder it is to ensure quality. Also, if everyone receives notices of each pin from all contributors, at some point this can become overwhelming unless you filter those notifications. All the more reason to be selective about whom you invite to collaborate with you.

Each person on a group board is only able to edit her own pins unless she created the board. As the board creator, you can edit any pin, remove someone else's pin if you deem it inappropriate, or remove a person as a collaborator. Each person, even a board creator, can only moderate comments on his own pins. If someone comments inappropriately on a collaborator's pin, you can only report it to Pinterest.

Benefitting from Pinterest Integration

Pinterest is a vibrant community of users who communicate and respond through images. Build a strong following by being active and consistent with your pinning. Pinterest can also enhance your other online marketing efforts and social networking. Isolating Pinterest from other networks limits many opportunities to increase engagement both on Pinterest and on your site, blog, and other social networks.

Inspiring others to pin your images

Take a look at your website through the eyes of a Pinterest enthusiast. Make sure your website is Pinterest-ready to add to your opportunities for engagement using Pinterest. Although you could choose to block others from pinning images on your website, the more engaging approach is to make sure that your website contains compelling and pin-able images.

If you really want to block others from pinning the images on your website, add this code into the head of any website page: `<meta name="pinterest" content="nopin" />`. We don't recommend that you do this unless you have a sound business reason to do so, such as a copyright issue with the images on your site that limits where and how you can distribute them or simply a desire to maintain more control over your images.

Some initial ways to ensure you have pin-worthy images on your site include

- **Getting visual:** Illustrate every article, blog post, or page with images, keeping in mind the types of images people enjoy pinning on Pinterest.

- **Using large images:** Embed images that link to larger versions at least 600 pixels wide. Any height works on Pinterest, but thumbnails on boards appear as 192 pixels wide, so consider how the image looks in a smaller format as well.

- **Making pin-specific images:** Create images for your website made with the main purpose of being pinned. Create quote images or how-to images. Even if these types of images aren't what you'd typically create to illustrate your content, the more your images look pin-able, the more likely people will pin them.

- **Asking for pins:** Encourage your website visitors to pin your image by overtly stating that your images are pin-able or asking them to pin them.

To further encourage your visitors to pin from your website or blog, install Pinterest widgets. Use the widget that adds a Pin It button to your website or blog so all someone has to do to generate a pin is click the button.

Add a button on your website that lets people know you're on Pinterest and requests that they follow you there. You can also install a widget that pulls in your most recent pins to display directly on your website or blog.

Create tall, skyscraper-style images combining a number of images stacked on top of one another to create a narrative. This popular type of image is often used for step-by-step how-tos such as how to create a paper peony. Figure 11-17 shows how a tall, vertical image visually breaks down a step-by-step process.

Make complementary boards on Pinterest to correspond with other content you've created elsewhere. If you write a blog post on a particular topic, enhance that post with a board to be a visual archive linking to related material.

Figure 11-17:
A tall, how-
to image.

Look for every opportunity to let others know that you're pinning and that you want them to pin what you publish. Being clear about your intentions and your expectations on your website or blog about Pinterest invites others to engage with you through pins. Encourage your community to connect with you on Pinterest so they can follow along. Make it simple to pin images and video from your site with a single click.

Linking Pinterest to Twitter

Consider linking your Pinterest account to Twitter if you use Twitter frequently as a platform for engaging your audience. Pinterest provides you with fresh content to tweet, and tweeting your pins can provide you with an additional source of potential Pinterest followers. By linking Pinterest and Twitter, you build your community and increase your opportunities for connection.

If you didn't link Pinterest and Twitter when you first set up your Pinterest account, you can do it at any time by following these steps:

1. **Log in to Pinterest through the website (**www.pinterest.com**) or mobile app.**

2. **Access your account settings by clicking your name in the upper-right corner of the Pinterest page you're on and choosing Settings (if you're on the website).**

If you're using the app, tap Profile⇨click on the gear on the upper-left corner of your mobile screen and choose Account Settings⇨Account Settings.

3. **Toggle the Twitter slider to On.**

   On the website, the slider is under Social Networks and next to Log on with Twitter. On the app, the slider appears under Twitter Settings. Cut the connection by toggling the slider to Off.

4. **Authorize Pinterest to access your Twitter account by accepting the permission request from Twitter that pops up on your computer or your mobile screen as Pinterest attempts to connect both accounts.**

5. **Save profile changes by clicking the Save Settings button on the website or clicking the Done button on the mobile app.**

After you link your Pinterest account to Twitter, your pins do not automatically post to Twitter. When you click on your pins or anyone else's pins, you'll see a share arrow button on the upper-right corner of the pin to share on Twitter, Facebook, via e-mail or to grab the pin's embed code.

Pin images that you capture on the fly using your smartphone and the Pinterest mobile app. Using the mobile app, you can choose to post your pins simultaneously to Twitter to increase their reach right before you post your pin.

A byproduct of tweeting your pins may be retweets of your pins on Twitter, but only if you manually tweet your pins from either Pinterest or Twitter. People who use Twitter and Pinterest are more likely to retweet a pin when they recognize the link in the tweet as a pin. When people search Twitter for Pinterest, your pins show up because the word *Pinterest* is in the URL of the link in your tweet.

Craft short pin descriptions if you plan to cross-post your pin to Twitter so the content fits in a tweet. At least put the most important text at the start of your description in case Twitter cuts off the rest.

People who don't use Pinterest may retweet your cross-posted pin because of the message conveyed in the tweet. If you say you're drooling over a chocolate Snickers cheesecake pin, even the most inexperienced Pinterest users on Twitter may click or share it. If they click the link in your tweet, they arrive at your pin and can now connect and interact with you on Pinterest.

Integrating Pinterest into Facebook Timelines

When you first set up your Pinterest account, you had the option of linking it with Facebook. As with Twitter, by linking Pinterest to Facebook, you increase opportunities for people to see that you're on Pinterest and to follow you and interact with you there. The current limitations with this feature however, is that Pinterest links with your personal Facebook Timeline versus your Facebook business Page.

That said, if you use your Facebook Timeline for personal branding, Pinterest integration is a great way to enhance your Timeline. Linking Pinterest to our Facebook Timelines works for both of us because we reveal more personal aspects of our lives as part of our brands. Our Facebook friends are a mix of real-life friends as well as business colleagues. If a personal touch works for your brand, linking Pinterest to your personal Timeline is a no-brainer.

Choose the option to link Pinterest to your personal Facebook account or go even further and choose to Link to Timeline so your pins are automatically added as a status update. To link Pinterest to Facebook or unlink it, follow these steps:

1. **Log in to Pinterest through the website** (www.pinterest.com) **or mobile app.**

2. **Access your account settings by clicking your name in the upper-right corner of the Pinterest page you're on and choosing Settings (if you're on the website).**

   If you're using the app, tap Profile⇨click on the gear on the upper-left corner of your mobile screen and choose Account Settings⇨Account Settings.

3. **Toggle the Facebook slider to On.**

   On the website, the slider is under Social Networks and next to Log on with Facebook. On the app, the slider appears under Facebook Settings. Cut the connection by toggling the slider to Off.

4. **(Optional) Add to Facebook Timeline by using the Post your activity to Timeline slider (on the website) or Publish to Facebook Timeline on the mobile app.**

   Choosing this step makes your pins and Pinterest activity appear prominently in your Facebook Timeline.

5. **Authorize Pinterest to access your Facebook account by accepting the permission request from Facebook that pops up on your computer or mobile screen as Pinterest attempts to connect both accounts.**

6. **Save profile changes by clicking the Save Settings button on the website or clicking the Done button on the mobile app.**

You can undo these connections at any time — switch the slider to Off.

Be careful not to spam your Facebook friends with pins. If you automatically cross-post, keep this in mind when you pin. Pins showing up frequently on Facebook can seem a lot more intrusive than frequent pinning directly to Pinterest.

When you pin and post to your Facebook Timeline, your Facebook friends see that pin in their News Feeds. They can immediately like or comment on your pin directly from the feed or your Timeline. Your pins and likes also appear in your Activity panel on the right side of your Timeline.

For more details on how to link Pinterest to social networks, see the book *Pinterest For Dummies* (John Wiley & Sons, Inc.).

You can also control the connection between Facebook and Pinterest on the Facebook side by going to your Account Settings on your Facebook Timeline and clicking Apps. Then click Edit next to the Pinterest app to remove the app.

Integrating Pinterest into Facebook Pages

Chances are you're looking for ways to engage people on your company's Facebook Page. You can provide new ways for your fans to interact leveraging your Pinterest pins. As of this writing, you can't directly integrate your Pinterest account into your Facebook Page through either Pinterest or Facebook. You can always post your pins as status updates. Or you can use a third-party application to add Pinterest to your Page.

Use an iframe app service that programs one HTML document inside another such as Woobox (www.woobox.com) or ShortStack (www.shortstack.com) to make a custom Facebook app for your Page featuring your pins. Services such as these allow you to embed your actual Pinterest page into Facebook using their software, usually for free. A third-party solution is a pretty good work-around for Pinterest's limitation integrating with Facebook Pages. In Figure 11-18, Monogamy Wines enhances its Facebook Page by displaying its Pinterest boards within the Woobox Pinterest app.

Figure 11-18:
A Pinterest account pulled into a Facebook Page.

At the time of this writing, Facebook blocks the ability to pin images from its site. You can bypass this restriction on your Facebook Page by using a third-party application called Pinvolve (`http://apps.facebook.com/pinvolve`). Pinvolve creates a separate app on your Page that turns the images you've posted to your Page Wall into pin-able images. It also imports your Pinterest images and Instagram images into the same app. Using the Pinvolve app gives your Facebook fans new ways to interact with you and spread your messages by letting them tweet your posts in the free version or pin your Page posts if you are using Pinvolve Pro ($5 per month).

Chapter 12

LinkedIn

....

In This Chapter

▶ Expanding your network with LinkedIn

▶ Enhancing your company presence on LinkedIn

▶ Leveraging LinkedIn conversation tools

▶ Establishing your LinkedIn community

....

*E*very business is built on relationships. Whether it's relationships with your vendors, customers, employees, or the general public, your business runs and grows based on the relationships you form and cultivate over time. LinkedIn is focused on the professional relationships that you foster in business.

LinkedIn helps you first and foremost establish a professional presence online and build and strengthen the connections you have to other professionals. But its beauty is so much deeper than that; LinkedIn also offers you tools to showcase your business as well as create a platform to build a professional community.

What we like most about LinkedIn is that it doesn't try to be everything to everyone. Even as Facebook's popularity exploded, LinkedIn didn't say, "To heck with focusing on business professionals. Let's be a jack of all trades." Sticking to its guns has made LinkedIn the most powerful business-oriented social network around.

Although LinkedIn can be useful for business-to-consumer (B2C) marketing, it's especially useful for business-to-business (B2B) marketing and social media engagement.

Setting Up Your LinkedIn Profile

The value of LinkedIn begins with providing you the ability to build your professional résumé online and to connect with your business contacts. Your main presence on LinkedIn is your profile, essentially an enhanced résumé.

Creating a new public profile

First impressions count, so don't scrimp on the information you add to your LinkedIn profile. LinkedIn offers a variety of features on your profile to showcase your expertise and experience and allows you to interact with others. As you fill out your profile, LinkedIn prompts you to continue optimizing your profile until it's 100 percent complete.

Your public LinkedIn profile (see Figure 12-1) is visible to anyone, even if they aren't logged in to LinkedIn. You can control what parts of your profile are included in the public view in your settings, as we discuss in "Editing and enhancing your profile," later in this chapter.

Figure 12-1:
A LinkedIn
profile.

Your LinkedIn profile consists of

- ✔ **A snapshot:** This text appears at the top of every profile and includes your name, location, current title, links to your websites, and a cursory view of past positions, education, and recommendations. Think of the snapshot as the elevator pitch of your elevator pitch — the ten-second glimpse of who you are and what you do.

- ✔ **Your photo:** Although optional, we highly recommend that you include a clear, professional-looking photograph of yourself on your LinkedIn profile to appear more accessible. A close-up headshot to your shoulders with a friendly and relaxed smile is ideal and inviting to encourage others to interact with you.

- ✔ **Activity:** Publish status updates in the field at the top of the LinkedIn home page when you're logged in to your LinkedIn account. Your updates appear in your activity feed and are one of LinkedIn's main engagement and community-building features. Although visible to you at all times, the activity feed is only viewable on your profile by others when they are logged into LinkedIn.

✔ **Background:** You can rearrange any of the Background sections to highlight one over the other. Background sections include

- *Summary:* Craft a professional 30-second elevator pitch for this section.

- *Skills and Expertise:* The key skills you add for yourself are displayed here along with endorsements from others. Once you approve endorsements, endorsers show up on your profile with tiny thumbnails of their LinkedIn profile photos next to each skill they've endorsed. Note that you can move the Skills and Expertise section higher or lower in your profile. We suggest keeping it higher on your profile to encourage additional endorsements.

- *Experience:* Like in a traditional résumé, detail your work experience in reverse chronological order, with the most recent appearing at the top.

- *Education:* List your educational background in reverse chronological order.

- *Additional Information:* This section consists of your Websites, Interests, Groups and Associations, and Honors and Awards. The more you add to this section, the more reasons people find to be in touch with you.

✔ **Recommendations:** You can display both recommendations from others about your work and your recommendations of others. See more about engaging through recommendations in "Giving and receiving recommendations," later in this chapter.

✔ **Connections:** If you opt to make your LinkedIn Connections viewable by others, photos of some of your Connections appear on your profile with a link to all of them. Because of the emphasis on professional networking, showing your Connections helps facilitate contacts and introductions.

✔ **Groups:** Logos for some of the groups you've joined on LinkedIn signify your affiliations and link directly to the groups where you're a member. Being a member of a specific group can encourage connections and interactions based on similar interests.

✔ **Following:** This section has links to news and companies you follow. See more about Company Pages and posting company news in "Communicating through Your Company Page," later in this chapter.

Simply signing up for a LinkedIn account and entering your employment and education history isn't enough to get noticed or to stimulate engagement with others. Look at every feature listed above as a potential starting point for engagement. Give people as many clues and cues as possible to showcase who you are and what you do and provide a variety of reasons and ways to connect. We provide some tips in the following section.

Editing and enhancing your profile

LinkedIn provides numerous ways for you to customize your profile even down to your communications preferences. In Edit mode, you can modify how you want others to contact you. You can also modify the types of contacts that interest you such as career opportunities, expertise requests, or consulting ventures. The more options you provide, the more chances someone has to interact with you.

When you edit your public profile settings, opt to include more information rather than less to give others a variety of reasons to engage with you. Search engines index LinkedIn accounts, giving you yet another reason to add more information about yourself and your work to your profile.

When you first sign up for a LinkedIn account, choose your *vanity* or personalized custom *URL* for your LinkedIn profile so you have a more branded link to provide others. Ideally, use your name, but if that's already taken, add your company name, a relevant keyword, your location, or some other identifier such as `http://linkedin.com/in/JaneDoeCEO` or `http://linkedin.com/in/JohnDoeFL`. You can also add your custom URL later, in Edit mode. To go to Edit mode, click the Edit link to the right of the current URL under your profile photo.

You can add links to videos, images, documents, and presentations throughout your profile to attract more attention and encourage more interactions.

Enhance your LinkedIn profile by adding a link to a video, image, document or presentation. If you sign up for a free account at SlideShare and upload your PowerPoint presentations and PDF files, you can then embed them into your LinkedIn profile to add visual interest and demonstrate your expertise. LinkedIn supports files from many other multimedia websites including Pinterest for images, YouTube for video, and SoundCloud for audio. Adding presentations and documents into your profile provides richer engagement opportunities. See Figure 12-2 for an example of the SlideShare presentations embedded on a profile.

Figure 12-2: Embedded presentations on LinkedIn pull in multimedia such as slides from your SlideShare account to add visual interest.

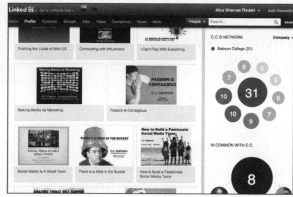

Reaching Out and Connecting with Your Peers

Although Facebook Pages can be effective B2C marketing tools and Twitter works well as both B2C and B2B outreach platforms, LinkedIn is definitely geared more toward both B2B marketing as well as Peer-to-Peer (P2P) networking. Your profile on LinkedIn is the hub for connecting with others, both your actual LinkedIn 1st-degree connections as well as your network of 2nd- and 3rd-degree connections.

LinkedIn offers specific features that help you interact with other members on LinkedIn or that help them reach out to you. Table 12-1 shows the different LinkedIn features you can use for P2P engagement depending on if you're actually connected with someone or not.

Table 12-1	LinkedIn P2P Engagement Features
When Connected	**When Not Connected**
Send a message	Send InMail*
Suggest a profile update	Ask for more information
Recommend	Get introduced
Endorse skills and expertise	Search for references
Share profile	Share profile
Save profile into Profile Organizer*	Save profile into Profile Organizer*
Export profile to PDF	Export profile to PDF

Available only in paid accounts

You get the most value out of LinkedIn when you connect with people whom you actually know. LinkedIn works well for warm leads, but only when you're connected to people who know and trust you and are willing to facilitate introductions to their connections that in turn expand your network.

Make sure you personalize the invitations you send through LinkedIn — or any other social network for that matter — to connect with you. Don't rely on LinkedIn's canned invitation message as your introduction or you risk seeming impersonal or even lazy.

It's against LinkedIn's user agreement to invite people you don't know to your network.

Don't spam others, and don't try to hide your intentions or you may offend others or violate the LinkedIn user agreement. Most people are wise to unsolicited sales pitches couched as friendly greetings. Be clear and straightforward when contacting others on LinkedIn and on any social network.

Engaging in reciprocal interactions

Some of the key P2P engagement features on LinkedIn are reciprocal, such as these:

- ✔ **Messages:** You can send messages to your connections, and they can send messages in return.

- ✔ **InMail:** InMail is an internal e-mail system for LinkedIn members with paid accounts. You can send messages to people with whom you are not connected if you are a paid subscriber to LinkedIn, and they can respond to you. (LinkedIn pro accounts start at $24.95 per month with a discount when paid annually.)

- ✔ **Recommendations:** You can recommend a connection, and they can recommend you back. Making a sincere recommendation of someone's work may result in a reciprocal recommendation. Don't give kudos if you don't mean it. See "Giving and receiving recommendations," later in this chapter.

- ✔ **Endorsements:** The endorsement feature is a quick way to recognize someone's skills. Your photo appears on his profile as an endorser once he approves your endorsement, so use this feature thoughtfully. The person you've endorsed is notified and can also reciprocate.

Other P2P engagement features on LinkedIn are handled via your home page where you can see updates such as posts by you and others and announcements about your connections connecting with others, similar to your Facebook News Feed. We discuss engaging via your LinkedIn home page later in this chapter.

Joining LinkedIn Groups

LinkedIn offers ways to connect with other people beyond your own connections and their connections through LinkedIn Groups. Think of LinkedIn Groups as online forums where you can engage in professional networking while joining conversations on topics relevant to your interests. See Figure 12-3 for an example of a LinkedIn Group home page.

Because LinkedIn has a professional focus, most LinkedIn Groups are oriented toward business, career, and organizational topics. Many established real-world groups like professional networking organizations and trade associations take advantage of these web-based groups to regularly engage with their members beyond the typical monthly in-person meetings.

Companies also use LinkedIn Groups to build communities, interacting with their business customers on a regular basis, such as banks offering advice to their small business clientele, or marketing companies engaging clients, vendors, and prospects in dialog about marketing trends.

Voices.com, for example, is an online marketplace for voice-over talent. Its open LinkedIn group is a place where voice-over professionals can discuss industry trends, work opportunities, and learning resources, and also where company representatives can join to find voice-over talent for their business needs. Figure 12-3 shows the home page for the Voices.com group. If you are interested in topics related to the voice-over industry and were to join the group, you'd have the opportunity to network with a diverse group of professionals and have something in common with them. If someone was interested in hiring a voice-over professional, she could also join the group to find suitable talent.

Figure 12-3:
Discussions
in the
Voices.com
LinkedIn
Group range
from tips
and advice
to technical
questions
where
industry
peers can
exchange
information.

Finding pertinent groups

You can find groups by conducting a search on LinkedIn using the drop-down menu on the upper-right side of the site. The default search category is People, so choose Groups from the menu options. You can search by topic of interest or by an organization or business name. Another way to find groups is to watch your LinkedIn updates and see when your connections join groups. The action of joining a group is an action that is broadcast to others unless you choose otherwise. If you see one of your connections join a group you can click the group name to check it out.

In the drop-down menu under the Groups section across the top of LinkedIn's site, you can select Groups You May Like for some suggestions of groups based on content in your profile as well as groups in which some of your connections are members. The more active groups rise to the top of the list.

Joining and participating in a group

To join a LinkedIn group, after you're on the group's home page, click the Join button. If it's an open group, you are added as a member immediately. If not, you have to wait until the group moderator approves your request.

When you are a member of a LinkedIn Group, you can

- ✔ **View what's happening.** In this view, you get a general overview of activity taking place in the group, including a slide show rotating recent posts at the top. Most Popular Discussions are listed under that.

- ✔ **View the latest discussion.** Choose to view this stream to see a list of only the group discussions in the order of more recent first. Use this view to participate in the most current discussions.

- ✔ **Start a discussion.** Similar to posting to any group, type in and submit a conversation starter in the blank field at the top of the home page of the LinkedIn Group.

- ✔ **Start a poll.** When starting a discussion, you have the option to embed a quick poll to group members. A quick poll is a great way to do quick research or start a conversation. The poll feature is supported only through Groups.

- ✔ **Peruse the members list.** You can see who is in the group, and the listing is ordered based on your connection to other members with 1st-degree connections at the top. You can also search the group members list.

- ✔ **Follow and unfollow other members.** By default, you follow members who are also your 1st-degree contacts in LinkedIn. You can also follow other members so you see their discussions on your home page, including top influencers in the group who provide the most content.

✔ **Read or add promotions.** You, other members, or the group organizer can add promotional messages in this section, which is optional and controlled by the organizer.

✔ **Post or peruse jobs.** You, other members, or the group organizer can post job listings and discussions on the Jobs tab that automatically expire after 14 days.

✔ **Search the group.** You can search the group by keywords or view only polls, discussions, and manager's choice based on content featured by the group organizer. You can also view group content by discussions you've started, discussions you've joined, and discussions you're following.

✔ **View group updates.** This features the latest group activity, so you can see the most current conversations to join as well as who has recently joined.

✔ **Review your group activity.** This shows your most recent updates or actions in the group. Check this to get a sense of how much you're engaging.

✔ **Modify your settings.** This includes receiving an e-mail digest of activity in the group to alert you when someone posts content or an action that could lead to engagement. You can also adjust your settings to allow messages from group members, increasing the likelihood of networking and business opportunities.

✔ **Join a subgroup.** Subgroups are optional additions to a LinkedIn Group to split members off into smaller groups more focused on specific topics.

Being part of a LinkedIn Group is similar to being part of any online community. Follow the community guidelines, add value to the conversation, and be respectful to get the most value of your interactions within the group.

Communicating through Your Company Page

Company Pages are newer offerings from LinkedIn, and not everyone is leveraging these free tools yet. In the past, you could list your company in LinkedIn's company directory, but these listings have been expanded to include a multipage presence. Figure 12-4 shows the PGAV Destinations Company Page, customized with a cover image; PGAV Destinations posts regular updates to the page ranging from company to industry news.

Figure 12-4:
A Company
Page on
LinkedIn.

Creating a Company Page

LinkedIn offers Company Pages similar to Facebook Pages. Initially, businesses could list their companies for free in LinkedIn's company directory. More recently, LinkedIn expanded a business presence on their service through Company Pages that showcase company news and information and include status updates.

A LinkedIn Company Page has the following sections:

- **Home page:** Visitors land on a main page when they click your company name in your profile or do a search on LinkedIn. The page is similar to Facebook's Page Wall with a cover image, a way to post status updates with an update feed, as well as tabs for information about your company.

- **Careers:** You can post job openings on this tab. If you have team members, they can update their LinkedIn profiles with your company name to appear on the Careers section as your employees.

- **Products:** You can list your products or services in this tab to give others more background about your company and what you offer.

To connect your LinkedIn profile (see "Setting Up Your LinkedIn Profile," earlier in this chapter) with your Company Page, edit your current employment. When you type in your company's name, a pop-up menu appears with a list of companies with LinkedIn Company Pages. Choose your own company name to create a link from your profile to your Company Page. Your team members can do the same to appear on your Company Page.

Making the most of your Company Page

Just as your audience can follow your LinkedIn Company Page for the latest news and job openings, you can do the same for your competition, keeping tabs on their progress, what they are doing well, and where you might take the lead.

Add your LinkedIn Company Page to your editorial calendar for social content and conversations. Cultivating an active Company Page is similar to cultivating a community on a Facebook Page. It takes time, attention, consistent posting, and moderation. Posts to your Company Page should include valuable news and information that others want to read, act on, and share.

You can share updates beyond just your Company Page. When you post, you also see the option to share an update to one of the groups you belong to or to share the update via a message to specific connections.

Some of the other things you should share on your LinkedIn Company Page include company news (new products, services, or hires; open positions; discounts, promotions, or sales), media coverage of your company (articles or articles in which you've been quoted), company content (slide presentations, white papers, or articles your company has published), and company conversation (general questions; commentary on industry news and current events; and polls, surveys, and questionnaires).

The best content for your LinkedIn Company Page is any information that appeals to or is useful to your target audience. Include links in your posts to your website and include easy ways for people to contact you. Your Company Page should be a professional presence that stimulates business inquiries.

Stimulating Interactions through Updates

The LinkedIn home page (see Figure 12-5) that you see when you first log in to your account operates similarly to the Facebook News Feed. You can see posts from your connections on the service, and you can interact with them through their activities on LinkedIn. You can also post updates of your own.

Figure 12-5:
The default
LinkedIn
home page
contains
posts by you
and your
LinkedIn
connections.

Engaging with others on LinkedIn generates messages in your activity stream that act as signals to others to what you're doing. These signals can also prompt additional interactions as you use LinkedIn each day.

Some actions that automatically post to your LinkedIn activity feed include

✔ When you like something someone has posted

✔ When you share something someone has posted

✔ When you connect with someone on the network

✔ When you post to another service that you've connected to LinkedIn

Optional actions that LinkedIn posts to your activity feed are when you make a recommendation, update your profile, or join a group.

Click on your name in the upper-right corner of your profile, and then click Settings. In Settings, you can choose to turn activity broadcasts on or off announcing to everyone actions such as when you change your profile, make recommendations, or follow companies. The Turn On/Off Your Activity Broadcasts and Select Who Can See Your Activity Feed options are under Privacy Controls. Selecting the check box turns activity broadcasts on, and deselecting it turns them off. Making activity broadcasts about your actions on LinkedIn public is a personal choice based on the image you want to project to others.

At the top of your home page, LinkedIn recommends content that might be of interest to you. Check this section regularly to find relevant content that you can share with your connections.

Use LinkedIn Signal (www.linkedin.com/signal) to filter news updates to find the most relevant content to like, comment on, and share. You can filter by network, industry, company, time published, group, school, location, seniority, and update type. Relevance increases the potential for engagement. You can also search by keyword.

Posting compelling content

Be proactive and strategic about what shows up in your news feed by posting regularly to it. Post a combination of information about your professional work, news from your company, and industry news. Determining what to post to your LinkedIn activity feed should be based on

✔ Your professional goals

✔ Your audience — in this case, your connections

✔ The image you'd like to convey

✔ The actions you'd like others to take, such as reading your content, spreading your messages, contacting you, or hiring you.

To make your updates on LinkedIn more compelling, you can use links that expand with a preview and can include an image if the host website is set up properly. You can also attach files of your own to your updates including images, Word documents, PDFs, and PowerPoint slides. Control the appearance, quality, and value of your LinkedIn updates by attaching your own files to them. Figure 12-6 shows how to enhance a post by attaching a Word file. The file then automatically converts to a PDF.

Click to attach a file.

Figure 12-6:
You can attach a file to your post.

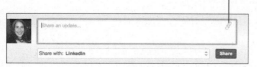

Even if you post regularly to your Company Page, you most likely have far more connections through your own personal profile than your Company Page has followers, at least to start. Share what you post onto your Company Page to your personal profile to increase attention for your company's news.

Posting updates through your Group or Company Page can help garner more attention for either of those features. If you post content within a public LinkedIn Group, it can show up in your activity feed and others can like it directly on the feed or share it from the feed. If they try to comment on it, however, they are led to the post on your Group's page. To comment on the content, they have to join the Group. Even if they don't join at that time, they still see your Group and can consider joining at a later date.

Interacting with others in the feed

To interact with others based on what they share to their activity feeds, you need to keep an eye on your LinkedIn home page for updates. You can toggle your views to focus on particular topic areas and points of conversation. Look for news and activities that warrant a Like at a minimum or take more time to post comments on other people's updates. If their content is compelling, you can share it to your own feed.

By default, when you log in to your LinkedIn account, you see the most recent updates on your LinkedIn home page. You have the option to change what you see on your home page by clicking All Updates on the top-right side of the page, directly under the open field where you post your own updates. You can sort the content you see into different categories including top and recent posts; by source such as your company and co-workers or your connections; and content you've shared, posted to groups or just your updates. You can even customize your content view based on only new connections, just job opportunities, or trending news.

Taking a proactive approach can show people that you're paying attention. Your actions on other people's content can get you noticed, and others may return the favor, amplifying your messages to their connections.

If you are handy with RSS feeds, you can generate an RSS feed for your Network Updates at the bottom of the drop-down menu under All Updates.

Taking Advantage of More LinkedIn Features

Engagement happens more frequently when you know your audience and post the right kind of content that attracts their attention and gets reaction. Using the right tools on the right networks can also help you up your engagement with your connections. On LinkedIn, you can consume information using various tools, but you can also provide information in a variety of ways.

Whether you're giving recommendations to others, answering questions to showcase your expertise, or forming a LinkedIn Group to build and communicate with your targeted community, pick the tools that will best serve your audience and achieve your goals. Using these tools in combination can also be powerful, but don't bite off more than you can chew.

Giving and receiving recommendations

We talk about the value of giving kudos to others as a way of engaging in a valuable and meaningful way online. *Recommendations* are the LinkedIn version of kudos that let you give and receive detailed recommendations from other LinkedIn members.

Recommendations are different from endorsements (see "Providing endorsements," later in this chapter) in that the former include a more in-depth description of you and your work from people with whom you've worked. Figure 12-7 shows sample recommendations. When you give someone a recommendation or endorsement, she has the option of featuring it on her profile for others to see — or not.

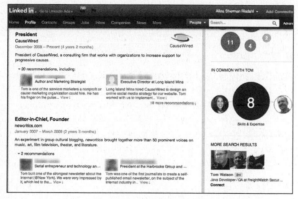

Figure 12-7: Sample recommendations.

Making a recommendation

To recommend someone, follow these steps:

1. **Go to the person's profile who you'd like to recommend.**

2. **Hover your cursor over the button with the upside down triangle to the right of the Send a Message button.**

3. **Choose Recommend from the drop-down menu.**

4. **Select the appropriate option for how you know the person you're recommending:**

    • *Colleague:* You've worked with him at the same company.

    • *Service Provider:* You've hired him to provide a service for you or your company.

- *Business Partner:* You've worked with him but not as a client or colleague

- *Student:* You were at school when he was also there, so you were a fellow student or teacher.

5. Fill in the recommendation form.

The form asks for the following specific information:

- Position you are recommending her for.

- Service category.

- Year you first hired her, if applicable. You also have the option to note if you've hired her more than once.

- Choose three attributes that best describe her. These include: great results, personable, expert, good value, on time, high integrity, and creative.

- Fill in a written recommendation that's specific but brief.

6. Review your recommendation and make changes as necessary.

7. Click the Send button to send it to the person you're recommending.

Indiscriminately endorsing others can affect how others perceive you and could dilute the value of your recommendations. As with any kudos you give, your recommendation or endorsement of someone else also reflects on you, so do so with care.

Asking for recommendations

Asking for recommendations may feel uncomfortable, but on LinkedIn, it's part of the typical networking process to seek recommendations from people who are familiar with your work. To ask for recommendations, follow these steps:

1. In the LinkedIn navigation bar, hover your mouse over Profile and click Recommendations.

2. Click the Ask for Recommendations link in the Recommendations section.

In this section, you can also manage recommendations others have given you and peruse recommendations you've given to others.

3. Choose a job position on your LinkedIn profile.

You can also add a school you attended, if relevant, although most people recommend one another based on jobs.

4. Enter which of your connections can provide information about your work in that position.

You can add up to 200 connections.

5. **Edit the default request.**

   We highly recommend personalizing your request message rather than sending the canned version.

6. **Click Send to submit the request.**

   If someone recommends you, you will receive an e-mail from LinkedIn with the recommendation text.

7. **Click the link provided in the e-mail.**

   You will arrive at a page on LinkedIn where you can approve the recommendation and add it to your profile or opt to keep it hidden.

Thanking someone who recommends you on LinkedIn is a nice touch.

Attract attention for your profile, your Company Page, or anything else you'd like to promote by advertising on LinkedIn. This is similar to how you'd advertise on Facebook. Target your ads geographically and by occupation so you reach a targeted audience such as senior-level management at healthcare companies or managers at insurance agencies. Choose an image and text for your ad, and set your daily ad budget and the duration of your ad run.

Providing endorsements

Endorsements are different from Recommendations. Recommendations are longer form testimonials that you can request and then choose to put onto your profile. Endorsements are a quick and simple way of giving someone kudos for specific skills. Both require approval before they appear on a profile. When you give someone an endorsement on LinkedIn, your profile photo appears on his profile next to the skill you've endorsed, as shown in Figure 12-8.

Figure 12-8: A sample endorsement section.

When you're logged in to your LinkedIn account, you periodically see a prompt to endorse others with a single click. Each time you click to endorse someone, additional suggestions appear until you decide to stop. The ease of this particular LinkedIn feature has drawn some criticism from professionals who feel there's no real weight or value in simply clicking to endorse someone without taking the time to add relevant context.

Forming and managing a LinkedIn Group

LinkedIn Groups are by default open to the public but can be made private. Groups provide you with moderating tools to cultivate conversations between people with shared interests.

The main features of LinkedIn Groups are

- **Discussion:** The home page of your group is where the main discussions take place.
- **Members:** You can choose to follow other members so you can see their updates on your home page.
- **Promotions:** Members can share news, links to articles, promote products or services, and post anything that isn't a general topic for conversation.
- **Search:** Use this feature to find discussions on specific topics and also access the member search function.
- **Jobs:** This isn't a default feature; however, you can add this feature to give members the ability to post job openings for the benefit of other members.

You can form subgroups within your LinkedIn Group to offer more granular discussions on specific topics. LinkedIn subgroups have similar features to the main group including discussions, jobs, and digest e-mails. You can find out more about the ins and outs of LinkedIn Groups in LinkedIn's Help Center (http://help.linkedin.com).

Moderating a LinkedIn Group is similar to moderating any online community. You should have community policies in place and use the moderation tools at your disposal to keep the conversation appropriate and on-topic to provide the most value to your group members.

Naturally, we can cover only so much in one chapter, so we would be remiss if we didn't tell you that Joel Elad explains LinkedIn extensively in *LinkedIn For Dummies,* 2nd Edition (John Wiley & Sons, Inc.). Check out a copy if you decide this social media engagement tool is going to be a priority for you.

Going mobile

You can access your LinkedIn account using the LinkedIn mobile app. You can peruse top news and recent updates; like, comment, and share updates from others; share your own updates; edit your profile; manage your messages; interact with your groups, jobs, and companies; all on the tiny screen of your smartphone. The app is available for iPhone, iPad, Android phones, BlackBerry, and Windows phones.

Gauging LinkedIn Results

Success with LinkedIn depends on using it often. Too many professionals set up their LinkedIn profiles and then sit back to wait for something to happen. If you connect with others thoughtfully, post regularly to your profile and Company Page, and also participate in a few LinkedIn Groups relevant to your business or industry, you'll reap the networking and marketing benefits of LinkedIn. Determine how well you're doing with LinkedIn through a combination of qualitative and quantitative metrics.

Tracking interactions

Although LinkedIn offers some concrete numbers depending on the features you use, you should also be tracking interactions including

- **Connections:** Instead of focusing on how many connections you've amassed, examine how many connection offers you've sent versus how many have been accepted. The more thoughtful you are about connecting with people you know, the more likely they'll accept your connection offer.

- **Recommendations and Endorsements given and received:** Track these manually. You will receive e-mail notices when others endorse or recommend you. For more information, see "Providing endorsements" and "Giving and receiving recommendations" earlier in this chapter.

- **Links clicked:** Track clicks on links you've used in your LinkedIn posts using a URL shortener like bitly (www.bitly.com) or a management tool like HootSuite (www.hootsuite.com). You may be posting, but gauge if people are responding to what you post.

- **Number of mentions:** Use LinkedIn Signal (www.linkedin.com/signal) to search for your name, your company name, or any other keyword related to your company to see how many times others have posted about you.

✔ **Number and quality of inquiries:** You may be getting a lot of messages in your LinkedIn inbox, but are they quality inquiries or requests to connect? Track how many of these connections are turning into real business, but remember that it takes time to cultivate any connection.

With a paid version of LinkedIn, you can see who has viewed your profile and use this information to potentially follow up to do business. With the free version, you can peruse a list of the people whose profiles others have viewed in addition to viewing yours. You cannot see who viewed your profile with a free account.

Analyzing engagement

In addition to scanning your own profile activity to get a sense of how proactive and interactive you are on LinkedIn and how responsive others are to you, here are some other numbers you can track to see how well you're leveraging LinkedIn engagement features each week or month:

✔ **Number of updates you've posted:** Note how many people are liking and commenting on your updates.

✔ **Number of updates from others you've shared:** Share what others are posting as another way to connect with your network.

✔ **Number of discussions you started in Groups:** You should also participate in discussions started by others.

✔ **Number of answers you've submitted:** You should also pose questions in the Answers section.

Checking the business benefits

All of your effort is commendable, but you should also assess how well your LinkedIn presence is serving you and your company by tracking the following:

✔ **Direct inquiries to do business:** Although it's nice to receive requests to connect, the more valuable inquiry is one to actually do business with you.

✔ **Number of introduction requests passed along for you:** Take advantage of one of the best ways to get warm leads and introductions to other LinkedIn members who can open new business opportunities for you.

✔ **Number of introduction requests received:** Especially note if these introductions lead to any solid business.

✔ **Growth of your network:** Expand your network thoughtfully so that each connection can potentially be a conduit for new business and genuine contacts.

Using analytics tools

Table 12-2 breaks down the different analytics you can obtain directly from LinkedIn based on the feature you're using.

Table 12-2	LinkedIn Analytics	
Feature	**Type of Measurement**	**Stats**
Company Page	Page Insights	Views, visitor demographics, unique visitors, clicks
Groups	Group Statistics	Number of members, comments, demographics (seniority, location, function, industry), growth and activity
Profile	Profile Strength	Rates how complete your profile is
Ads	LinkedIn Ads	Number of impressions, clicks, CTR (click-through rate), average CPC (cost per click), total spent

You can also use third-party social media management tools to track the interactions with your LinkedIn updates. Buffer (www.bufferapp.com), for example, records the number of comments, likes, potential (number of connections), re-shares, and clicks each item you share through its application gets. Hootsuite (www.hootsuite.com) also provides tracking for LinkedIn updates posted through their tool.

Chapter 13

Google+

In This Chapter

▶ Finding out how Google+ can help your business

▶ Getting started with Google+

▶ Interacting with other Google+ users

▶ Hanging out, circling, and building a community

This chapter explores the ever-expanding features of Google+, the social networking platform (also known as G+) developed by the big search-engine company Google. Think of G+ as being a cross between Facebook and Twitter, providing the longer-form posting of Facebook with comments directly attached to posts, and the ability to group content as you can with Twitter Lists.

Trust us when we say Google is not satisfied being like Facebook or Twitter and is working nonstop to be different and better. At this writing (Global Web Index, January 2013), Google+ is the No. 2 social network, with an estimated 343 million active users, compared with 693 million on Facebook and 288 million on Twitter.

Checking Out the Benefits of Google+

Google wants to make sharing easy and natural no matter where you are online and its suite of online communications tools dominate the Internet. Google+ is still a work-in-progress, and the company seems to be pretty responsive to feedback from users regarding features. The main features of G+ are

✔ **Profiles:** Like all the other social networks we discuss in this book, G+ starts with your individual profile, including a photo, occupation, skills, and employment details. Google profiles are for individuals and contain many of the same features as other social network profiles, such as a photo, an About section, and a content stream. See Figure 13-1 for an example of a G+ profile.

Figure 13-1:
A Google+
profile.

✔ **Circles:** A G+ Circle is a grouping of your connections. You can circle connections such as business contacts, work colleagues, or personal friends to direct your posts to specific people or to filter your home page content stream and see only posts from specific circles.

✔ **Communities:** Like Facebook or LinkedIn groups, this newer feature is ideal for group discussions and collaboration.

✔ **Photos:** Upload, organize, share, and even edit images using the G+ suite of photo tools. G+ is a visual network, so photos are showcased nicely with a slide show feature.

✔ **Events:** Invite others to your event, and you can add the event to everyone's Google Calendar.

✔ **Hangouts:** Organize face-to-face video conferencing with up to ten people, including screen sharing and Google Docs integration.

✔ **+1:** You can publicly recommend a page on the web by clicking the +1 button that appears either on the site or on Google. +1ing — as Google refers to the action — is similar to clicking a "like" or "favorite" button.

We discuss all these features in this chapter.

Getting Your Feet Wet on Google+

Setting up a Google+ account starts with signing up for a Google account, which is your single access to all Google sites and tools. To sign up, you fill out a standard registration form in which you enter your name, a username, password, birthdate, and gender.

You are also asked to include your mobile number and current e-mail address, meaning something other than a Gmail account. If you already have a Gmail account, then you can log in to all Google products using that account, including Google+.

After you sign up and sign in, you're ready to move to the next step: creating your profile.

Building your personal profile

When you first set up your G+ account, you are given a chance to fill in your profile. As with setting up a profile in any social network, we recommend filling out as much as possible from the start. You can also return to your profile settings by clicking on the Profile icon to the left of your G+ Home page.

As you build your profile, you are prompted to enter the usual information such as an introduction or bio with a photo, your occupation, employment, education, and contact information. G+ also provides a field for a tagline and "bragging rights" or your accomplishments. You can control visibility for all elements of your G+ profile except Tagline and Photo.

To make your profile easier for people to find, make it visible in a search by selecting the Profile Discovery option. You should also be able to claim or change your custom Google+ URL in the same section of your profile.

The Google+ registration page also includes several optional fields: Relationship, Looking For, Birthday, and Gender. You can fill them out or not; it's up to you. Make your choices based on what works for your public image as a representative of your company.

Google+ vanity or custom URLs for your personal G+ account or business page are rolled out by Google over time. If you don't see a blue Claim URL button at the upper-right side of your page when you set it up, you might see it later. In the meantime, you can use a site like GPlus.to (http://gplus.to) to claim a shorter URL.

After you verify your website can be — or is — listed on Google's search engine, add this line of code to your site:

```
<a href="https://plus.google.com/[yourpageID]" rel="publisher">Find us on
        Google+</a>
```

To find your G+ page URL, go to your page and copy the web address straight from your browser address bar. Then link your website to your Google+ page by editing your profile and clicking Website, then adding your website URL to your G+ profile. Google does the rest.

Setting up a Google+ business page

Although you may already have a personal presence on Google+ through an individual account, Google encourages you to set up a business page. A G+ page looks similar to a personal G+ profile, but is for a brand, organization, or company. You can have a company profile and post updates to your content stream. See Figure 13-2 for an example of a G+ page.

Figure 13-2: Beth's Cafe in Seattle has a Google Local Place page.

Pages require a personal profile to "own" a business page, but the identity of the page owner remains hidden to page visitors. After you complete the initial page setup, you can add other managers, similar to Facebook Page administrators (admins).

Some main differences between G+ profiles and pages are

- **Restricted circling and sharing:** Pages can't add people to circles until those people first add or mention the page. As an individual with a profile, you can circle anyone and any page. Also, pages can't share to extended circles. They are limited to sharing to their direct circles.

- **No instant chat:** If you have enabled the instant chat function as an individual on G+, you will see your connections who are currently online on the right side of your home page and can message them directly. Pages do not have access to individuals via chat.

- **+1 restrictions:** Pages can't +1 content on the web, even if there is a +1 button because it will always show up tied to your personal profile. Both profiles and pages can +1 content inside Google+, such as posts, photos, and videos.

  Pages contain the +1 button so people can endorse the page itself. On profiles, only content you post can receive +1s.

✔ **Administration:** Pages can have multiple managers. Profiles are for individuals so unless you give someone else access to your personal Google account, only you can manage your profile.

Think about your Google+ page as another way to increase your company presence online, giving you more opportunity to show up in relevant Google searches. Your Google+ page also enhances any advertising you're doing or plan to do with Google.

Setting up an effective page

To create a new page on G+, you can either go to www.google.com/+/business or click the Pages icon on the left side of your G+ Home page. To set up your page, you need to do the following:

1. **Choose an appropriate type of page.**

   If your business has a physical location where customers can frequent, for example, select Local Business or Place when setting up your G+ page to have your page show up in Google Maps. Google+ prompts you to enter your phone number so it can find you through your phone company listing. Other Main categories are Product or Brand; Company, Institution, or Organization; Arts, Entertainment, or Sports, and Other.

2. **Choose a category.**

   When you select Company, Institution, or Organization, you then have to pick an appropriate category for your page such as Media, News and Publishing, or Travel and Leisure.

   You can't change your category after you create your page, so choose wisely.

3. **Add info and agree to Terms of Service.**

   Fill in your company name, a website, and specify whether your page content will be appropriate for all G+ users or restricted to specific ages such as over 18 or over 21. Alcohol companies must select Alcohol-related. Select the check box to agree to Google's Terms of Service, and then click the Continue button.

4. **Add your "story," contact information, and change your images.**

   Enter a short statement — limited to ten words — about your company that gives people a clear first impression. This feature is not available to Local Pages. You're also prompted to change your cover that appears at the top of your page as a banner.

Hover your cursor over the rectangular image at the top of your page and click Change Cover Photo. Click Upload on the left, then click Select a Photo From Your Computer if that's where your photo resides. You can select photos and cover images that you've already uploaded to your page. Once uploaded, click your cover image and drag it to reposition it as needed. Cover image sizes can be as large as 2120 x 1192 pixels or as small as 480 x 270 pixels.

Upload your page's profile image that is 250 x 250 pixels. As with any social network, pick an image that best represents your company and looks good at a reduced size. This could be your company logo or another image consistent with your brand.

At any time you can return to Edit mode to continue modifying your profile by clicking on the About tab on your company's G+ Home page. The sections within the About tab — People; Story; Contact Information; and Links — are editable by clicking the Edit text link below each one.

5. **Add admins to your page to help handle page management.**

   Add admins on the Settings page: Click the gear button under the right corner of your cover image or in the drop-down menu in the upper-right side of your G+ page. Click Manage; then invite other page managers by entering their e-mail addresses in the open field and clicking the Invite button. You can also transfer page ownership from here.

Start posting to your content stream to attract attention. See "Posting multimedia" later in this chapter.

If you don't have a lot of people in your page's circles yet, start circling strategically. Since you have to wait until someone circles you back before they can see your posts, you should post an invitation to your new G+ page publicly through your personal profile for a wider reach. If you want a more targeted reach, send your announcement to specific circles of people within your personal profile.

Getting Google authorship

You can verify that you're the author of content on sites you either own, control, or where you have an e-mail address matching the domain of the website. The theory behind claiming authorship is that your name and photo could appear in Google Search when associated with the content where you are the verified author.

Note that Google is careful to state that claiming authorship doesn't guarantee that your name will appear in Google Search. Still, if you're publishing content on the web, attaching that content to your G+ profile and vice versa can only improve how people find and connect with you.

To claim authorship, visit `https://plus.google.com/authorship`.

Getting into the Flow of G+

As we mention earlier, Google+ is similar in certain ways to both Facebook and Twitter. A main difference among the three networks is that only G+ lets you filter streams of content by particular groups based on the circles you've created and the people and pages you've designated into those circles.

For a while, G+ was the only service to let you sort your contacts into groups to target the posts you published. Now Facebook lets you group your friends and then post targeting Public, Friends, Friends except Acquaintances, Only Me, and Custom. The Custom options on Facebook and G+ are similar, allowing you to name specific people to add or exclude from your targeting. Customizing and targeting your content is still a core aspect of Google+.

Leveraging long-form publishing

Google claims that you have no limits to the number of characters you can use in your posts on the service. Most people, however, still post shorter updates with just a few sentences. Others treat the G+ platform as an alternative to a blog, posting on average between 400 to 600 words.

When you have more to say, you can do it on G+ easily. Only the first portion of your post shows up, but after someone clicks the link to read more, the entire post opens. Information designer and consultant Dave Gray created the long-form post shown in Figure 13-3, discussing G+ benefits such as long-form posting.

Figure 13-3:
A long-form post discussing long-form posting.

In terms of readability and people's attention spans, more words aren't necessarily more effective.

When you post, you can put an asterisk (*__Aliza__*) on either side of a word to make it bold, and underscore (_Danielle_) when you would like to italicize a word. Use these styles to help your text stand out in the G+ stream.

Posting multimedia

Just as visuals win on Facebook Pages, photos and videos are important to attracting attention, generating +1s and comments, and garnering those coveted shares on Google+. Text alone as a post may disappear in someone's content stream with so many eye-catching things to look at and react to as the stream moves by.

Photos and video

Author C. C. Chapman engages frequently on his Google+ profile and posts a variety of content from other sources including articles, blog posts, and video. He also provides links to his own blog posts and includes a lot of his own images in those posts. Figure 13-4 shows how he uses visuals.

Figure 13-4:
C.C. Chapman's use of video in his G+ account adds visual interest to his content stream.

Documents

On G+, you aren't limited to photos and videos. You can enrich your updates with your Google documents, spreadsheets, presentations, forms, PDFs, and any other file types supported in Google Drive. People in your circles can then open and interact with these documents directly in your stream without having to leave G+. You can set any file you want to share to Public On the Web or Anyone With the Link.

Slide shows

When you upload photos to G+, especially as photo albums, people can view your images as a slide show. Use high resolution images to take advantage of the bold and dramatic interface of the slide shows with your images appearing in a large format on a black backdrop. See Figure 13-5 for an example of a G+ slide show on the web.

Figure 13-5:
Google+ lets you display photo albums in slide show format.

Interacting in the stream

Google+ enthusiasts will tell you that one of the things they love about the platform is how active their streams are and how much G+ users participate. Although we tend to agree with this, the truth is that your G+ stream is active only if many people have circled your page and if you are very active on the network.

When you first log into G+, you're accessing as yourself — an individual — by default. You can easily access your page and use G+ as your page in several ways: Click the Pages icon on the left side of your G+ Home page and click Switch to Page. Or hover your cursor over the Pages icon to see a list of the G+ pages you've created.

Another way to enter Page mode is on the upper-right side of your G+ screen; click the upside down triangle to the right of your profile photo and select your Page. The Manage Your Pages screen, shown in Figure 13-6, displays the pages you've created, as well as the pages you manage along with some cursory stats for each page. If you manage more than one G+ page, they all appear here. You can also create a new page from the Manage Your pages section.

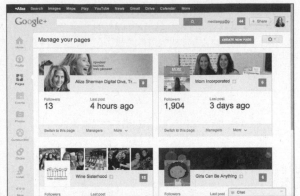

Figure 13-6:
The Manage
Your Pages
screen.

Once you are accessing G+ as your page, you can be active in a number of ways similar to individuals, including by

✔ **Posting regularly:** Whether you post text, photos, or videos, or whether you post your own content or links to other people's content, developing a regular rhythm for posting on G+ is key to successful engagement. To get noticed, G+ requires more frequent posting than a Facebook Page, but not necessarily as much as needed on Twitter, although it couldn't hurt.

✔ **+1ing other people's or pages' posts:** The +1 on Google+ is similar to the Like on Facebook. It's a quick acknowledgement and positive endorsement of content or a page.

✔ **Commenting on other people's or pages' posts:** Be thoughtful and noncommercial with your comments, adding to the conversation in an appropriate way.

✔ **Sharing other people's or pages' posts:** Share posts that your following will appreciate and that reflect well on your brand. Sharing makes a more meaningful gesture that can lead to an actual connection.

✔ **Targeting and tagging people and pages:** Send posts into the streams of specific people or pages for greater custom targeting of your messages.

By adding the + sign or @ sign in front of a person's name or company's name, you *tag* them so their name is a link in your post and the mention appears in their streams. They'll also get a notification depending on how they've configured their notification settings. You can only @ mention people who are on Google+. You can share your posts with people who aren't members of G+ by entering their e-mail addresses after the + or @ signs.

If you are only a manager for a G+ page and not the creator, you won't see the page show up when you hover over your Pages icon unless you're operating as the page. You will, however, see all the pages you've created and the ones you manage on the Manage Your Pages section.

After you're operating as your page, your personal identity isn't visible when you post. When interacting as your page, you can do nearly everything you can as an individual G+ user with the exception of not being able to invite individuals to instant chat with your page. As a page, you can post, create photo albums, edit photos, and upload video.

Building your page audience

Building your page audience goes hand in hand with populating your page with content. As you reach out and direct people to your page, you want to make sure interesting content is there to prompt them to circle your page and engage with you. Like any presence you build in social media, you need to implement a combination of tactics to help people find your page, profile, or account while giving them compelling reasons to connect with you.

To start, fill out your page profile so your G+ page looks professional and complete. Add your company name, add images to customize it, fill out the About section to give people relevant information about your business, and provide more ways and reasons to connect with you.

Some other ways to get people to your Google+ page include

- **Inviting others to G+:** When your page is ready, post an invitation with a link to your page on your G+ profile as an update. Use a third-party social media management tool such as Hootsuite Pro to schedule regular — but not too frequent — posts to your personal G+ account reminding people that you have a business page.

- **Embedding the G+ badge:** Install the G+ badge on your website or blog so your visitors and customers can add your page to their circles directly from your site. The badge lets Google track your +1s from your own site and your G+ page, and higher +1s can have a positive effect on your Google rankings.

- **Linking to your page:** Look for places besides your website and blog where you can link to your G+ page, such as in your profiles on other social networks and in your e-mail signature.

- **Sharing your page by e-mail:** Expand your reach beyond G+ to build awareness of your page. Use your other channels and communications tools, including your e-mail newsletter, Facebook Page, Twitter account, and YouTube channel to announce the launch of your G+ page and repeat that message where and when appropriate.

- **Sharing your page via social network posts:** Pepper in occasional posts on your other social networks to let your audience know you have a page on Google+. Being connected to people in several places where they spend their time online can help you engage them.

Although it may be tempting to circle everyone who circles you, note that some — or many — of those who have you in their circles may not be the appropriate audience for your page. For example, they may be in another country, and if your business serves only a local or U.S.-based clientele, those fans may not be a fit. Or if you're trying to reach new moms for example, an older male executive may not be your audience. Take a look at their G+ post streams or their profiles to gauge if they're the right audience for your page.

To further build your page circles, while in Page mode, search for keywords pertaining to your business. For example, if you're a wine company, you can search for *wine* and find posts from people or pages you aren't following. Circle individuals with care and thoughtfully comment on their posts. Follow other pages of companies that are complementary to your business.

You can choose to show or not to show the people and pages you've circled or who has circled your page on your page's profile. To reveal or hide this information, go to the About section of your profile; then click Edit under the People section of your profile. Your choices include which of your circles to show and if the public or just your circles can see that. You can also view who has circled your page in this section and opt to make that list visible or hidden. Once you've saved your changes and leave the About section, you're out of Edit mode.

Expanding Your Google+ Engagement

For all intents and purposes, using G+ as your company page is similar to using the network as an individual. You want to be friendly, attentive, responsive, and interesting. The main difference between interacting as your page or as an individual is that you will probably want to be more strategic as your page and more aware of consistent messaging and branding. The more you reach out to others on G+, you'll get a greater response and form stronger connections.

Circling your connections

Google is the first major social network to provide the ability to share your messages with specific audiences. As a page, you can create circles of your connections based on any criteria you want. Some examples of circles are team members, vendors, fans, competitors, and other relevant groupings. You can also manage the posts you see in your home page stream based on these circles. Figure 13-7 shows an example of the Circles page.

To be able to engage with others on Google+, you need to circle them and they need to circle you back. When you circle them, you see their posts in your content stream. If they don't circle you back, they won't see your posts.

In a way, circling is like following on Twitter. You can follow someone else and see her content, but until she follows you back, the communication is mostly one way.

Figure 13-7:
Create and
manage
your page's
circles on
your Circles
page.

You can reach out to the people you follow by giving a +1 (like a YouTube Thumbs Up or Facebook Like) on their posts or commenting appropriately. By doing so, you're getting onto someone's radar, and your profile photo and name are visible to the other person. They can still however, choose not to circle you.

Connecting with groups in Hangouts

With your Google+ account comes the ability to participate in or organize a videoconferencing meeting with up to ten people called a Hangout. Pages have the same ability as individuals to create and participate in a Google Hangout. See Figure 13-8 for an example of a Hangout.

You can use Hangouts for virtual team meetings, tutoring, interviews, viewing YouTube videos with others, troubleshooting support, consulting, webinars, and presentations (to limited audiences).

Starting a Hangout

You can launch a Hangout easily by clicking the Hangout button on the upper-right corner of your G+ screen from the home page, your Page's profile, Explore (the area streaming popular content on G+), and Events and Communities (see more about Google Communities later in this chapter). You can launch a Hangout as a Page or as yourself as an individual. We recommend building your company's brand and using Hangouts as a Page publicly. You can also initiate a more private Hangout amongst your internal team.

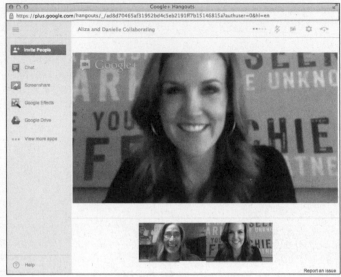

Figure 13-8:
Google+
Hangouts
can bring
together
up to ten
people in
videocon-
ferencing
mode.

Take advantage of Hangout collaborative features including screen sharing, Google Docs collaboration, presentation viewing, and group diagramming. After you are inside a Hangout, you can click the Add App button and view the various apps that you can add. You can also take screenshots of your Hangout using the Capture button to the left of your screen with the camera graphic.

If someone can't join your Hangout through G+, you can call the person and conference her in. Just click the Invite button and then click the +telephone link. Calls to the U.S. and Canada are free through VoIP (Voice Over Internet Protocol) technology, which allows you to make calls over the Internet. International call rates are low, according to Google.

Scheduling Hangouts with Google Events

Use the G+ Events feature to promote your public Hangouts. You can also use Events to invite people to any online or offline event. If your event is offline, you can allow attendees to contribute photos from the event to a shared photo album. If you or they are using the Google+ app at the party, you can also add photos to the shared photo album in real time.

You can schedule regular Hangouts and use Google Events to invite people to them and place them on everyone's Google Calendar if they have a Google account.

Broadcasting interactively with Hangouts On Air

To take your hangouts to the masses, switch on the Hangouts On Air feature. This enhanced hangout option broadcasts your Hangout live to your Google+ profile or page stream, your YouTube channel, and your website or anywhere else you embed the viewer. Like regular Hangouts, Hangouts On Air include text chat so a broader audience can join the conversation and interact even if they are not participating via video. See Figure 13-9 for an example of a Google+ Hangout On Air viewed on YouTube.

Figure 13-9:
Digital media consultant Lynette Young's Women of Google+ show has boosted her professional profile.

To share your Hangouts more broadly, check the Enable Hangouts On Air button as you start a Hangout. While you are broadcasting, you'll be able to see how many viewers you've gained. When you sign off the air, a recording of your public Hangout is automatically uploaded to your YouTube channel. The archived video also appears on your original G+ post when you announced the Hangout.

At the time of this writing, Pages could not participate or organize a Hangout on a mobile device. Both pages and profiles can start a Hangout from a computer, but only individuals can participate in Hangouts through their mobile devices. If you want to start a Hangout for your page, connect to G+ via a computer.

Video is a powerful medium, and you can use live and archived Hangouts On Air for a variety of purposes where using video for public viewing by a larger number of people makes sense. Ideal uses for Hangouts On Air include presentations and webinars, live shows, town hall-style meetings, press conferences, performances, and other events.

Leveraging the power of +1

Google+ gives people a way to endorse web content and to give it their version of "like" or "thumbs up" through their +1 buttons. The +1 button appears throughout Google's suite of tools including Google.com search results; Google+ pages; and G+ posts including videos, articles, comments, and photos.

People can +1 your page directly or through the content you post to your page. In a more pervasive way, they can +1 your page if they see it on other sites on the web — either owned by Google or in the Google Display Network and through Google search results.

When someone is signed in to Google+ and then clicks the +1 button, Google includes annotations in search results that can show up for his connections, letting them know that he's endorsed something. Similar to how Facebook shows people if their friends have liked the page of an advertiser right within an ad, Google shows people's +1 activity to their connections.

As a business, the integration of the +1 button means that you can incorporate other people's endorsements for your company and content into your advertising and outreach. As you promote your company, people can see when their connections have given your page or your content a +1.

You can leverage the +1 feature several ways, including

- **Adding the +1 button to your website or blog:** You can generate code for a G+ button for your business and embed it into your site or blog, allowing your visitors to add you without having to travel away from your site or blog. Google provides the code and graphics for a variety of +1 buttons for your website or blog; see Figure 13-10.

- **Connecting your website and G+ account:** Connect +1s for your website with +1s on your Google+ page and your Google ads. After you create your G+ page, add a line of code on your site to connect them so Google can begin tracking your combined +1s.

- **Using social extensions:** *Social extensions* let you link recommendations about your company and content from others to your AdWords campaigns. When you connect your Google+ page to your ads, Google can show your customer endorsements for your business in combination with your ads. A +1 on your ad applies to your Google+ page's +1 count. The reverse is also true, so +1s from your Google+ page are applied to your AdWords ads. Although AdWords campaigns cost money, any +1s you accumulate on your page or ad through your ad campaigns doesn't cost anything extra.

Figure 13-10:
Examples of
the variety
of +1 but-
tons Google
offers.

Collaborating in Google+ communities

A new feature offered to companies with G+ pages is the ability to form an online community and invite others to participate in it. The community can be a place for discussion and to post photographs, events, and other content. Figure 13-11 shows an example of a G+ community with updates from members that can be +1'd, commented on, or shared — just like profiles and pages.

Figure 13-11:
A G+
community.

The goal of communities is to bring together an affinity group for conversation and collaboration. Anyone can join other communities forming on G+ ranging from industry networks to cause-related groups. Communities take a lot of time to manage, whether you're building one on your G+ or your Facebook Page, Twitter, LinkedIn, or any other social network.

G+ communities are similar to Facebook or LinkedIn Groups in that they are all geared toward deeper discussions among group members. Each is useful for bringing together like-minded individuals or actual clubs, organizations, or groups that have already formed and are seeking an online forum where they carry out ongoing discussions.

The main difference that separates G+ communities from Facebook or LinkedIn is the ability to categorize discussion content. When you create your community, you can add discussion categories such as Photos, Reviews, Q&A, or Tips. As people post to the community, they can select the appropriate category and then anyone in the community can sort content by category. Other than this feature, G+ communities are more similar than not to Facebook and LinkedIn Groups.

To create a G+ Community, click the Communities button on the left side of your G+ screen. To attach it to your G+ Page, make sure you're in page mode before clicking the Create Community button in the Communities section. You have the choice of creating a Public or Private community. If public, you can choose to let anyone join, or have a moderator approve before letting someone join. If private, you can either opt to hide it from searches, or allow it to be found but require that people ask permission to join.

Your community's privacy setting cannot be changed after you choose Public or Private, so select with care based on the goals of your community.

After you set up your community, Google+ prompts you to

- ✔ **Write a tagline.** Make it short and compelling.

- ✔ **Pick a photo.** The optimal photo size is 250 x 250 pixels (like profile photos). Otherwise, you have to crop the image.

- ✔ **Complete the About section.** Google also encourages you to include community guidelines in the About section.

- ✔ **Add a few discussion categories.** The category feature is a major difference among G+ communities and Facebook or LinkedIn groups. You can pre-establish categories that community members can choose for their posts and more easily filter posts based on category.

After you create a community, Google+ immediately prompts you to invite others to it. If you're acting as your page, you can invite only people in your page's circles. After you create a community through your page, you can personally join the community (via your profile) and make yourself and others community managers; then you can invite people to the new community in your personal G+ circles. If you've formed the Community as an individual, you can also join the Community as your page and then give your page manager status.

Managing a community takes a lot of time and attention. Not every company needs an additional community beyond the ones that organically form in social networks. Carefully consider if a more active community is right for you before embarking on more intensive community-building.

Chapter 14

Location-Based Services

In This Chapter

▶ Blending online and offline outreach

▶ Building connections around locations

▶ Growing communities with images

▶ Enhancing real-world events with mobile marketing

*T*his chapter details how you can hold the power of community and social media engagement in the palm of your hand — literally. An amazing thing happened in the past decade: Our telephones became more portable and more powerful than you probably ever imagined. With smartphones, we're carrying mini computers around, not to mention still and video cameras, audio recording devices, and myriad other tools that use a variety of software applications.

The increasing ubiquity of smartphones brings a seemingly endless supply of mobile applications you can download for free, or for a small fee, that perform many different functions. Some of those applications lead to social networks accessed primarily on mobile devices instead of through the web. These social mobile networks often use the GPS feature in smartphones as an integral part of their services. All of the popular web-based social networks that have corresponding mobile apps can also tap into your location coordinates. In this chapter, we focus mostly on the social networks predominantly based in mobile apps, which we call *location-based services* (LBS).

Bridging the Real and Online Worlds with LBS

Social mobile networks give you a whole new way to engage with your customers and prospects. You may have been told that reaching others in their e-mail inboxes or through their favorite social networks on the web is a more intimate way to communicate and connect with them. Making contact through someone's smartphone or other hand-held mobile device ups that intimacy even further.

A location-based service is a social mobile network that ties directly into your mobile device's Global Positioning System (GPS) coordinates and uses your location to tag your photos and your posts. Location and place are an integral part of how these services work. Practically every social mobile network prompts you to give permission to access your location to unlock functionality tied to where you are at any given moment.

Using LBS means you can connect and communicate with others, combining both a physical location and a mobile device. Location plays a major part in the functionality of an LBS, so look for ways to tie in places to your social media engagement messaging and outreach.

Choosing an LBS (or two)

Here are some of the popular and newer social mobile networks that rely on or incorporate your location:

- **Foursquare** (`https://foursquare.com`): If you have a business with a physical location, you can claim the actual address on this service based on the GPS coordinates, allowing your customers to *check in* there. People nearby can discover your establishment and read tips or recommendations. The service also includes gaming features and badges. It combines check-ins, tips, deals, and images. This service is available — and most commonly used — on smartphones: iPhones, Androids, BlackBerry, and Windows Phone.

- **Path** (`https://path.com`): This service aggregates check-ins, photos, videos, music, movies, and other moments that you create on Path or by importing content from other social networks. It emphasizes smaller connections — limited to 150 people — so it's more suitable for communicating with niche groups. You can use this service on iPhones and Androids.

- **Foodspotting** (`www.foodspotting.com`): Use this app to take photographs of meals at eating establishments and to find places to eat by perusing snapshots of dishes served nearby. Even if you aren't a restaurant, you can build your reputation by sharing great food images and reviews that tie back to your brand. This service is available for iPhones, Androids, BlackBerry, and Windows Phone.

- **SCVNGR** (`http://scvngr.com`): You can build games or challenges that others can play based around locations — think scavenger hunt. As a business, you can brand experiences that other people can enjoy. It's available for iPhones and Androids.

For a related suggestion, see the sidebar "Engaging with geocaching," at the end of this chapter.

✔ **Yelp** (www.yelp.com): Yelp (see Figure 14-1) started as a web-based review site where users could leave reviews of businesses. Its mobile app also includes discovery of places nearby with the reviews. As a business, you should review what people are saying about you. The app is available for iPhones, Androids, Windows, BlackBerry, and Palm.

Figure 14-1: Yelp is both a review website and a social mobile app.

 In addition to LBS, you can market to and engage customers through their mobile devices in other ways. *Near field communication (NFC)* lets two devices (a data chip and a smartphone, for example) in the same area communicate with one another. And location-based advertising (LBA) uses *geofencing,* in which virtual boundaries trigger pop-up messages on people's mobile devices when they are moving within specific locations. Learn more about these topics in the book *Location Based Marketing For Dummies,* by Aaron Strout (John Wiley & Sons, Inc.).

Setting up an LBS account

As a business, you can establish presences on LBS as an individual representing your company or a "personality," as the company itself, or both.

 We recommend that you set up both company accounts and personal accounts and limit the number of people who can post to your company account. In social media engagement, you want to infuse your brand with personality and presence so that people want to connect and interact with your company. Having a brand presence on LBS is a perfectly acceptable way to demonstrate aspects of your brand that can attract customers and prospects and deepen relationships.

Personal accounts

Using an individual, personal account on any LBS is convenient and easy to set up. Also, people like to first and foremost connect with other people. A personal photo in a profile is much more approachable than a company logo.

If you go the individual route, you may end up with less company branding and some brand confusion. You also have to be careful not to use your personal account in a personal manner that may not properly reflect your brand image. If you want team members to participate on behalf of the brand, you don't want them to use your personal account, but setting up multiple personal accounts for people who are supposed to represent your brand means more accounts to monitor.

Business accounts

Using an LBS as a company keeps your brand image consistent and carries it over into the new social mobile space. There is a lot to be said about branding consistency in social media engagement. Because most LBS are not set up specifically for companies, you may have to finesse some of the profile elements to convey the personality of the brand and not an individual person behind your brand.

Going the company or brand route can be problematic if you or your team members also have personal accounts on the same service. For the most part, LBS are not set up to accommodate multiple accounts on the same mobile device. In order to toggle between a personal and company account, you have to log out of one and log in to the other. You can get into some hot water if you forget which account you're logged in to at any given time and post something inappropriate to your company account.

Making Connections with LBS

Although most LBS tap into your mobile device's GPS, each one tries to differentiate itself by using location data in different ways. Each service allows you to connect with others in the same way web-based social networks do. LBS have similar connection, conversation, and community-building features described throughout this book, such as profiles, friends, liking and favoriting, and comments.

The difference between LBS and other types of smartphone apps that allow you to have a profile and connect with others is that it incorporates GPS as a basis for connection, discovery, and tagging posts to tie them to a place. Other social networks and mobile versions of social networks, such as Pinterest and LinkedIn, don't make active use of location data.

Checking in to locations to engage others

The act of checking in to locations may seem like a strange activity, but millions of people do it every day as a way of connecting with others and announcing what they're doing and where. Even if people are not actively checking in to a place using an app with a check-in feature, they might post from a location — your physical business location — and tag their post or even their photograph with GPS data. Many share these check-ins and geo-tagged posts and photos on several social networks, including Facebook and Twitter.

People check in to locations for a variety of reasons:

✔ **Letting their friends know where they are:** When someone is frequenting your establishment, encouraging them to check in can increase exposure to your brand and location.

✔ **Organizing impromptu meet-ups with connections based on proximity:** As a business, you can benefit from additional foot traffic when someone uses an LBS to gather others to your location.

✔ **Broadcasting their activities as part of their general social network sharing:** Check-ins share your location name, increasing your brand exposure.

✔ **Leaving tips, kudos, or critiques of businesses they frequent:** Use check-ins as a customer service and marketing tool by noting what people like or where they may have a complaint and taking action to improve their experiences.

✔ **Accessing specials and deals from companies leveraging LBS marketing:** Stimulate interactions with customers by tying deals and offers into popular LBS.

✔ **Competing with their friends for status:** This includes top positions on leaderboards, or badges, or kudos.

For details on how to use check-ins for promotions, see "Offering deals driven by check-ins," later in this chapter.

GPS location isn't highly accurate for indoor spaces. If you're looking to create check-ins within an indoor space, ByteLights (http://bytelight.com) are LED lights that help feed data about a customer's movement and activities within a confined space. The company's technology claims one meter of accuracy, which is far closer than typical GPS provides.

Discovering others nearby

Several LBS take professional networking to a whole new level using *proximity,* or notifying you when people you know through social networks are nearby. Apps that point out proximity to people, places, and things are also known as *geosocial discovery apps.*

Apps such as Banjo (`http://ban.jo`), Highlight (`http://highlig.ht`), and Sonar (`http://sonar.me`), all available for iPhones or Android phones, announce when people you might know are nearby. Highlight tells you when your Facebook friends and other Highlight users are physically close to you. Sonar uses data from your Facebook, Twitter, Foursquare, and LinkedIn accounts while Banjo accesses data from Facebook, Twitter, Foursquare, LinkedIn, Instagram, Vimeo, and Google to determine relevant connections. The app Here On Biz (`http://hereon.biz/`) taps solely into your LinkedIn account.

Using geosocial discovery apps can be helpful for real-world networking; you can meet social networking connections in person or meet friends of your connections through the serendipity of being nearby. Although you can link geosocial discovery apps to your company's Twitter and Foursquare accounts, you can't link them to your company's Facebook Page or LinkedIn Company Page — only to your personal Facebook and LinkedIn accounts.

Tying images to places through geotagging

Although some apps use active check-ins or automatically add geographic information to tie posts to physical locations, some also use geotagging to tie images, particularly photographs, to places. Some of these apps incorporate geotagging into main features on the service while others let you decide when to tie images to a location.

In addition to Foodspotting (mentioned earlier in this chapter), there are a number of LBS that center around geotagged photographs and content including

- ✔ **Instagram** (`http://instagram.com`)**:** Instagram describes itself as "a fun and quirky way to share your life with friends through a series of pictures." As a business, you can build a community by *lifestreaming* images to showcase your brand's personality and provide a more intimate look at your company. You can take photos, filter them, label them, and share them with your followers who can "like" them or comment on them. You can also integrate Instagram with other social networks as we detail later in this chapter. It's available for iPhones and Android phones.

✔ **Trover** (www.trover.com): With this app, people find and explore places and hidden gems around the world. Even if you aren't a company with a physical location or have anything to do with travel, you can create lists of local businesses as resource guides and build your brand and reputation on the network, exposing your brand to new people. It's available for iPhone and Android.

✔ **Wyst** (http://wyst.it): Use this app to leave notes and photographs at specific locations to be accessed by others using the app when they're in the vicinity. As a company, you can publish helpful notes around your local location or other places to build your brand and showcase your expertise. If you're a business with a physical location or if being local is important to your business, this type of activity makes sense. Even if you're traveling on business, you can "leave behind" virtual posts for other Wyst users to find. It's available for iPhone only.

As a business, you can use mobile photo sharing apps that use geotagging to tie images to your location or to tie your images to locations that others can discover in a search or when in close proximity to the location where your images are tagged.

Watch that you don't accidentally reveal your location when you don't mean to do so. As you set up social mobile networks on your smartphone or mobile device, make sure that you check settings and permissions within the app or on your phone to limit the use of your location data. Settings vary by each app and each type of phone.

Using LBS for Promotions

Not all LBS offer business features. Most are geared toward the individual user and aren't tailored for companies or brands looking to engage with others through social mobile networks. Most LBS don't offer separate or enhanced features for businesses like Facebook offers Facebook Pages, but they also don't forbid companies from setting up personal accounts for their brands or businesses.

Most LBS don't have features to accommodate companies or brands like LinkedIn, Pinterest, and Google+ offer with distinct Business Pages. Many newer social mobile networks tend to focus first on individual users to quickly build a large base that, in time, will be attractive to companies. Foursquare is an exception because it rolled out features to support companies fairly early in its development.

Pushing messages to people on their mobile devices can come across as creepy or invasive. Make sure you get people's permissions before adding them to your mobile or location-based marketing programs. Compiling your own mobile marketing list or using reputable LBS that people willingly join and are comfortable using reduces the chances that you'll turn them off with your mobile actions.

Doing business with Foursquare

Foursquare offers businesses free tools for attracting, retaining, and rewarding customers.

Claiming your business

If you have a physical location for your business such as a retail store or restaurant, start by claiming your business on Foursquare at `https://foursquare.com/signup`. Use Foursquare's search function to check if your business is already listed. If so, you can claim it by clicking the Claim Here link under the text Do You Manage this Location? Follow Foursquare's step-by-step instructions to claim your business.

If your business is not already listed, you can first add it while you are physically at your place of business and then follow the instructions to claim it.

Using Foursquare for business

After you have a claimed business location on Foursquare, you can update your listing and post updates from your location. You can also offer specials to attract customers and post events taking place at your location. Offer rewards to loyal customers — the *mayors* — who check in to your establishment often. Only one person can be mayor of an establishment at a time.

As shown in Figure 14-2, Foursquare also provides analytics for your claimed business. You can see check-in activity, including number of check-ins and how many were broadcast to Facebook, Twitter, or both. You can also see information about the mayor of your location and top visitors. Foursquare also sends weekly e-mails with the most recent tips and photos submitted by your customers.

Change your specials often enough to keep repeat customers interested, and be clear about what you're offering and how customers who check in can access or claim the offer.

Tell your customers that your business is on Foursquare and encourage them to check in. You can order a free window cling to put into your establishment's window to signify that you're on Foursquare. Foursquare also lets you set up events at your location so customers can check in to an event at your establishment.

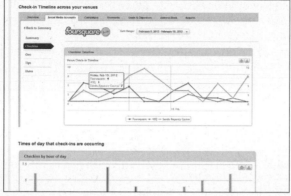

Figure 14-2:
Foursquare's dashboard provides data about your business and customers.

Tapping into the power of Instagram

Instagram is a wildly popular social mobile network that, until the end of 2012, existed only on smartphones. The value of Instagram's super loyal user-base and photo-sharing community was confirmed when Facebook bought the company for $1 billion. Photographs are a powerful part of online story-telling, and we talk earlier in this book about how images are an important part of social content and social media engagement.

Sharing photos on popular networks

Use Instagram to take, filter, and share images on popular social networks in addition to the Instagram community. You can set up an account on Instagram as your company in the same way you'd set up a personal account.

As a business, you can use Instagram to tell stories about your company, product, or services. Some ideas for images you can post include

- ✔ Behind-the-scenes at your company headquarters or locations
- ✔ Events you host or attend
- ✔ Images from your business travels
- ✔ Product images
- ✔ Images that portray themes in line with your brand messages
- ✔ How-to or demonstration shots
- ✔ Images with quotes

You can use mobile apps such as Overgram for iPhone or Phonto for iPhone and Android phones to add text to your photos to create popular quote images. You can add text on top of photographs you've taken and post directly to Instagram. Other apps let you create text-only images for Instagram such as Whims for iPhone and TextCutie for Android.

See "Linking LBS for integrated posts," later in this chapter, for a breakdown of other networks that you can connect to your Instagram account.

Using Instagram for promotions

In addition to tying Instagram into your social networks, you can incorporate the app and its photo-sharing capabilities into promotions and contests.

In early 2012, retailer Tiffany & Co. began a campaign called True Love In Pictures. People were invited to take photos of themselves with their significant others. If they used Instagram to submit images, they were instructed to use the hashtag #truelovepictures and other hashtags. The company created a microsite called `WhatMakesLoveTrue.com` as a destination about the art of romance. The site, shown in Figure 14-3, included a gallery of photo submissions. The site included filters that users could add to their own photographs as well as a tool to add photo captions and prompts such as "True love lasts forever when _____#TimelessTrueLove." The site also lets users send a Love Note with their images. Couples visiting the company's New York City, London, and Tokyo stores could take pictures in photo booths at each location and upload to the website.

Figure 14-3:
Tiffany & Co. posted users' photos on a website created for a specific promotion.

Use the Statigram contest toolkit (`http://statigr.am/instagram-contest-toolkit`) to organize, implement, and track a photo contest on Instagram. Tie the photo contest to a place, use a hashtag to tie the images together, and leverage the images on other social networks. Instagram users will spread the word about the contest and extend your brand to their followers simply by entering.

Linking LBS for integrated posts

Depending on the LBS you're using, you can connect it to other LBS. Most services let you connect to other services, and then give you the choice with each post if you'd like to broadcast more widely.

Using one LBS to post to several others is a common way to cross-post to get more use out of the content you're producing while engaging in social mobile networks. By providing your followers across multiple platforms with content, you create more touch points to stay top of mind with them. Although you may have some overlap of audiences, chances are most people won't be on all the services you're using. Even if they are, you're reaching them in different ways on different services at different times.

Table 14-1 shows some of the most popular LBS and the services they can connect with for broader posting. Connecting to Facebook and Twitter is common; however, the connection to Facebook goes to your personal Timeline, not your Facebook Page. Two social networks that work well with many LBS are Flickr, a longstanding social network for photo sharing, and Tumblr, a multimedia blogging platform that continues to grow in popularity.

Table 14-1		Connecting LBS				
Service	*Facebook*	*Twitter*	*Foursquare*	*Flickr*	*Tumblr*	*Instagram*
Foodspotting	x	x	x	x	x	x
Foursquare	x	x	-	-	-	-
Instagram	x	x	x	x	x	-
Path	x	x	x	-	x	-
Trover	x	x	-	-	x	-
Yelp	x	x	-	-	-	-

The apps that connect to Facebook are connecting with your personal Facebook Timeline and not your Facebook Page. You can still repurpose the images you take and upload to these services onto your Facebook Page. The most straightforward way is to upload the images you've taken for these services that are also saved on your phone. You can also take a screenshot of some of your check-ins and posts and upload them to your Page.

Use the tools at IFTTT (If This Then That, http://ifttt.com) to link apps that aren't typically linked. Use this website to create formulas or "recipes" that let you choose one social network, LBS, or website, and specify an action that will take place. An action could be when you post a photo to Instagram using the tag #social, it posts to your Facebook Page. For another example, when you check in on Foursquare with a photo, it's posted to your Tumblr.

We talk earlier in this chapter about using Foursquare and Instagram for promotions and customer loyalty programs. You can incorporate other LBS into promotions in similar ways. Some services build in tools that let you create deals or offers and tie them into your location. You can also tie rewards to actions that bring people to you through an LBS, such as "follow us on Instagram, and we'll pick a random winner each month to receive these cool products."

As long as you have a presence and a following, or connections in an LBS, or an audience primed and ready to join those services and engage with you on them, you have the potential to draw people in to participate in activities such as contests. When they participate, their actions can help spread the word about your brand and boost your outreach in new forums.

You can run online/offline promotions and activities using the mobile apps for popular social networks and tie them into your Facebook Page Timeline or Twitter, LinkedIn, Google+, or Pinterest (and so on) accounts. The more popular the app, the more likely people already have it on their mobile devices, and you've skipped the extra step of asking them to download a new app.

Offering deals driven by check-ins

As we mention, not all LBS have set up specific features for companies or brands. Although most also don't forbid you from creating a presence for your brand instead of for you as an individual, the limited features and support for businesses can be challenging if you're trying to use the service for promotional purposes.

LBS rely on location, and when you create a promotion, you want to tie it to a place that either you own or can control, even for a short period of time. If you do not have a business with a physical location where others can visit and check in, you could still create a location or promotion at a trade show, conference, or other event as long as you plan for something with a short duration.

Tying your promotions to a more public space can be an interesting way to engage people who are using an LBS and pass through an area that you've tagged. Tagging spaces, however, could involve getting permission from the owners of the space. In most cases, however, tagging places with virtual data such as offers and challenges should not create a conflict, although this fact may change as more people and companies use geotagging, geofencing, and geo-apps.

Table 14-2 lists LBS that do offer businesses ways to leverage the check-in feature to provide users with a special offer or experience.

Table 14-2	Check-Ins and Offers		
Service	*Check-In*	*Proximity*	*Business Options*
Facebook Places	x	-	Check-in deals
Foursquare	x	x	Check-in deals, mayor perks
SCVNGR	x	-	Challenges, treks, rewards
Yelp	x	-	Check-in offers

Don't tag your competition's space. Although there are no legal precedents at this time about creating virtual tags or uploading photos, comments, or tips about your business at the location of your competitor, at the very least you'll create bad blood. There may be no rules dictating ownership of GPS coordinates, but use the Golden Rule when dropping geocontent in places you don't own. Don't do anything to someone else you wouldn't want them to do to you and your space.

Newer deal and offer platforms are surfacing to leverage consumers' greater comfort with marketing and commerce on their mobile phones. Some newer mobile platforms that let you create special offers for others include Gyft (http://gyft.com), Apple's Passbook (http://support.apple.com/kb/HT5483), and Google Wallet (http://www.google.com/wallet/).

Adding Mobile to Your Engagement Mix

Adding mobile marketing activities to your social media engagement can happen using other mobile tools and platforms in addition to LBS, so we cover just a few to round out your social mobile engagement mix. The main difference between LBS and other mobile marketing tools is community. LBS have features that let you build communities because they're social networks on mobile platforms.

Other mobile marketing tools are not about forming communities but reaching your communities through their smartphones and mobile devices via texting or SMS, the phone's web browser, or using other apps. A common benefit of LBS and other mobile marketing outreach is that it adds new ways of engaging with customers and prospects in more personal and intimate ways.

Reaching customers through SMS marketing

We talk about the importance of opt-in e-mail lists for marketing and engagement with customers and prospects. Another type of opt-in or permission-based list that you can explore is a mobile marketing list. Getting permission to send your customers or prospects text messages or SMS (short message service) is a forward-thinking move toward mobile marketing.

You can compile your mobile marketing list in a variety of ways including

- A sign-up form on your website
- Posts on Facebook leading to a Facebook app with a sign-up form
- Calls to action on your social networks leading back to a web-based, mobile-friendly form
- Signs at your business location using QR codes to lead to a form (See the next section for more information about QR codes.)
- Point-of-sale forms that customers can fill out
- Verbally requesting permission to sign up your customers

Retailer REI used a service offered by Placecast called ShopAlerts (`http://placecast.net/`) to create location-based messaging and time-based messaging pushed to customer mobile devices. Customers had to first provide their mobile numbers and give permission for REI to engage with them through SMS. Then Placecast helped REI build virtual boundaries near its stores that triggered messages to customers who had opted to receive texts. The messages helped drive customers to REI stores when they were nearby.

Food company Udi's Gluten Free prompts customers to give it their mobile phone numbers in its contact form and includes a check box for receiving mobile updates with special offers and seasonal promotions on its site and shared on other sites and blogs, as shown in Figure 14-4.

If you create a mobile app for your location or business, you can include pop-up notifications that are triggered when people are close to particular GPS coordinates. For these notifications to work, people must first download your app, then give the app permission to tap into their phone's GPS, then allow notifications. Once over those humps, you can push messages to them based on specific locations. You can also advertise on other people's apps that sell push notifications as part of their advertising services.

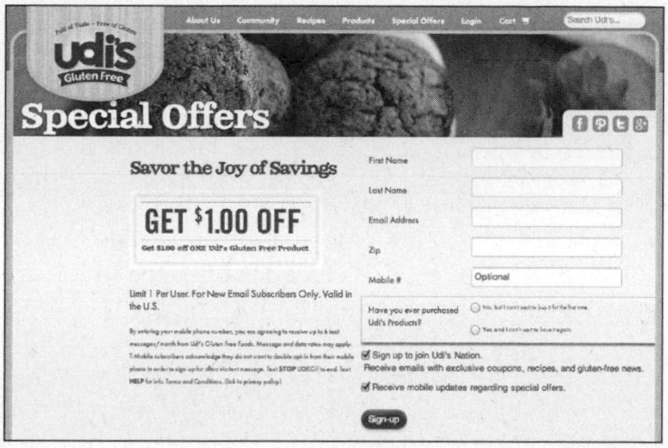

Figure 14-4:
This oppor-
tunity to
sign up to
receive
mobile
updates
comes with
a coupon.

Using QR codes for location-based marketing

QR codes or quick response codes were originally created by Toyota as two-dimensional black and white bar codes for its inventory tracking system. Today, these codes can come in a variety of shapes and colors as long as they maintain the key "hotspots" of the code. The codes can represent text and numbers, including website URLs.

A QR code is read by a QR code scanner app that you download to your smartphone. After you scan a code, it can either trigger an action or lead to a destination site. You scan a QR code to go on a social network, access additional information and resources including videos, make a purchase or donation, or take other online actions that can be completed easily on a smartphone.

QR codes can appear on a variety of real-world items and act as a bridge between the offline and online spaces. Using QR codes can help you interact with customers and prospects even when they aren't necessarily online but still have their smartphone with them or easily accessible. Some of the places where you can place a QR code include product packaging, signage, clothing, and marketing collateral.

The key to successfully integrating QR codes into your marketing mix is to carefully consider the destination where the code leads and making sure it's mobile-friendly. Even the actions you want people to take should be easy to do on a smartphone or the small screen of any mobile or Wi-Fi–enabled device. Don't require too much typing or too much reading. Think fast, easy, one-click, short, and sweet.

Laptop Lunches uses a QR code on its cardboard packaging that wraps around its colorful plastic bento-style lunch boxes. The code leads to a very mobile-friendly site with images of bento-ware lunch ideas. The images are large, and the content is mostly visual without requiring much text to get the information across (as shown in Figure 14-5). At a glance, busy parents can get inspiration for their children's lunches that fit perfectly into Laptop Lunches' bento-ware.

Figure 14-5: Laptop Lunches opts for large images with little text to provide meal tips and ideas for kids' lunches via SMS messaging.

Although it may seem clever to put a QR code on a billboard, keep in mind that the chances of someone in a car being able to scan the code from the road, much less do so safely, are slim. A QR code on a poster at the airport or on a bus or subway makes more sense because people have time to safely pull out their phones and fire up their QR code scanners.

When you use QR codes at physical locations, include a call to action. "Scan this code and be entered to win a prize" or "Scan this code to follow us on Facebook" may seem obvious, but most people need you to spell out for them why they should fire up their QR code scanner and scan your code. Also determine what QR code scanner you'll use and recommend to your customers and prospects.

Some QR code scanners offer QR code services such as mobile landing sites for QR codes and custom-designed QR codes. Scan (http://scan.me) for iPhone, Android, and Windows Phone offers free mobile sites. Paperlinks (www.paperlinks.com) for iPhone offers a paid service for mobile sites and can provide custom-designed QR codes in a variety of shapes and colors that can also include your company logo or other objects or images in the code. Work with a designer skilled in QR code customization to ensure the design doesn't interfere with the code scanning.

Don't use QR codes that are too small to function or too dark to scan. Your QR code should be no smaller than 1-x-1 inch square and preferably larger. Make sure the background of your code is much lighter than the code itself for optimal scanning.

Geolocating and geotagging

We'd be remiss if we didn't mention how Facebook uses geolocation for its Facebook Places feature. Although this isn't a main aspect of its overall service, and Facebook is also a web-based network, its initial Places service was competitive to Foursquare in particular when it first rolled out, even though now it's integrated with Pages. Plus, Facebook offers businesses options for reaching its customers through this feature, unlike many of the newer LBS.

Facebook Places lets users add a location to their posts so if they are at your place of business, they can tag their posts with the location. In the past, companies could set up a Place on Facebook. Now the Place feature is combined with a company Facebook Page if you've designated your Page as a business establishment with a location. For people to be able to check in to your place of business, select Local Business or Place when setting it up and add your business address.

Even if you don't have a Facebook Page, people can still check in to your location by adding a new location as they try to check in. Clearly, having your own Facebook Page facilitates this process and adds the number of people who have checked in to your location. Figure 14-6 shows this number next to number of Likes and people "talking about this."

People can check in to Facebook Pages with locations when they're nearby. Even if you've never made a Facebook Page for your business, people may still be able to check in there by creating a new location when they check in.

In addition to Facebook, you can use the mobile apps of other popular social networks to add location or geotagging to your posts and images including Twitter (Chapter 10), Google+ (Chapter 13), and Flickr (www.flickr.com).

Engaging with geocaching

Another activity that combines GPS coordinates and offline and outdoor activities is called *geocaching.* The concept of geocaching — also called "waymarking" — is that participants around the world hide and seek out containers called *caches.* Each cache is usually in a sturdy, waterproof container and at a minimum has a log book so each person who finds it can sign the log book before hiding it again.

Often, people add other items to a cache: small, portable trinkets or items that can fit easily in the container. If someone removes something from the cache, it's common that she replace it with something else for the next person.

Businesses can participate in this popular activity and engage avid outdoor enthusiasts and active individuals by creating and hiding your own caches, which could include branded or promotional items. Use a GPS coordinates tool such as GPS Compass, Free GPS for iPhone, or CacheSense and c:geo for Android to record the coordinates and provide them to others in a variety of places including social networks, on your website or blog, in forums for geocaching enthusiasts, and on offline signage.

Figure 14-6: The number of people who check in appears at the top of your Facebook Page.

Creating hybrid online/offline engagement

A natural fit for creating engagement that crosses from offline to online and back are applications like SCVNGR (mentioned previously) that tie to GPS coordinates linking to online content. The online content then leads to instructions for offline activities such as scavenger hunts, quests, and other challenges.

The key to successful hybrid online/offline mobile-powered campaigns that tie into your overall social media engagement is careful planning, including

✔ Your main goals and the goals of your campaign

✔ The audience you're trying to reach

✔ The specific action or actions you'd like them to do

✔ The destination site or sites that will house instructions, resources, or related information

✔ The online and social mobile tools and platforms you'll use to carry out the campaign

✔ The online and social mobile tools and platforms you'll use to promote the campaign

✔ The offline tools and materials you'll use to promote the campaign

Map out the entire process from start to finish for how your social mobile initiative will work. Plan the fewest steps possible to complete a successful hybrid activity or campaign. You'll more likely have fewer participants if your activity or promotion is long, arduous, confusing, or convoluted.

You'll have more success with fewer barriers to entry such as making sure that at least both iPhone and Android users can participate unless you are specifically targeting one platform over the other. If your activity requires that people download an application, make it easy to do so and consider providing additional incentive such as random drawings with prizes.

Part V
Leveraging Audio and Video for Engagement

To learn how to build your YouTube community with annotations, go to www.dummies.com/extras/socialmediaengagement.

In this part . . .

- ✔ Become familiar with audiocasting and videocasting to enhance your engagement efforts.

- ✔ Enhance your social networking with audio and video.

- ✔ Get more marketing mileage from well-produced and engaging videos on YouTube.

Chapter 15

Audio and Videocasting

In This Chapter

▶ Building your audience with audio

▶ Appealing to your community with multimedia

▶ Mastering the use of streaming video

Speech is power; speech is to persuade, to convert, to compel. It is to bring another out of his bad sense into your good sense.

—Ralph Waldo Emerson

Ralph Waldo Emerson wasn't talking about social media engagement or your desire to introduce your brand to a new audience when he first uttered these words in the mid-1800s, but there's more than a kernel of truth in his words. Speech is powerful, whether you communicate in person or embrace multimedia and social media to share your message.

In this chapter, we discuss the deeper character and personality you give your brand by putting a voice, a face, or both to your business. Though it may seem that audio and video broadcasting don't fall into the category of conversation, they do. Yes, you want your audience to listen, but when done right, audio and video online is much more than one-way communication. Let us explain how and why, and the best ways for you to use these tools to maximize your impact.

Enhancing Your Marketing with Audio

Quite simply, messages can be conveyed with multimedia in a completely different way than with the written, tweeted, or "Facebooked" word. By producing audio and video, you produce shareable content. Use audio, video, and combined forms of multimedia to grow your audience and to communicate in a memorable fashion.

Audio — and video, as we explain later in this chapter — is uniquely positioned to make content relevant to what matters most to your audience: them. You open up a dialogue, share valuable information, and encourage your community to react or act, just like you would be doing if you were using text.

With audio and video, however, you can do something the written word alone often can't do: form a more personal connection. (In the case of video, you form a more face-to-face connection than words could ever do.)

You have a variety of options to reach your target audience. The most common are audiocasting, usually called podcasting; teleseminars; and webinars. Here are some of the marketing benefits of audio:

- **Appealing:** Online digital audio is reminiscent of radio, a familiar communications, informational, and entertaining medium. People are comfortable listening to audio.

- **Popular:** According to PodcastAlley.com, a podcast directory, more than 91,000 podcasts existed as of December 2012, and more than a quarter of the U.S. population has listened to at least one show.

- **Low bandwidth:** Although audio files require more bandwidth than text and images, they're less intensive than video, making them easy to upload, host, access, and consume. Segments can be five to ten minutes or up to an hour, and usually require far less editing than video.

- **Low cost:** Audio can be very low-cost to produce. Because most podcasts and audio files are offered for free, they are attractive to your audience as valuable content they can listen to and share.

- **Low production:** Like online video, audio doesn't require high-end production value to be appealing. You don't need to produce radio-quality audio to have a successful online podcast.

- **Embeddable:** You can embed audio files into your website or blog, or you can add them to — or link to them from — the social networks you use.

- **SEO-friendly:** The more places your audio is listed, archived, and tagged, the more opportunities people have to find you in search engines. A description of the audio you upload along with your name, topic, and business name is easily searchable and can help build your audience.

- **Portable:** After your audience downloads the audio, they can listen anywhere, anytime — in their cars, while they prepare dinner, as they finish that last bit of work, or spend time on the treadmill.

Audio lets you share your personality with others. People can hear the tone of your voice and other vocal inflections, creating a deeper connection with your audience in a different way than text. See Chapter 6 for more about connecting with your audience.

Using podcasts to build an audience

The term *audiocast* — or *podcast* as we call it from here on out — refers to digital audio content that you can listen to online through your web browser on your computer or download to a mobile device like an MP3 player or a smartphone. The ability to download a podcast makes listening on the go simple.

As we mention in Chapter 3, podcasts can be delivered in a variety of ways: live streaming that's often recorded; recorded in advance and then broadcast later; embedded on a site or social network for instant or on-demand replay; or archived on a network like iTunes for individual download or subscription.

Deciding what — and how — to podcast

Podcasts can take the form of a radio broadcast, a seminar, a performance, an audiobook, you name it. Anything that can be published as text can also be produced as audio. And of course, any audio that can be recorded can be made into a podcast. We talk more about video podcasts later but for now, know that podcasts can be produced in audio, video, or both.

Before you decide what your podcast is about, download other podcasts first. Look at the list of popular podcasts, but also search for podcasts created by companies in addition to individuals to see how you might format a podcast for your business. Some of the most popular podcasts including TED Talks, NBC Nightly News, and The Today Show are all available via audio and video podcasts and can be listened to or viewed on your iPod, iPad, iPhone, or Apple TV.

People are often delighted to do audio interviews because they require very little physical preparation, don't require travel, and can be done from anywhere by phone. Giving someone else the opportunity to share her knowledge on your podcast is a win-win for both of you.

If you're looking for a little something extra, you can produce *enhanced podcasts,* especially audiobooks, that include photos, hyperlinks, and even chapter marks. If someone downloads your enhanced podcast from iTunes, he sees everything he needs to navigate the chapters, hyperlinks, and artwork in a menu bar.

Getting a podcast off the ground

Getting started with a podcast is relatively easy. The low barrier to entry is one of the many reasons podcasts are quite popular. If you're anxious to get started, you can begin with software like Apple's GarageBand, a microphone for less than $100, and free online podcast-publishing software such as SoundCloud (`http://soundcloud.com`), Podcast Generator (`www.podcastgen.sourceforge.net`), and PodOmatic (`www.podomatic.com`). These services provide all of the initial resources you need, including the RSS feed for submitting your podcast to iTunes (see the next section) that will be necessary once you feel you are ready for this step.

Distributing your podcast

When you're ready to share your podcast, and you have used a podcasting service or tool to generate the feed, head to iTunes to submit it. Submitting your podcast to the iTunes Store starts with a valid iTunes account; then you must have your podcast RSS feed to start the submission process. Here are the steps to adding your podcast to iTunes for easy downloading and subscribing:

1. **Launch iTunes.**

   If you don't yet have iTunes, you can download a free version and sign up for a free account at http://apple.com/itunes.

2. **At the very top of the iTunes page, click Podcast on the navigation bar to go to the podcast section.**

   You must be logged in to your iTunes account.

3. **Click the Submit a Podcast link in the right-hand sidebar.**

   The podcast submission page appears.

4. **Enter the RSS feed URL for the podcast you've created and click Continue.**

   You can find the feed through the podcasting service you used. See Figure 15-1 for the submission screen.

   The RSS feed you want to use when submitting your podcast to iTunes is an XML file. Although you can generate this file from scratch, it's a long and tedious process. You're better off using a podcast-publishing tool that generates this file.

5. **Fill in the submission form.**

   You are taken to a review page where iTunes prompts you to upload artwork and enter your name, the name of your podcast, a short description, a long description, and an iTunes category. Note that some podcasting services may prompt you in advance to add all of these things, or your RSS feed may already contain some or most of what iTunes needs. iTunes prompts you for missing information.

6. **Submit and wait.**

   Expect about one to two days of processing time for iTunes to approve your podcast.

7. **Market when ready!**

   After your podcast is live on iTunes, you can begin marketing it by sharing a link to it on your website, blog, and social networks.

You can also publish your audio podcast to a WordPress blog. WordPress automatically generates an easy-to-find RSS feed that you can then use in iTunes. Just add **/feed** to the end of your blog URL. You can also create a feed by using a tool like Google FeedBurner (http://feedburner.com).

Figure 15-1:
Submitting
your pod-
cast to
the iTunes
Store.

Growing your podcast audience

Here are some tips for growing your podcast audience:

- ✔ **Content is king.** Creating shows that bring listeners back again and again is key. Think how-to's, tips, and tricks. Content that can still be relevant a year from now is your goal. You want your audience to be able to listen today, next week, or four months from now and still be moved.

- ✔ **iTunes reviews are gold.** Ask for feedback. And then ask again. The power of positive feedback cannot be underestimated. The reviews seen on iTunes will be some of the first impressions potential new listeners get of your podcast. You want good feedback and as much as possible.

- ✔ **Commitment matters.** To hook your audience, you need to appear regularly. Whether it is every Tuesday or Mondays and Fridays. But once you tell your audience what to expect from you, you must deliver.

- ✔ **Spread the word.** Yes, tell your fans on Facebook about your podcast. Yes, tell your audience on Twitter. Yes, shout it from the rooftops on Google+. But don't forget the power of your e-mail list, as well. A regular announcement with a link can be extremely valuable.

- ✔ **Popularity counts.** That means you want popular guests: Tim Ferris, Seth Godin, and Scott Stratten are a good way to catch your audience's attention, but don't rely on the 'big names' alone to do the marketing for you. You must still publicize your podcast as you would any other show.

✔ **Saying thank you is powerful.** A small gesture can go a long way. Thank your community regularly for being a part of the work you do. Srinivas Rao from Blogcast FM believes in the personal touch of taking the time each day to acknowledge new subscribers. Remember that using audio is just one way to connect with your audience online; it isn't the only way.

Publishing audio from a mobile device

Maybe creating a full podcast sounds too complicated for you. Maybe you want to give audio a shot, but don't want to invest in any technical equipment just yet. You can open dialogue between you and your community using audio easily and with minimal expense.

Reach into your pocket or purse and grab that smartphone or mobile device of yours. This little tool you're holding, the one that makes social media engagement so accessible and portable, can be your perfect audio tool.

If you're using an iPhone, tap the Voice Memo icon (looks like a microphone) that's located in the Utilities folder. You can also download any number of apps that can get you started, like Audioboo (`http://audioboo.fm`) or Chirbit (`http://chirbit.com`, Figure 15-2). Both are available on iPhone and Android. Start with short bursts of audio that provide useful information to your audience. You can quickly record, save, and share them on the go. Later you can embed or add those segments to some of your social media platforms.

Figure 15-2:
Chirbit allows you to upload audio directly from your mobile device or webcam, share via your social media platforms, and embed in your site or blog.

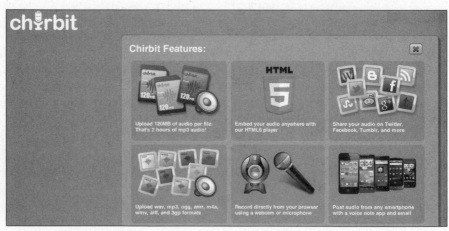

Business podcast hits 1 million mark using SME

Srinivas Rao launched Blogcast FM in 2010 after what he calls a "fortunate accident." He began by creating audio interviews to satisfy his insatiable curiosity about people and their business success, to provide insightful information for his audience, and as a way to drive traffic to his blog, The Skool of Life (www.theskooloflife.com). After about three months, a friend recommended that Rao spin the series into a regular podcast. As of the beginning of 2013, the podcast gets 1 million downloads a month. You read that right — 1 million.

Rao says his audience consistently uses three words to describe his show — actionable, insightful, and useful. The best thing about those three words from a marketer's perspective is that they prove that his audience finds value in what they're hearing. This level of engagement highlights the success of podcasts: Audiences don't hesitate to come back or to share what they enjoy or find useful to their daily lives and business success.

Adding audio to your social network

Although it's indeed delightful — and in many ways sounds incredibly fancy — that your podcasts or other audio can live on iTunes for all the world to see, you don't want to forget the many other opportunities to engage with your audience on your social networks.

To leverage the audio you're producing, you can

✔ **Share it.** From your page on iTunes, you have the option to share to Facebook and Twitter, e-mail the show's link to a friend, or simply copy the link so you can paste it elsewhere online. See Figure 15-3.

✔ **Embed it.** After you publish your podcast, you can use the embed code by placing it on your blog, Facebook, LinkedIn, or Google+. If you're feeling sassy, you can even create a board on Pinterest focused entirely on your new series. You get the embed code on whichever site you used to host your actual audio content.

Figure 15-3:
On this
iTunes
page for the
Freakonomics
podcast,
you can
share the
audio con-
tent in a
variety of
ways.

Offering Teleseminars and Webinars

Webinars and teleseminars are other ways to engage your audience and offer meaningful, quality content. The difference between the two audio delivery forms is distinct. A *teleseminar* is an audio-only session or conference via phone or computer. A *webinar* incorporates visuals such as PowerPoint slides that require you to be in front of your computer to participate.

Seeing the benefits of webinars and teleseminars

Both of these options offer benefits to your business or brand:

- **Trust:** Build trust by offering your audience information and inspiration they need. If your audience trusts you, they'll continue to rely on you for information and products.

- **Expertise:** Webinars and teleseminars highlight your expertise. Show off what you know. Answer the questions your community wants answered.

- **Connection:** Hearing your voice on a teleseminar — or even seeing your face if video is part of a webinar — allows your community to develop a connection with you. Whether you like it or not, it isn't always the best product that wins. People are more likely to purchase from brands that get the connection factor. See Chapter 6 for more on connecting with your community.

- **Growth:** A growing customer base signals success. If attendees enjoy your webinar, share their experience, return and bring others with them, your community continues to grow.

✔ **Revenue:** It would be silly if we didn't mention making money here, right? You can charge for teleseminars and webinars for what you show and tell. Building that trust and connection can pay off.

Although your decision to choose one over the other may come down to your preference, comfort level, and an assessment of the content you share, the distinct differences between the two may sway your opinion.

Choosing between webinars and teleseminars

Here are some distinct differences between webinars and teleseminars to help you decide which format is better suited for you.

Whichever you choose to produce, allow time at the end of the session for attendees to ask questions. Though it may be a slightly more complicated process on a teleseminar, Q&A allows you to engage with your attendees. Note that some teleseminar systems allow attendees to "raise their hands" via a button on their phones to make Q&A more organized.

Advantage: Webinar

A webinar is the better choice when you need the following features:

✔ **Show and tell:** The visual aspect of the webinar — including slides, videos, images, charts, and even streaming video so you appear in the presentation — creates a personal connection between you and your audience. It's a real seminar on the web.

✔ **Real-time interaction:** Attendees ask questions either verbally or via real-time text chat. You, as the leader of the webinar, can poll your audience and ask them questions. Keep in mind though, unless your teleseminar has a web-based dashboard, it can be chaotic when attendees try to interact verbally.

✔ **Networking:** Without dashboards or web-based communications tools that let you and your attendees interact, teleseminars are more isolating experiences. Some webinar software even allows attendees to create their own profiles to facilitate personal branding and connecting.

✔ **Technology showcase:** Let's face it — a webinar is simply a fancier technology. As a business or brand that can master this type of format, you show your clients you're savvy.

✔ **Feature set for attendees:** In addition to slides, webinars can contain video clips or live streaming video, polling, and real-time text chat.

Advantage: Teleseminar

By contrast, a teleseminar can be a better choice in the following ways:

- ✔ **Ease of use for attendees:** To participate in a teleseminar, all someone has to do is pick up a phone and dial. The more technically capable could call in via their computers, but hands-down, teleseminars are much easier for attendees than webinars, which can require downloading and installing software to participate.

- ✔ **Preparation time:** Compared with the visuals needed to produce a quality webinar, including slides and possibly video, a teleseminar is purely audio based, so you spend less time preparing.

- ✔ **Ease of access:** To participate in a teleseminar, you need only a phone line, compared with a computer and internet connection for a webinar.

Equal advantage

Webinars and teleseminars are equal in the following ways:

- ✔ **Cost:** Both are low-cost to produce. Although, there's a slight tip to teleseminars, which can include the cost of the phone call or the conferencing call system (depending on what system you use), but services for a high-tech webinar tend to be higher.

- ✔ **Recording and replay:** The good news is both teleseminars and webinars can be recorded, archived, and replayed later.

Selecting the right tool

To get started with teleseminars or webinars, there are a variety of online options ranging from completely free to a regular monthly fee:

- ✔ FreeConference (www.freeconference.com).

- ✔ FreeConferenceCallHD (ww.freeconferencecallhd.com)

- ✔ InterCall (www.intercall.com)

- ✔ MeetingOnNow (www.meetingonnow.com)

- ✔ InstantConference (www.instantconference.com)

- ✔ Cisco WebEx (www.webex.com)

- ✔ GoToWebinar (http://gotowebinar.com)

Beware of extra or hidden costs. Read the fine print from each service to make sure that the pricing is straightforward and obvious. Also keep in mind that if you use your telephone instead of your computer to place calls, you may incur long distance fees or eat up your mobile phone minutes.

Getting More out of Multimedia

What? You want to know more about video, too? You are clearly a business owner after Danielle's heart. It's her favorite medium in the world of social media engagement. In talking about multimedia, we touch on video, but delve into it even more deeply in Chapter 16 when we go over YouTube.

A 2011 study by Frank N. Magid Associates (`http://magid.com/sites/ default/files/pdf/metacafe.pdf`) indicates eight of ten people on the web watch online video every week. Additionally, 46 percent are watching user-generated content instead of news, music videos, or television clips. This means they watch what you create, or they would be if you were creating it.

So get moving!

Conferencing with video

The number of platforms available for you to reach out and talk to your community, to interview experts, and to connect with those around you astonishes even the most experienced in the social media space. It seems that there is a new way to engage almost weekly.

Videoconferencing is often on a considerably smaller scale than the teleseminars and webinars we discuss earlier in this chapter. A more intimate use of video creates an opportunity to garner more face-to-face time with specific people. In the following sections, we cover a few of the most popular video-conferencing products.

Skype

Skype (`www.skype.com`) first appeared in 2003, but video calls weren't officially introduced until late 2005 and early 2006. Skype was originally created to allow free audio and video calls through the Internet using Voice Over Internet Protocol, or VoIP. Today, Skype is one of the most popular videoconferencing tools, creating connections among family, friends, teachers, and students. Even companies use it for everything from meetings to interviewing job candidates to making presentations, without the associated travel costs.

In just the last two years, Skype's usage has nearly doubled to more than 700 million minutes every day — nearly half of those on video calls. It's no wonder Skype interviews are now a regular sighting on news and entertainment programs as a way for people in far-flung places to join the conversation. See Figure 15-4.

Figure 15-4:
Oprah uses Skype to bring readers into the conversation with author Eckhart Tolle during her web series about his book, *A New Earth.*

Skype has a screen-sharing feature so you can show someone else what's on your computer screen. Use the screen-sharing feature to enhance your two-way videoconference call and show something more clearly with visuals.

Skype videoconferencing is limited to two people in the free version or up to ten people in the paid version, and requires you to download the software. You can also access Skype via your mobile device to use videoconferencing as long as you have a video camera built into your device.

If you use a Mac, Call Recorder for Skype (`www.ecamm.com/mac/call recorder`) lets you record videos on Skype to archive and let your audience replay later on your site, blog, or on your social platforms. This is a paid option. A popular PC solution for recording Skype calls is Pamela for Skype (`http://Pamela.biz`).

Google Hangouts

Skype isn't the only solution in town. Google Hangouts, part of Google+, are another videoconferencing solution. You can chat face-to-face and hold a virtual meeting on Hangout for up to ten people entirely for free. You don't have to download any software with Google Hangouts. Although you cannot access Google Hangouts via your mobile device, you can broadcast the entire thing to the world via YouTube using Hangouts On Air. See Chapter 13 on Google+ (`www.google.com/+)` for more details on Hangouts.

iMeet

Another virtual conferencing solution is iMeet (`http://imeet.com`), which offers phone conferencing; videoconferencing for up to 15 people at once; no software downloads; the ability to share a screen or upload, share, and collaborate on a document; and easy access from a smartphone. iMeet subscriptions start at $19 per month, so you can see that different videoconferencing solutions have a range of costs and features.

Engaging with live streaming video

Going live with video is a way of inviting the world around you — or your community specifically — to sit down and connect with you in real time. Some benefits include the chat commentary, the connection with the audience, and the ability to actually hear from your community.

For businesses, the benefits of live streaming video include

- **Transparency:** You can't hide when you're on live video. If an audience member jumps into the conversation to ask you a question — either via chat or when permitted on camera — you build trust by responding directly.

- **Pure engagement:** Live video gives you the opportunity to share information in real time, ask questions, and to hear what your audience has to say. See Figure 15-5 for an example of engaging with live video.

- **Expanding your stage:** By opening yourself up to a live event, you are live everywhere. The world is your stage. This kind of exposure can grow your audience.

Figure 15-5: In November 2012, ABC News, Yahoo!, and Google Hangouts hosted a conversation with moms about the Presidential Debates.

- **Archiving Content:** Most platforms allow you to record your live event for later use with the ability to embed the saved video on your site, blog, or social networks. Live video content doesn't have to disappear, but can be repurposed and used to attract attention and generate revenue.

Tools for live streaming video include Google Hangouts (discussed earlier in this chapter), Spreecast (`www.spreecast.com`), Ustream (`www.ustream.com`), Livestream (`www.livestream.com`), Veetle (`http://veetle.com`), and Qik (`http://qik.com`).

The moment you go live on a Google Hangout, your video is recorded and automatically saved to your YouTube account. Make sure you check the recording settings on whichever live video-streaming tool you use so you don't lose the video you produce.

Showing on the go: Mobile video

Smartphones are now equipped with video, and many tablet computers also come with a camera and video capabilities. You can capture video on the fly wherever you are and upload quickly and easily to video-hosting sites including YouTube (Chapter 16) and Flickr (`http://flickr.com`).

Mobile apps also make it easy to record and upload quick videos to online communities like video-based social networks:

- **Magisto** (`www.magisto.com`): A video community with the magical ability to transform videos you take into a completed project in minutes. This app was launched in early 2012, and in a year's time had more than 15 million videos from 3 million users. You can share videos via Facebook, Twitter, YouTube, or e-mail. This app is for iPhone and Android devices, and online.

- **Viddy** (`http://viddy.com`): If you like the Instagram photo community, you'll probably like Viddy. This app is a video community and connects with your personal Facebook Timeline. It's for iPhone only.

- **Socialcam** (`www.socialcam.com`): Another mobile video community site. Easily share video on Facebook, Twitter, YouTube, e-mail, and by SMS. It's available for iPhone and Android.

- **Tout** (`http://tout.com`): This video app is more like Twitter, allowing only 15-second video uploads. You can share on Facebook, Twitter, or embed the video widget on your site. It's for iPhone and Android.

- **Klip** (`http://klip.com`): If Viddy is like Instagram and Tout is like Twitter, then Klip is like Pinterest. You can upload videos to Klip including using URLs to your videos already on YouTube. You can also record from your smartphone or webcam. This app is for iPhone and Android.

- **Vine** (`https://vine.co/`): This app allows you to make 6 second video clips and post them to your social networks. The videos are created only when the user is tapping the screen — giving the completed project a stop-motion effect. This app is currently available only for iPhones.

Chapter 16

YouTube

In This Chapter

▶ Producing memorable, shareable content

▶ Increasing your number of subscribers

▶ Mastering the technical side of YouTube

▶ Building a community video experience

*O*nline video: It isn't simply the quickest way to learn "Gangnam Style" (to date, the most-watched YouTube video of all time, with 1.2 billion views and counting), to keep up on the latest *Les Misérables* Flash Mob Wedding video, or to view quirky cat videos. Video is an opportunity to connect with your audience on a personal level — to make them laugh, to teach them something new, and to engage in some very basic, but honest, show and tell. In front of the camera, it's just you and your viewing community.

We aren't talking about creating a one-time hit video that drives clicks; instead, we're talking about motivating a community to keep you in their video sights permanently. Reports say that two thirds of the world's mobile data traffic will be video by the year 2016. Will you be along for the ride?

Using Video to Build Community

In 2011, the sixth year of YouTube's existence, 48 hours of video were uploaded every minute. By 2012, 72 hours of video made their way onto YouTube every 60 seconds. So what's happened in these past few years? You started watching. And your friends did. You shared what you loved. The brands you trust hopped in and started to broadcast. Then you began to share their content as well. YouTube is now a community-oriented platform and social network similar to some of the others we discuss in this book.

By now, you know a community cannot exist as a one-sided conversation. If your audience shows up and you're nowhere to be found, they leave. If they appear and your content is inconsistent or irrelevant — same result — you're on your own.

Although some of the same community-building basics apply — establishing a presence, building trust, listening carefully, and reacting accordingly (see Part II for a refresher) — YouTube has its own unique way of doing things. That's what we discuss in this chapter. You want a community that isn't expecting you to produce a video that entertains them for a few seconds, but is expecting content that continues to engage them so they never miss what you have to say.

Capturing your audience's attention

We have a friend who runs a series of successful one-day conferences for beginning bloggers. Bloggy Boot Camp is the brainchild of Tiffany Romero and Francesca Banducci. Tiffany commands the room the moment she wants her audience's attention by saying, "If you can hear me, clap once!" She pauses to wait for the response that always follows: a clap and then silence. She repeats, "If you can hear me, clap twice!" Two claps and another round of silence follow. Tiffany is to a live audience what you want to be to your online video viewers. The beginning of your video is your "clap." From that moment, you have their full attention. Your goal is to keep it.

YouTube works best not for that single amazing viral video, but for the channels producing an amazing viewing experience for their communities on a regular basis. You want people to watch and to continue watching. Stopping by your channel is great, but staying for the stories you tell in each of your videos is the longer-term goal.

Think of YouTube as an opportunity to show and tell in a way you can't with any other platform. According to Nielsen Wire, more than 147 million Americans watch video on the Internet. Those are eyeballs you want. Consider these best practices to capture your YouTube audience's attention:

✔ **Create regular content.** You must update your YouTube Channel regularly. It's up to you whether you post a new video every Monday, Wednesday, and Friday, or only once a week. However, your audience must know what to expect from you, and you must stick by whatever commitment you decide to make. A YouTube Channel last updated six months ago might as well not exist.

Post or share in plain sight when you plan to update your YouTube page — either in your banner or in your channel trailer — so your audience knows what to expect from you and when.

✔ **Remember that first impressions rule.** The first ten seconds of your video are crucial, as well as your screenshot (the picture visible when your video isn't playing). Compel your audience to click Play and then to stay with you. Be funny and engaging, and give your audience a feel for what to expect. The first impression is more important than how long your video is.

✔ **Know that production value matters.** If your audience cannot see you or hear you, they will click away instantly. It doesn't matter how compelling your content may be; you must ensure a certain level of quality. Lighting, sound, the framing of your shots, a still camera, and even some editing keeps people engaged.

Use YouTube's video editing tools to edit, make minor adjustments, or add some special effects to your video. You can trim videos to a specific length, combine multiple videos, add music from a library of approved songs, or even include custom special effects (www.youtube.com/editor).

✔ **Use annotations.** *Annotations* are text content that you can lay over your video, including a link to any page within YouTube and a call to action. Annotations can prompt your viewers to subscribe to your YouTube Channel, such as your video, or link to another one of your channels. Keep annotations small and unobtrusive to offer a small nudge in the right direction. Figure 16-1 shows how to encourage a Thumbs Up by using an annotation. A Thumbs Up is a simple way for a viewer to say 'I like this video.'

We cover annotations in more detail in "Using annotations and thumbnails," later in this chapter.

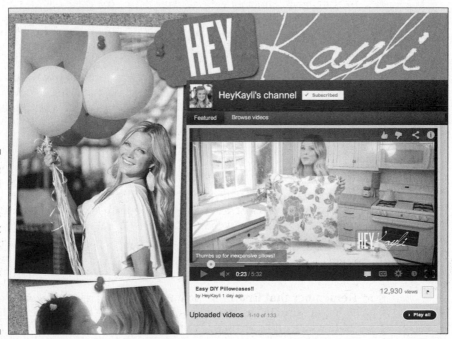

Figure 16-1:
HeyKayli uses annotations throughout her videos, encouraging viewers to like the videos and subscribe.

- ✔ **Make content meaningful.** Your videos should answer a question, solve a problem, or make people laugh. You want your audience to look out for your videos and want to see more. Create content that is helpful, interesting, or intriguing in some way.

- ✔ **Create playlists.** To make it easy for your community to navigate your channel, group similar content in a YouTube video playlist. For more details, see "Creating a playlist," later in this chapter.

- ✔ **Buy an ad.** You have several ways to buy advertising on YouTube, including Promoted Videos that show up on the right side of a similar video, and inline ads where your short video "commercial" appears before someone else's similar video.

Optimizing your YouTube Channel

You want your audience to dig deep when it comes to spending time on your YouTube Channel. To entice them, you need to be branded, you need to be consistent, and you need to take advantage of all of the technical tools the platform puts at your disposal. You don't need us to tell you that your main page on your YouTube Channel is one of the first impressions you make on your audience.

Here are some ways to use YouTube's tools to optimize, or make the most of your channel and increase engagement:

- ✔ **Brand your channel.** You want people who visit your channel to know, without a doubt, they are visiting you or your business. When they click on your main page, everything they see, hear, and feel, reminds them of you, from the colors, to the verbiage to the pictures you choose to represent you.

 In early 2013, YouTube changed the look and feel of the main page, streamlining the change across all channels to ensure all pages would be equally visible and branded on all devices.

 The new One Channel option, shown in Figure 16-2, allows you to create a branded banner across the top of the page as well as a personalized trailer to welcome people who have yet to subscribe. Use these options to sell yourself. This is more than a typical bio; this is your chance to tell people why they should watch you as well as what to expect from your videos. You also have room to include links to all of your other social media engagement platforms.

- ✔ **Set expectations.** In addition to telling your audience when you will update, tell them what to expect from your content. If you plan to do classes on selecting seasonal produce, for example, list this information in the short bio form on your YouTube trailer. The first 45 characters of your description are visible whenever a new viewer discovers your channel, even on a mobile device, so make them compelling.

Figure 16-2:
Danielle's banner is branded, showing her name, her face, and how frequently she updates her channel.

✔ **Prioritize playlists.** Keeping your audience around as long as possible is a priority, so make your content as user-friendly as possible. Playlists let you group your videos together into categories such as recipes and business tips. We discuss playlists in "Creating a playlist," later in this chapter.

✔ **Feature other channels.** We could simply say use good karma to boost engagement, because featuring other YouTube Channels on your page lets your audience know who in the online video space is in your community, who you recommend, and who recommends you. In the new One Channel layout (see Figure 16-2), the Featured channels you select show up on the right side of your YouTube channel's page.

Anytime people subscribe to your channel, some of your featured channels are also recommended to them. The same is true in the reverse: Anyone who features you is recommending you to new subscribers.

✔ **Call your viewers to action.** Tell your viewers what you need from them by including a call to action. This is as simple as asking your viewers to like or share your video or to subscribe to your channel by mentioning it in your video or using annotations (see "Using annotations and thumbnails," later in this chapter). When viewers take any of these actions, these actions are broadcast to their viewers in your Channel Feed (see the next point), which is much like your Timeline format on Facebook. This, in turn, helps your audience to grow as *you* are then visible to a whole new set of eyeballs.

✔ **Keep an active Channel Feed.** Your Channel Feed is the pulse of your activity on YouTube. When you post, comment, or like a video, or subscribe to a channel, those actions show up in your activity feed. If you're extremely active on YouTube, consider adjusting your settings so you don't overwhelm your subscribers.

Creating a playlist

Playlists (see Figure 16-3) make it easier for your viewers to find the related content from you. Because videos play right after the other, your audience sees more of your videos in one sitting.

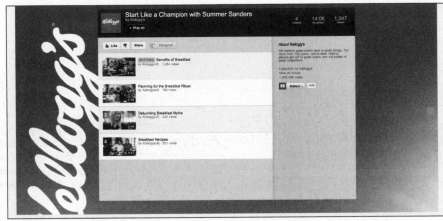

Figure 16-3: Kellogg's YouTube page has playlists highlighting Olympic athletes.

Creating playlists also makes your content more searchable because your videos can be discovered not only individually, but also as a collection. If you create a playlist called Salad Recipes, for example, the videos are optimized in search engines not only for each specific recipe video, but also as the entire playlist.

To create a playlist to increase views and engagement, follow these steps:

1. **Log in to your YouTube account.**

2. **Click Video Manager in the top-right corner.**

   All videos you have uploaded appear.

3. **Click Playlists on the left side of your screen under Video Manager.**

   Any previous playlists you have created appear.

4. **Click the New Playlist button on the right side of the screen.**

5. **In the Playlist Title and Description dialog box that appears, title your playlist and describe its content; then click Create Playlist.**

6. **In the Editing Playlist box that appears, click Add Video by URL.**

   A box to add the URL will appear mid-page.

7. **Copy the URL of the first video you want to include in your playlist.**

8. **Paste the URL of the video into the Video URL box and click Add.**

   You'll see a green bar that says 'Video successfully added!'.

9. **On the right side of the page, click Public and Allow Others to Embed this Playlist.**

10. **Click Save.**

    All the videos you selected are grouped in a playlist and will play automatically one right after the other when a viewer clicks on any within the grouped list.

Maximizing your subscriber base

There's tremendous value in building your subscriber base and in increasing your community. The more subscribers you have, the more people who see each video as you post it and have the opportunity to share your video content. Sitting idly by and hoping people will stumble upon your channel is not the answer.

Fortunately, we do know a few tricks to help you increase your exposure and get more people to click Subscribe.

Don't offer incentives to people to like your videos or subscribe to your channel. If you do, you'll be in violation of YouTube's terms of service and community guidelines. You are certainly safe to ask or encourage people to like your videos or subscribe, but you can't offer prizes or hold giveaways of any kind.

The three keys to building your subscriber numbers are consistency, strong content, and communication. Set a schedule and force yourself to stick to it. Your subscribers need to know what to expect from you. Posting weekly is optimal, but it's more important that your audience have faith in your consistency. Pepsi, for example, posts two to three times a week, depending on the time of year. This consistency, combined with quality content, made Pepsi one of the biggest brand channels of 2012, according to Digiday, a media company and digital media community.

Interacting with the YouTube community

You wouldn't be reading this book if you didn't place high importance on engaging with your community. Mastering that interaction with your YouTube audience requires a different set of tactics and practices from the other social networking platforms we discuss in this book:

✔ **When people comment on your videos, reply.** The three main reasons to reciprocate are

- You build relationships with members of your community.

- You show you value the feedback. If someone doesn't like your video, he'll often let you know. Anonymous feedback is not uncommon. Consider the tougher criticism an opportunity to look for ways to improve what you do. However, do try to let excessive negativity roll off your back. You can't take it too personally.

- The more frequently you comment, the more visible you are to your subscribers. Each time you reply to a comment, your video reappears in your subscribers' feeds and your Channel Feed or home page.

Consider responding to comments a few at a time so that your video reappears a few different times throughout the day on your subscribers' main feeds. Not everyone is online at the same time, so this tactic allows a greater number of people access to your content on a regular basis.

✔ **Be a commenter.** Don't simply wait for people to comment on your work. Take an active role in your community. Identify those creating valuable content. March your happy self out into the wide world of YouTube and start commenting on other individuals' and brands' videos and clicking Like or Thumbs Up. If they are seeing your name or brand for the first time, they will hopefully be intrigued enough to visit you, watch some of your videos, and subscribe.

✔ **Subscribe.** While you are out watching, liking, and commenting, determine which channels you would like to visit regularly and click Subscribe. Some of those channels may eventually be ones that you feature on your own channel.

✔ **Remove offensive comments.** You have no obligation to keep offensive comments visible on your YouTube Channel. Taking the time to remove every comment that you don't love is a waste of your time, but true spam, hatred, personal attacks, or anything else offensive can easily — and should — be taken down. As administrator of your channel, you have the tools to moderate comments.

Don't let spammers hijack your YouTube Channel. Allowing spam and hateful words to take up real estate can turn fans away and lead people to believe you don't care about your channel. Block commenters who are repeatedly offensive. You can also flag for spam or simply remove their comments (see Figure 16-4).

Figure 16-4:
Remove anything that includes hateful or offensive language by making a choice from this drop-down menu.

Standing Out on YouTube

Millions of people produce videos every day, and thousands of those videos are good. You watch them, smile, laugh, and cry; the video ends and you move on. Certainly not every video can be a viral video and, in fact, very few are. Setting out to create a viral video is a lesson in futility.

What you want for your video is the "Watch this!" factor, even if it isn't shared a million times. Any sharing at all is the chance to expose new people to your brand. Any one person who likes what she sees can potentially reach dozens, hundreds, or thousands of others simply because she shared your video. When this happens, you want to understand the qualities of that shared video so your next video and the one after that keeps people sharing.

Producing video content that keeps people watching

You've had those days when you just can't escape that video. You know the one. The one that everyone is sharing. That popular video of the moment is on Twitter; it's dominating your Facebook feed; it's the topic of conversation at the work cocktail party; and even your mother calls you to tell you about it.

In October 2012, nearly 8 million people watched the live YouTube stream of Felix Baumgartner jumping from a platform nearly 128,000 feet above Earth, becoming the first person to break the sound barrier outside a vehicle. That video holds the record for the most concurrent views ever on YouTube.

As Baumgartner crushed that barrier, so did sponsor Red Bull, which was in control of the event; its logo was visible every small step of the way. To date, the Red Bull Stratos playlist, with 23 videos, has 69 million views total, with just one of the videos in that list topping 32 million (see Figure 16-5).

Figure 16-5:
The Mission Accomplished video has been viewed more than 32 million times.

What made this YouTube campaign such a success? It built suspense, it was live action, and it involved branding.

Another extremely successful YouTube campaign was Old Spice's 2010 Old Spice Guy campaign, which began with a video of actor Isaiah Mustafa wrapped in a bath towel and came fully to life as he responded by video to tweets from social media personalities across the country. The video campaign was full of humor and quickly evolved into something extraordinary, garnering more than 236 million views on YouTube and more than 80,000 Twitter followers in just two days. Old Spice had both a viral video and an astronomical increase in sales.

Mastering metadata

Suppose that your first few videos don't go viral (and there's a 99.9 percent chance they won't). You need to work to bring your audience to your video and channel. Much like inviting people to your blog through search engine placement, or starting a conversation on Twitter, or posting something to Facebook, getting your video out there needs to start with you.

Because YouTube is the No. 2 search engine in the world, it makes sense to master the way people find you when they search online. This is where your title, tags, and description come in.

Your title, tags, and description, or *metadata,* are indexed in YouTube's algorithm based on content. Videos are found based on promotion, ads, search, and other related videos. If you aren't entering this information properly, you miss valuable opportunities to be found.

For help, use keyword-generating tools like Google AdWords to find popular, relevant search terms to drive traffic to your videos. You can access this free tool at `https://adwords.google.com/o/KeywordTool`.

Title

Titles are the first things viewers see, but they aren't only first impressions. Video titles are also key to placement within the ranks of search, so they must be good. Here are some tips for titles:

- ✔ **Grab viewers' attention.** Make the titles compelling and clickable.

- ✔ **Maximize search potential.** Choose keywords carefully and strategically.

- ✔ **Be honest.** Don't mislead your audience with false titles or phrases.

- ✔ **Put the topic first and the brand second.** Begin with the subject or keywords and then include the brand or show title (see Figure 16-6).

Figure 16-6:
The episode (topic) title is followed by the show title.

✔ **Follow up.** Dig into any older videos you've published, and update titles for relevancy to gain additional views.

Tags

Tags help you categorize your videos, grouping your videos into the relevant topics online. Depending on how well you tag, you can determine if you're linked to trending topics. Here are some guidelines for tagging your videos:

✔ **Include a mix of broad and specific tags.** Here's an example of a broad/specific mix: Politics, Presidential Debate Denver, Mitt Romney, Barack Obama, Election 2012.

✔ **Add consistency.** Have a standard set of tags for your channel that apply to every video you publish. For example: business advice, business tips, and social media and business.

✔ **Don't go overboard.** There is no must-have number of tags, but do reasonably cover all areas of your topic.

We've found that 15 tags is a good amount.

✔ **Include the title.** Make sure the title of your video is also in the tags.

✔ **Use quotation marks.** Put any phrases in quotes, such as "Mickey Mouse" and "Walt Disney World."

✔ **Prioritize.** List your tags based on importance, with the first ones being the most relevant.

Don't put tags where they don't belong. If you do, you could hurt your search ranking or risk the removal of your videos. The only place to include tags is in the Tags metadata section. Don't even think about putting them into the description or YouTube may penalize you.

Description

The first few sentences of your description matter most because they are the only ones fully visible when a viewer first clicks to your video. The description helps persuade a potential new viewer to watch. Here's what you should include in your description:

✔ **Keywords:** Include keywords from title and tags but not your actual tags.

✔ **Links:** Include clickable links to other sites and social networks.

✔ **Time codes:** If the video is long, consider including time codes, or particular moments in the video — 1:22 or 3:16 — that point to certain highlights in the video to entice people to keep watching.

Using annotations and thumbnails

Video annotations are text and picture overlays enhancing your videos to boost your subscribers, likes, viewership, and engagement. These lines of text that appear over your actual videos are exclusive to YouTube and prompt your viewers to like or click Thumbs Up for your content, keep them watching longer, and push them to other videos on your channel.

Best uses for annotations

Some of the most effective uses of annotations include

- Adding a Subscribe button
- Adding fresh content to old videos
- Encouraging a Thumbs Up or Like
- Asking a question to engage your community
- Linking to other videos or playlists on YouTube
- Highlighting certain moments or time codes in the video

When it comes to using annotations, use your best judgment. Don't spam your viewers with too many, or they will feel pressured to do too much. They should be able to enjoy the experience of watching your video without feeling bombarded.

Make sure any annotations you use are legible, and try to avoid using the lower third of the video because most advertisements are placed there, so any annotations would be obscured.

Types of annotations

As for the actual types of annotations, you have a few options:

- Customize your annotations based on size, shape, or color.
- Determine whether to include a link.
- Add a speech bubble to add a little creativity to the video.
- Use a spotlight to highlight an area, making it clickable. The text is visible only when the viewer moves the cursor over it.
- Play with the different types of annotations to determine what strategy works best for you.

TIP

Adopt an annotation strategy: Use the same annotations in each video whether it's a call to action for subscribers or likes, or a prompt for viewers to watch a previous favorite video. Repetition in marketing is critical, so repeating your annotations can help get them noticed and used.

Best uses for thumbnails

Another important element you should never ignore is the thumbnail for your video. The thumbnail shot of your video is a teaser for what your audience can expect of your video. Ideally, you want a shot that looks good both large and small. If you or someone else is in the video, you want a thumbnail in which you or she isn't caught with closed eyes and mouth wide open. Your thumbnail should reflect the story you're about to tell in the video. ConAgra Foods' Child Hunger Ends Here campaign released a video by country band Little Big Town. Viewers are instantly drawn to the video by the thumbnail of the band performing (see Figure 16-7).

Figure 16-7:
A perfor-
mance
thumbnail
draws
viewers in.

childhungerendshere uploaded a video 4 months ago

Little Big Town on performing "Here's Hope"
512 views

1:16

WARNING!

Don't upload a false image to entice viewers to watch. Showcasing something that doesn't actually exist in your video leaves you with many, many disappointed viewers who may leave negative comments.

Extending Your Reach with Video

Make your video work for you in more than one way. While the YouTube community is strong and spending time nurturing those relationships can be extremely important, you want the value of your video to live well beyond the walls of this platform. The more people viewing the video you create, the more your video engagement continues to grow. We're talking about extending your power of your video to a larger audience. And while you're out building your community in person, why not learn to do a little video on the go?

Embedding and integrating your videos

When your videos are posted to YouTube, your work isn't done. Taking the additional time to embed those videos on other platforms can increase your reach exponentially. A good example is the Make it Count Nike video, shown embedded on Facebook in Figure 16-8. By taking the video from its home on YouTube and placing it in front of its Facebook audience, Nike started an entirely new conversation — generating hundreds of comments and thousands of likes. By embedding the video in a new location, more fans saw the video and had a chance to talk about it.

Figure 16-8: Nike's ad campaign was liked more than 19,000 times and received nearly 700 comments on Facebook.

YouTube makes it easy for you to embed your videos on virtually any platform — you can put them on your blog or Facebook, or share them on Twitter. You can even set up a board on Pinterest specifically to showcase your YouTube videos and pin videos straight from your channel.

To embed your videos, copy the URL from a specific YouTube video and paste it onto your Facebook Fan Page, into a tweet, or onto your blog post or web page. Grab the embed code by doing the following:

1. **Go to your YouTube Video.**

2. **Beneath the video, click the Share button.**

   You will see a box that says Share This Video with a URL.

3. **To the right of Share This Video, click Embed.**

   A box with highlighted code appears.

4. **Copy the HTML code into the box.**

5. **Paste the code into the HTML text portion of your blog post (or tweet or Facebook status).**

Take the time to share your videos beyond YouTube for greater exposure so not only your current audience and community sees it, but also other people who may be seeing you for the very first time. These people are potential new subscribers and prospective customers.

Taking advantage of video responses

A creative way to join a conversation on YouTube and to increase the chance of people seeing your videos is to use the video response feature. Instead of posting a traditional comment, respond to a video with your own video. When you do this, you put yourself in front of a whole new community and gain more exposure for your video channel and your brand.

For example, say there is a hot debate about homeschooling, and you have an opinion. Plenty of videos pop up online on the topic. You want to add your voice to the conversation, so you do the following:

1. **Create your video response to a hot topic.**

2. **Upload it to YouTube, including title, tags, and description.**

3. **Find a video you would like to respond to with that video response.**

4. **Click the Comment box as though you are going to type a comment.**

5. **Below the Comment box, click Create a Video Response.**

   All the videos you have ever created will appear within a box that says, 'Select the video you want to respond with'.

6. **Choose the video you want to use and then click Use the Selected Video.**

You may occasionally see an approval notice that tells you your video will be posted after it has been approved by the Channel owner of the original video that inspired your response. Other YouTube users approve video responses automatically.

You can create video responses for your own content — this increases the chances you show up as a suggested video on the right-hand side of the screen for your own videos, thereby prompting viewers to check out more of your content.

Uploading video on the go

Maybe you want to take this whole YouTube business slowly or you're not quite certain you want to invest in a brand new digital video camera. The good news is that you probably have a suitable video camera on your mobile phone! Chances are it's all you need to get started. Both the iPhone and Android phones make it a snap to go from point, shoot, record, upload to publish in a matter of minutes. So, you can't use the lack-of-camera excuse to hold you back from leveraging video to engage online.

On both platforms, you can follow the sharing options after you record a video. Both iPhone and Android will allow you to enter a title, tags, and a description; opt to make the video public or private; and publish directly to YouTube.

At this time, both Windows and BlackBerry phones do not have a way to automatically upload to YouTube.

Analyzing your impact

YouTube makes it easy for you to monitor your influence online. Stats in the back end of your YouTube Channel track everything from overall performance to how many actual views your videos have received to how many minutes people spent watching your videos over the course of a month.

You can break down your analytics to the top ten most watched videos and find out at what point people stop watching certain videos — important information to know. You can also learn where your audience is in the world, if they came to you from another YouTube video or from an external site, and if they are male or female. You can even see what percentage of your audience is watching from a computer versus a mobile device. See Figure 16-9 for an example of YouTube statistics.

Paying attention to each of these statistics and adjusting accordingly can help you reach more subscribers and keep them around longer — and we all know that's the goal.

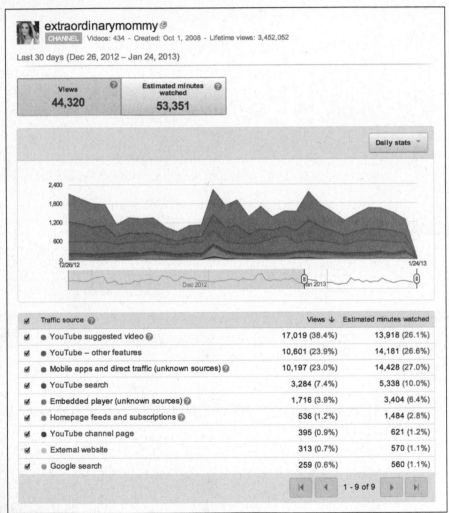

Figure 16-9: Danielle can see what percentage of her traffic is coming from within YouTube, from Google, and from elsewhere.

Part VI
The Part of Tens

Go to www.dummies.com/extras/socialmediaengagement to read about ten niche networks for social media engagement.

In this part . . .

- Find out how niche social networks help you zero in on specific audiences.

- Save time, money, and headaches by avoiding common pitfalls.

- Get the scoop from businesses that are experiencing tangible benefits from social media engagement.

Chapter 17

Ten Social Media Engagement Mistakes to Avoid

In This Chapter

▶ Skipping the planning step

▶ Leaving a robotic impression

▶ Focusing on yourself rather than on your community

▶ Posting erratically

▶ Failing to let your personality shine

▶ Neglecting to listen to your community

▶ Underestimating the effort involved

▶ Annoying your community with unwanted content

▶ Disregarding original material

▶ Making the same mistakes again and again

*W*hat fun would it be if we failed to list the pitfalls you must avoid when wading into the wide and wonderful world of social media engagement? There are many ways to plan how to do things well, yet just as many small (and big) ways to make a misstep. Plan ways to avoid making these ten mistakes as you plan your best strategy for engagement, and you'll be well on your way to success.

Flying by the Seat of Your Pants

Sure, you've been engaging your entire life, but social media engagement is a whole new animal, and it requires a plan. Running out to sign up for Twitter, Facebook, or Google+ with no thought to how you will dedicate time to connect with your community or respond to them after they realize that you're online would be disastrous. You must determine not only who will be in charge of your social media engagement but also which platforms are appropriate for your brand or business.

Take the time to put an action plan in place so that you're prepared to engage with your audience and ready to respond when they reach out to you — because they will, and they want to know that you're listening.

Operating without a plan can lead you down a path of missteps — one that can be detrimental to your business and brand reputation.

Using Too Much Automation

We understand that you may want to automate some content because you can't sit in front of your computer 24 hours a day, and it's certainly impossible to be on all your platforms at any given time. Do too much automating, however, and your community will peg you as a robot. If they respond to your automated content and you never reply, they eventually give up.

Take the time to balance the pins, videos, Facebook and Twitter posts you share, and schedule specific slots during the day when you follow up on the chosen platforms to ensure that you're engaging with your audience. The time you take to have a conversation, to respond, and to let your community know that you're listening makes all the difference in making real connections with real people.

Broadcasting or Sharing Only Your Content

We know you've had the experience of meeting someone new who can't help but talk on and on about himself. This behavior seems harmless at first . . . and then slightly annoying . . . and then intolerable. In terms of social media engagement, your audience is initially curious about you, but after being incessantly bombarded with your products and posts about how wonderful you are, they're first bored and irritated, and then they become turned off by your self-centered attitude. They'll deliberately make the extra effort to unfollow you while simultaneously signaling their action to all their friends.

Choose the alternative: Make your engagement a two-way street. Talk, share valuable content from other people, praise others, have conversations, and reply to comments and questions.

Your community is made up of people who care about how you treat them — not just what you offer as products or services.

Being Inconsistent

Suppose that you post five times on Monday and then post nothing again until Thursday. You post a video on Tuesday, update Google+ and Facebook on Friday, spend two hours on Pinterest on Sunday, and then disappear for a week, leaving questions unanswered and replies swinging in the social media wind. Your community of customers and prospects doesn't know what to think of your erratic behavior. Do you want to engage or not? Inconsistency will grow old quickly, and your audience will disappear as they realize that they can't rely on you to be present regularly. You'll come across as though you're not listening — and nobody likes to be ignored.

Instead, set a schedule. Choose the platforms that generate the most value for you and your brand, and then make a commitment to them. Make the time to engage. Consistency has its rewards, including stronger connections with others.

Lacking Personality

Human beings connect to other human beings. If people see you as simply a logo on a computer screen, it's difficult for them to connect with you. Social media must be social. You're naturally drawn to the people and relationships that make you laugh, that make you think, that bring out the best in you — as are your customers and prospects in social networks. Be personable. Be kind. Everything you say online reflects on you and your brand. Put someone at the helm of your brand engagement who is willing to push the envelope and able to come across as genuine, friendly, and approachable.

Keep in mind that you, as a brand or business, should determine ahead of time what brand personality will be reflected online: wise, witty, sharp, intelligent, humorous, earnest, or informative. After you make that decision, go for it!

Ignoring Feedback

Your community uses your social media platforms as a way to tell you that they love you — but also that they're disappointed in you. A simple thank-you for a compliment can go a long way. Acknowledging positive comments says to someone that you're listening, and being heard resonates with a person.

Alternatively, ignoring a customer's negative feedback can be detrimental to your brand. Know that your community watches to see how you handle both the good and the bad. Burying or dismissing the bad makes you appear as though you have something to hide. Handle online negativity with care and concern. Deal out in the open (for the most part) with complaints that are made publicly. Others will see your good customer service in action, potentially earning you a new, reinforced fan base and often turning a disgruntled customer into a happy and loyal one.

Give your community the opportunity to see you as a responsive brand with caring individuals behind the logo. You will be amazed at how closely your customer service interactions in social media are followed and even shared with others.

Assuming That Social Media Is Easy

Social media engagement, friends, is hard work. Creating a social media engagement strategy for your business or brand, putting it into action, monitoring it, engaging with your community, tweaking the plan, and ensuring that you're present takes time and effort, and a lot of it. To assume that you can invest just a little bit of time — that you can "dial it in" in less than an hour or two a week — will be the death of your efforts. Social media engagement, as a way to build your business, isn't a cakewalk. It's an ongoing learning process that is ever-changing. Every day, you schedule, implement your plan, and modify the plan based on your successes — and then you have (you hope) the benefit of seeing your hard work pay off. But you definitely don't have the luxury of sitting back and *watching* it happen for you.

Spamming

Spamming others is easily one of the worst errors you can make. Sending out link after link, e-mail after e-mail, or pin after pin of the same content or of commercials gets you nowhere. No one wants to be spammed by an endless stream of your sales pitches, or by your links or lists of why your audience simply *must* be following your every move. Always have your community's permission to send them your information, and remember how easily they can opt out of receiving it.

Whether you spam e-mail inboxes with unrequested content or cram your social network feeds with one-sided announcements, nothing turns off a potential fan or customer more quickly than spam. Just don't do it.

Posting the Same Content Everywhere

You can easily copy and paste your content from Twitter to Google+ to LinkedIn or cross-post the same content to all your social networks at one time by using a messaging tool. Your audiences on each platform deserve more than that, however. Fans who follow you on more than one network may quickly spot the repeats, making you appear lazy and unoriginal. Though the occasional cross-posting doesn't signal the end of the world, take the time to tailor your content for each network: What engages well on Facebook may need to be tweaked for Twitter. Being specific to each network requires more work and more effort, but the difference in the level of engagement is noticeable.

Repeating Mistakes

Pay attention to what is happening when you're engaging with your community online. You'll do some things well, such as post content that resonates with your audience, tweets that are retweeted, videos that are shared, and Instagram pictures that make your community giddy. And some of your messages will backfire, Facebook updates will fall flat, or employees will convey the wrong messages in your stream. Take note of what works, and do more of it. Note what didn't work, and avoid repeating those same errors. Have a plan for recovering from errors, notice when they happen, respond immediately and take responsibility, and then learn from your mistakes.

Chapter 18

Ten Businesses That Excel at Social Media Engagement

In This Chapter

▶ Understanding your audience's needs

▶ Honing your social networking skills

▶ Adopting the right attitude online

▶ Leveraging content to attract attention

*W*e evaluated several companies after speaking with a wide array of people and industry leaders who have tackled different platforms for social media engagement. Each company featured in this chapter has identified the channels where they have the most success and where they regularly engage with their communities for the best results.

These businesses all have a few characteristics in common: They create plans that work for their brands, they diligently monitor their activities, they adjust whenever necessary (based on the results they see), and they *engage*.

Wine Sisterhood

www.winesisterhood.com, www.facebook.com/winesisterhood

Women can join the conversation at the online community Wine Sisterhood (based in Napa, California) to discuss wine, food, travel, style, and entertaining. The group's mission is to entertain, educate, inform, and inspire women, and they do so on Facebook, Twitter, Pinterest, Instagram, Tumblr, Foursquare, and (more recently) Google+.

Tips

✔ **Know your audience, and know what inspires them to respond.** Wine Sisterhood realizes that humor goes a long way with their female audience and that quirky products or wine crafts are true crowd-pleasers.

✔ **Become more visual.** Wine Sisterhood emphasizes visual elements (rather than plain-text quotes or links) on its page.

✔ **Distribute duties to better manage the load.** Two team members, in two time zones, monitor comments and Facebook messages on the Sisterhood's Facebook Page several times a day, and they make a point to respond *within 24 to 48 hours* to all inquiries and requests.

Avoid this pitfall: Ignoring what your fans want. Whenever the Wine Sisterhood deviated from light-hearted and quick-witted Facebook posts and presented a more serious tone, their interactions dipped, with only a few exceptions, such as posts about major events (Hurricane Sandy, for example). Knowing its audience and delivering more of what they want maintains a high level of interaction and actions on Facebook.

Gauge positive results: Without a doubt, Facebook has delivered the greatest amount of traffic to its website and driven a good portion of its online wine-club registrations and online and offline wine sales. As of this writing, the company was gearing up to incorporate an online shop of wine-related and lifestyle products directly into its Facebook Page in addition to a social media-powered e-commerce site.

Mabel's Labels

www.mabelslabels.com, www.facebook.com/Mabelhood

Created by four Canadian moms with an eye for beauty and a mind for business, Mabel's Labels produces durable "labels for the stuff kids lose." In its tenth year, the company has grown from working in one person's basement to a 14,000-square-foot commercial space with 40 employees. Though the company started on Twitter, its Facebook community is 60,000 strong and growing. And now Pinterest has become a priority as well. For the brand, choosing one person to maintain its social media was crucial — it now presents a unified voice across all platforms as it continues to grow — recently making the move into Target stores.

Tips

✔ **Avoid using social media as a sales tool.** Be involved in conversations. Don't push your products — that's boring. If you engage with your community, they'll buy your products.

✔ **Use social media engagement as a customer service tool.** Though many brands delete negative feedback, use it instead as an opportunity to solve the problem publicly and gain a new fan base. Use the critique to show your customers that you don't hide behind mistakes — you're willing to fix them.

✔ **Don't waste time "toe-dipping."** People are talking about your brand and products. Either you're part of the conversation or you aren't. If you're nervous, begin by joining the conversation and then move to a second when you're comfortable.

Avoid this pitfall: Not being mindful of saying or doing something that would damage your brand. Julie Cole, cofounder of Mabel's Labels, puts it eloquently: "Social media is the voice of your brand. Every time you engage, you're either contributing to your brand or contaminating it."

Gauge positive results: Mabel's Labels keeps an eye on its links, Facebook likes, comments, shares, and overall statistics, but its true return on investment (ROI) comes in the form of in-person relationships. Cole registers hugs at conferences and events as indications that its social media engagement efforts are truly successful.

Girls Crochet Headbands

www.girlscrochetheadbands.com, www.facebook.com/girls crochetheadbands

The online boutique Girls Crochet Headbands (GCH) is filled with girls' fashion accessories, including bloomers, tutus, and headbands. Since 2008, it has served more than 2 million customers, a number that continues to grow because of the company's presence on Facebook (its preferred social media space). In mid-2012, GCH hired Shelly Kramer and her company, V3 Integrated Marketing to help it rebrand and create its new digital strategy, putting in place a social media team that also understands the brand — and engages daily with the GCH community. In the first seven months, the GCH Facebook community more than *doubled,* by using not only product promotions, coupons, and contests but also true conversation. Many posts are liked hundreds of times (and shared by the dozen).

Tips

✔ **Don't assume that you can follow only one formula.** Don't follow a posting "regiment," such as four tweets a day, three personal posts and one promotional post on Facebook. Treat your brand page much like you treat your personal page — engage honestly and authentically, and post a variety of content.

✔ **Build a community team that understands social media *and* your brand.** GCH's social team is not only comprised of people who get social media, but they are interested in the brand itself. Many are moms (as are the clientele), so the voice used to connect with the audience is genuine.

✔ **Post on weekends.** Social media isn't a 9-to-5 job. By ignoring the weekend, you miss an important opportunity to engage with potential fans and followers.

Avoid this pitfall: Getting started with social media engagement before you know what success looks like to you and your brand. You first have to ask *why* you even want to engage on social media. For Girls Crochet Headbands, customer service is a fundamental aspect of engagement — at least 50 percent of customers' questions are directed to its Facebook page — so one driving motivation to exist in that space is to engage with its customers and answer questions.

Gauge positive results: Though Pinterest and Twitter definitely attract attention from the social media team at Girls Crochet Headbands, if the group's efforts were split into a pie, Facebook would grab the largest slice. The team focuses its attention not only on the platform where its customers spend the bulk of their time but also on the one that generates the highest level of traffic and percentage of sales. For GCH, the winner in that department is Facebook.

Ramon DeLeon, Marketing Mind behind 6-Store Domino's Pizza Franchise, Chicago

www.twitter.com/Ramon_DeLeon

Ramon DeLeon, has always worked passionately to prioritize the use of common sense in business and to strive to *wow* his customers. His unique characteristic is that he knows *exactly* what his customers need to hear at any given moment. Ramon engages with them daily (some would say hourly) on Facebook, but mostly on Twitter, even creating videos when necessary. He and a store manager once responded this way to a tweet from a customer who was disappointed in an order: They first refunded her money and replaced the order, and then they apologized — in a video that has since been viewed thousands of times. Ramon, known for using (appropriately) the hashtag #ramonwow on Twitter, offers advice in the form of the acronym he lives by: RAT — Be Real, Be Accessible, Be Transparent.

Tips

✔ **Be real:** When you engage with your community, you need to focus on being *you* at all times — that's who your audience wants to get to know.

✔ **Be accessible:** You must have the proper tools (smartphones and apps, for example) to ensure that you're available and listening whenever your audience reaches out.

✔ **Be transparent:** Recognize that whatever you say can be used against you. Anything that you add to the social media space is open for scrutiny.

Avoid this pitfall: Wasting time without acting. The social media space is a busy one, and you can easily busy yourself with trivial tasks. Ramon explains: "Things are happening — don't wait. Don't let your job get in the way of your career. Done beats perfect. Trust yourself, and trust your instincts."

Gauge positive results: Ramon measures the success of his social media engagement by the number and quality of responses he receives from customers online and by the measurable moments of success in his stores. In early 2013, he received an award for leading sales in the Midwest region, and four of his six stores were in the top ten in the Chicago Area.

Cabot Creamery Cooperative

`http://cabotcheese.coop`, `http://pinterest.com/cabotcheese`

Based in Montpelier, Vermont, Cabot Creamery is owned by more than 1,200 dairy farm families, located in rural communities throughout New England and upstate New York. The farmers own and operate four facilities to produce award-winning, all-natural cheeses and dairy products, including the "world's best Cheddar." Cabot engaged on Pinterest early on, then suddenly website traffic coming from Pinterest spiked as the new social network grew in popularity. Pinterest proved to be a perfect partner for showcasing the lives of the Cabot farm families and the allure of the rural Northeast (especially Vermont) — and for featuring delicious recipes created using Cabot products. The Cabot cooperative honors community, and cooperation anchors its social strategy on behalf of the farmer-owners.

Tips

✔ **Appreciate.** Appreciate your fans honestly, by pinning, sharing, and commenting on their content.

✔ **Connect.** Nurture and build authentic, ongoing relationships with your followers. (Cabot's consumers are active in social media.)

✔ **Connect even more.** Use Pinterest as a vivid platform to deepen connections with consumers and content creators from other platforms by pinning content from their sites.

Avoid this pitfall: Trying to follow all your fans, all the time. Cabot has always followed all its fans in return for following the company. Team members realized early on, however, that they could follow specific (and pertinent) Pinterest boards in order to review and savor fans' recipes and content — and then share only the most complementary content.

Gauge positive results: Pinterest is the perfect platform to showcase the farm families who own Cabot, their cows, and (of course) their mouth-watering food. Pictures truly tell the full story, and quickly. The Pinterest community, which has grown continually and steadily, has become a helpful source of traffic to and from the Cabot recipes. Pinterest also affords a two-way path to bloggers and other content creators who enhance the farmers' products and purpose.

Nylabone

www.nylabone.com, www.facebook.com/Nylabone, https://plus. google.com/+nylabone

Putting their company on the cutting edge of social media is a priority for the folks at Nylabone, which has been entrenched in social media since early 2009. They began with Facebook and have now even adopted the brand-new platform Vine. The social media team strives to cover all its bases by developing a presence on any social media site where customers are spending time. Though Facebook is where they see their greatest level of engagement, they believe it is important to embrace new social media platforms that have less "noise" and where it's more cost effective to develop a community. For example, though Google + is one of the newer platforms, Nylabone has established a strong presence there, noting the opportunity to reach their customers and take advantage of the special features: Hangouts, Circles, and Adwords.

Tips

- **Observe results, and respond accordingly:** Ideas that you believe will be hugely successful sometimes aren't, and less appealing ideas can turn into gold. Be adaptable, and be fearless in applying new content ideas.

- **Add value:** Ask "What value does my content provide to a consumer following our brand?" For example, it may be entertainment, education, current events, coupons, or giveaways. Give people a reason to follow it by offering interesting and valuable content! (Don't post only about your own products or services.)

✔ **Follow our 70-20-10 rule for dedicating time on social media:** Spend 70 percent on entertaining your community with interesting and compelling content (as just described); 20 percent on asking consumers to share their photos or stories and thanking them for engaging with your brand (always respond to their questions!); and 10 percent on marketing your products and services. A *small amount* of obvious promotion is fun and inviting as long as it aligns with the theme of your content.

Avoid this pitfall: Inadvertently upsetting your online community. Do lots of industry research and figure out what the controversial topics are and try to avoid posting about those issues. Develop a Crisis Strategy for your brand so you know exactly how to deal with an issue (should any arise) in a timely manner. Addressing a negative post or situation can create a new positive relationship with your online community.

Gauge positive results: Nylabone measures SME in a variety of ways. They track online leads via brand community growth on Facebook, Twitter, other social media sites, and its e-mail marketing lists. Additionally, they measure success based on brand impressions, customer engagement, website referrals and conversions, and online coupons/offer redemption. Beyond that, they hope to gain a better understanding of their target market, gauge customers' product needs, connect with brand advocates, and generate a positive brand image.

MomBiz

http://mombiz.com, http://mombizcoach.com, www.blogtalkradio.com/mombizcoach

The coaching and training company known as MomBiz serves the global community of moms who are business owners. As the MomBiz Coach, Lara Galloway helps mom-entrepreneurs figure out how to survive motherhood, and even thrive in it, by creating and running businesses they love. For more than four years, the *MomBiz Solutions Show* podcast has provided information about successfully running a business that suits women's strengths, skills, and priorities. MomBiz uses Twitter, Facebook, YouTube, LinkedIn, Pinterest, and podcasting.

Tips

✔ **Market and promote your podcast.** To encourage your audience to look forward to hearing about a topic, let them know in advance that you plan to discuss it. Galloway uses e-mail newsletters, Twitter, and Facebook and Facebook groups to alert people to upcoming topics.

- ✔ **Ask your readers, listeners, and followers what they want to know about a topic.** For example, if Lara talks about the difference between blogging for fun and blogging for business, she asks clients about the topic and incorporates their answers into a podcast.

- ✔ **Archive and leverage your podcast.** When your podcast is complete, archive it and post it to your blog, your Facebook Page, and your other social networks and highlight some of the material you covered. Ask more questions to generate discussion so that people will listen to your podcast and give feedback.

Avoid this pitfall: Recording a podcast in a robotic voice, devoid of nuance. Rather than read a perfectly crafted script, let your audience hear you speak in a conversational style and even occasionally stumble over a word or phrase or make a mistake.

Gauge positive results: About 80 percent of Galloway's clients find her by way of her social media channels, especially Twitter and Facebook and her podcast on BlogTalkRadio. (Most clients have listened to every archived show from the past four years.) The podcast helps Galloway attract highly qualified — and even ideal — clients.

Blendtec

www.Blendtec.com, www.willitblend.com, www.youtube.com/blendtec

The Blendtec blender is the brainchild of Tom Dickson, a curious and inventive man who tirelessly demonstrates his product (while always working to improve it). This flair for show-and-tell is a natural fit for his company's foray into social media: YouTube. (It also engages heavily on Facebook, Twitter, and Pinterest.) The Will It Blend series — which showcases the marvel of his blender devouring products from crowbars to iPads and from glow sticks to golf balls — has garnered more than 80 million views (counting only the top ten blends!). A series of Blendtec recipes on YouTube has branched into other platforms featuring an entire social media team. On Pinterest, its recipes drive people to the company's website, and its Twitter feed offers product-support articles and recipe tips and tricks. The team's philosophy is to provide fans and customers with what they want, when they want it, and how they want it.

Tips

- ✔ **Provide the content that your audience wants — and can use.** By showing your community how your product works — and how well — you encourage them not only to buy, but to come back to your channels for inspiration. Think recipes and new products.

✔ **Provide excellent customer service.** In the age of social media, people often forego phone calls to ask questions on Facebook or Twitter.

✔ **Strategize your engagement based on the platform you're using.** For example, because Facebook posts reportedly have a longer life span than tweets do, try to post there twice a day; on Twitter, tweet between four and ten times a day.

Avoid this pitfall: Not finding out what your community wants from you. Blendtec gives customers more of what they want by listening to their feedback. They go the extra mile by allowing their fans on social media to evaluate new ideas. Blendtec then gains a sense of what its community believes will be awesome content.

Gauge positive results: The Blendtec team looks at the goals they have for the specific platforms. They know that its fans on Facebook are more likely to click a link and purchase a product from the site than its Twitter followers, so its Facebook strategy includes support and additional links; on Twitter, on the other hand, it focuses on providing information and support for customers and potential customers, including supplying links to its blog. For Blendtec, success means providing customers and potential customers with the content they want.

Chobani

http://chobani.com, http://instagram.com/chobani

Though Chobani, an American brand that makes Greek-style yogurt from natural ingredients, is active on Facebook, Twitter, Pinterest, YouTube, Vine, Tumblr, Foursquare, Yelp, and LinkedIn, the company uses Instagram to capture snapshots of followers using its products, for sharing sneak peeks into new products, and for looking behind the scenes at Chobani. They like to show that the company focuses on more than yogurt.

Tips

✔ **Monitor hashtags.** Chobani monitors several hashtags, including #chobani, #nothingbutgood, #greekyogurt, and #tastereal to ensure that it stays on top of relevant conversation.

✔ **Engage, engage, engage.** To show fans that the company is listening, Chobani engages with every post as it relates to the brand by liking or commenting on fan photos that mention @chobani or that use a relevant hashtag. Fans feel special when the company likes the images they post.

✔ **Plan content for engagement.** Chobani invests a significant amount of time and thought in its online content. The digital team makes unique Chobani creations and parfaits at its regular "creation hour" so that fans can see unique ways to spice up their Chobani yogurt. The company often reposts great-looking fan images and holds regular, Chobani-branded gear giveaways to give back to the community and increase engagement.

Avoid this pitfall: Being disingenuous in social networks. The best lesson Chobani learned on Instagram (and it applies to all social media platforms) is to be personable and genuine and show fans that you're human. Engage in conversations that are the most relevant to you and your brand so they match your brand's image and personality.

Gauge positive results: Chobani's best successes happen when it engages with unhappy customers. Its immediate, intimate responses keep fans coming back for more — and quickly clear up concerns or misconceptions while possibly building fans for life.

AJ Bombers

http://ajbombers.com, http://foursquare.com/ajbombers

AJ Bombers, a family-style burger restaurant with locations in Milwaukee and Madison, Wisconsin, uses many of the major social networks (primarily, Twitter, Facebook, Foursquare, Instagram, YouTube, and Tumblr) to engage with its guests — connecting with them even while they're dining at the restaurant and promoting to them when they're nearby.

Tips

- **Speak your customers' language.** Know your audience.

- **Focus on the community.** Keep the community of your customers in mind when building your customer base. AJ Bombers thinks of itself as "one of the crowd," and invites customers to be part of their crowd.

- **Highlight the actions of your biggest fans.** Cultivate engagement from your most enthusiastic customers, and recognize them publicly.

Avoid this pitfall: Assuming that everyone knows about a particular social network. In its first large-scale Foursquare promotion, four staff members were placed in a "Foursquare training area," where any customer who wanted to load the app to a mobile device could do so and learn the basics of how to check in. This effort was the key to the enthusiastic participation of many other guests.

Gauge positive results: AJ Bombers creates events incorporating Foursquare badges and then entices customers to its restaurant to gain access to the badges on their own Foursquare accounts. One Sunday event was centered around the Foursquare Swarm badge. Promoting the event in its social networks and restaurant location drew 161 people to check in and earn the badge. And, sales for the day increased by 110 percent.

Index

• A •

abbreviations
  CPA (Cost Per Action), 35
  CPC (Cost Per Click), 35
  CPM (Cost Per Thousand), 35
action in online communities, 19
action metrics, considering, 37
actions
  asking for, 115–116
  versus interaction, 121
  offering rewards for, 116–117
  taking via e-mail, 45
alerts, setting, 88–90
AllFacebook blog, 157
analytics tools, 83–84, 111
Angie's List website, 80
Apple's Passbook platform, 293
attraction metrics, considering, 37
audience. *See also* customers; people
  analytics tools, 111
  demographics, 109
  finding online, 109–112
  identifying, 109–112
  knowing, 78
  knowing market, 147–148
  listening to, 111
  online conversations, 110
  online presence, 109
  psychographics, 109
  reaching out to, 147–148
  researching activities of, 110–112
  satisfying needs of, 76–78
  search engines, 110
  social media channels, 110
  targeting, 148
audio
  adding to social networks, 309–310
  Audioboo app, 308
  Chirbit app, 308
  marketing benefits, 304
  publishing from mobile devices, 308

audiocasting, 60
authenticity, 68–69
AWeber e-mail marketing tool, 141

• B •

backlash, dealing with, 27–28, 31–32
Banjo app, using with LBS, 286
barriers to entry, overcoming, 27–29
Beckham, David, 125
benchmarks, 38
BigTent website, 152–153
bitly URL shortener, 40, 83, 194, 259.
Blendtec, 350–351
Blogcast FM, 309
blogs
  answering polls, 49
  e-mailing site owners, 49
  engaging through, 48–50
  enhancing for engagement, 154–156
  feedback forms, 49
  sharing with friends, 49
  signing up for offers, 49
  The Skool of Life blog, 309
branding documents, 34
brands, 17
  attracting people, 13–14
  clarity of voice, 19
  emphasizing, 125
  engaging people, 13–14
  finding voice of, 70
  humanizing in marketplace, 12–14
  tracking mentioning of, 37
  trusting, 71
Buddy Media vs. bit.ly, 40
Buffer tool, 83
  scheduling tweets with, 200
  using with LinkedIn, 261
  website, 194
business pages, promoting on
    Facebook, 164–165
ByteLights, using with LBS, 285

• C •

Cabot Creamery Cooperative, 347–348
calendar, 97–100
Campaign Monitor e-mail marketing
    tool, 141
Campaigner e-mail marketing tool, 141
capacity, 86
case studies
    AJ Bombers burger restaurant, 352
    Blendtec, 350–351
    Cabot Creamery Cooperative, 347–348
    Chobani Greek-style yogurt, 351–352
    Domino's Pizza franchise, 346–347
    Girls Crochet Headbands, 345–346
    Mabel's Labels, 344–345
    MomBiz, 349–350
    Nylabone, 348–349
    Wine Sisterhood, 343–344
causes, supporting, 135–136
Cedar Creek Center cinnamon rolls, 188
Chipotle content, 73–74
Chirbit app, 308
Chobani Greek-style yogurt, 351–352
Cisco WebEx tool, 312
Citysearch website, 81
clicks from newsletters, 144–145
clients. See customers
commenting
    Disqus add-on, 155–156
    expanding with apps, 155–156
    Livefyre add-on, 155–156
comments, responding to, 91–92
communications, importance of, 27. See
    also conversations
communities. See also online communities
    creating comfort in, 123
    cultivating, 15, 113–114
    human element, 123
    humility, 123
    kindness is king, 124
    listening in, 123
    listening to, 74
    protecting information in, 34
    silence is golden, 124
    tenets of behavior, 20
competition, 87–88

complaints, responding to, 76. See also
    negative feedback
connecting with people, 19
connections. See also engagement
    attracting, 108
    basis of, 111
    boosting, 115
    building, 108
    creating, 23
    strengthening, 108
Constant Contact tool, 45, 141
consumer needs, keeping up with, 10–12
Contactology e-mail marketing tool, 141
content
    quality of, 122, 124
    retweeting messages, 115
    sharing, 15, 115
    tailoring to audience, 77
contests
    guidelines, 134
    laws, 134
    prizes, 134
    Rafflecopter giveaways, 163
    rules, 134–135
    running on Facebook, 163
    spreading the word, 134
    third-party solutions, 163
    Wildfire promotions, 163
conversations. See also communications
    about one's brand, 76
    asking questions, 72
    avoiding insults, 128
    building social media presence, 71–72
    contributing to, 70–73
    creating incentives, 73
    differences of opinion, 128
    entering effectively, 149–151
    filtering, 30
    Google Alerts, 75
    hot-button issues, 126–128
    humor, 128–130
    investigating topics, 71
    meaningful, 73
    refusing to argue, 128
    responding to, 76
    sharing quality content, 73
    starting, 23–24, 125
    starting via e-mail, 45

stimulating, 124
trending topics, 126
wording statements, 127
Costolo, Dick, 208
CoverGirl brand identity, 70–71
CPA (Cost Per Action), 35
CPC (Cost Per Click), 35
CPM (Cost Per Thousand), 35
credibility
assessing, 81–84
building, 22
cross-posting, 171
customer feedback, receiving, 16
customer needs, knowing, 11–12
customer service inquiries benchmark, 38
customers. *See also* audience; people
appreciating, 41
determining use of Internet, 10–11
getting reviews from, 81
hearing praise from, 11
as individuals, 18
offering communications choices, 12
providing forums for, 12
qualities sought by, 18
respecting, 18
responding to, 12, 18, 76
rewarding, 18
strengthening connections with, 14–15

• *D* •

dashboard tools, 30
dialogue. *See* conversations
discounts
offering, 41
offering for action, 133
Disqus commenting add-on, 155–156
dlvr.it tool, 83
documents, branding, 34
Domino's Pizza franchise, 346–347

• *E* •

earned media, 70
eBay Stores website, 158
EdgeRank, 166–167
editorial calendar, 97–100

e-mail
actions, 45
as communications tool, 45
as conversation starter, 45
encouraging users to opt into, 45
importance of, 44
marketing tools, 45
sign-up form, 45
e-mail accounts, statistic about, 44
e-mail marketing
benchmark, 38
increasing reach, 143
increasing visibility, 143
offering extra value, 144
subscribers to fans, 142–143
tools, 140–141
e-mail newsletters, 142–145
Emma e-mail marketing tool, 140
employees
approved content, 20
being role model to, 21
chain of command, 20–21
frequency of participation, 20
hiring, 30
policing process, 21
response style, 20
tone of conversations, 20
using best judgment, 21
engaged communities, 16–17
engagement. *See also* connections; SME
(social media engagement)
asking for action, 115–116
asking questions, 123
continuous process of, 122
creating rules of, 19
encouraging, 124–125
forum for opinions, 112
guidelines, 34–35
increasing, 108
increasing revenue, 108
increasing traffic, 106, 108
longer-term goals, 108
participation ground rules, 112
policies, 34
quality of content, 122
reassessing for improvement, 39–40
receiving reviews, 108
setting strategies, 122

engagement *(continued)*
  short-term goals, 106
  specifying actions, 106
  timing, 102–103
  trends in numbers, 40
  using consistent process of, 29
  by way of inspiration, 130–131
  word-of-mouth communication, 106
engaging people, 13–14
Epiphanie Bags page, 172–173
Estes, Jen, 177
Etsy website, 158
Experian study, use of social
      networks, 10–11

• *F* •

Facebook
  adding to Twitter, 207
  AllFacebook blog, 157
  amount of content, 165
  amount of time spent on, 157
  asking questions, 162
  authenticity, 160
  chats, 51
  Checkins, 51
  Comments, 51
  Comments Box, 155
  comparing to Twitter, 53
  contests, 135
  conversations, 51
  establishing trust, 160
  follower loyalty, 160–164
  frequency of posting, 167
  interaction, 51
  Likes, 51
  listening and responding, 161
  Notifications option, 89
  number of users, 44, 51
  Pages algorithm, 165
  Pages Manager, 89
  personal Timeline, 51–52, 164–165
  Pinvolve application, 239
  post likeability, 162–163
  posting frequency in schedule, 102
  promoting business pages, 164–165
  quality engagement, 160
  reach of page posts, 166

responses to posts, 15
running contests, 163
Shares, 51
status updates, 51
sticking to schedule, 160
taking time, 162
target market, 160
Terms of Service, 53
tracking progress, 161
treatment of members, 158
Facebook advanced features
  Graph Search, 175–176
  scheduling posts, 172–174
  SEO (search engine optimization), 174–175
  tagging photos, 172
  tagging posts, 172
Facebook advertising
  CPC (Cost Per Click) bid, 177
  CPM (Cost Per Thousand), 177
  creating, 177
  goals, 177
  options, 176–177
  setting price, 177
  social widgets, 178–181
  targeting audience, 177
Facebook community, growing, 159–165
Facebook Developers page, 180
Facebook Gifts, selling products, 158
Facebook Groups, 46–47
Facebook Insights
  accessing, 181
  Engaged Users, 182
  measurement categories, 181–182
  Reach, 182
  Talking About This, 182
Facebook interactions, analyzing, 181–182
Facebook News Feeds
  adding visual elements, 169–170
  crafting engaging posts, 166–169
  cross-posting, 171
  drawing instant attention, 169
  driving traffic to pages, 171
  EdgeRank, 166
  getting pictures, 169
  mixing posts, 169
  photo posts, 169
  post frequency, 170–171
  post timing, 170–171

reaching out to pages, 170
running caption contests, 169
sharing images, 169–170
sharing personal news, 166
Facebook pages
customer support, 159
engaging with customers, 158
explained, 157
integrating Pinterest into, 238–239
providing news, 158
providing updates, 158
selling products, 158
setting up, 27, 51–52
sharing pictures, 158
sharing videos, 158
Facebook scheduler, using with
posts, 173–174
Facebook Timeline
explained, 157
integrating Pinterest into, 237–238
Feedly RSS feed reader, using with
Pinterest, 223
Flickr Creative Commons website, 28
followers
assessing interests of, 71
questioning, 112
on Twitter, 115
Followerwonk website, 71
Foodspotting LBS (location-based
service), 282
forums
forming, 151–152
hosting services, 153
Foursquare LBS (location-based service),
54, 282, 288–289
freebies, offering, 133
FreeConference tools, 312

● *G* ●

G+. *See* Google+
gDiapers mission, 160–161
geocaching, 298
geolocating, 297
geotagging, 286–287, 297
Girls Crochet Headbands, 345–346
goals
assessing capacity, 86–87
evaluating competition, 87–88

including in messaging map, 95–97
setting, 85–86
Google Alerts, 75, 88–89
Google Groups website, 152–153
Google Hangouts videoconferencing
tool, 314
Google Places for Business website, 80
Google Trends, 126
Google URL Shortener, 83
Google Wallet platform, 293
Google+
* (asterisk), 270
_ (underscore), 270
+1 button, 265, 278–279
+1 ratings, 59
benefit, 263–264
bold words, 270
Business Page, 60
business pages, 266–267
circles, 59, 264
circling connections, 274–275
claiming authorship, 268
commenting on posts, 59
communities, 264
connecting with groups, 275–277
documents, 270
Events feature, 264, 276
expanding engagement, 274–280
features, 58
GPlus.to, 265
Hangouts, 275–277
hangouts, 264
italics, 270
live-streaming video, 59
long-form publishing, 269
number of users, 58
personal profile, 265
photos, 264, 270
posting frequency in schedule, 102
posting multimedia, 270–271
posting to G+ streams, 58
profiles, 263
profiles versus pages, 266–267
setting up pages, 267–268
sharing posts, 59
slide shows, 271
targeting messages to groups, 59
text-chatting in Circles, 59
URL shortener, 265

Google+ *(continued)*
  video, 270, 277
  video-chatting in Google Hangouts, 59
Google+ badge, embedding, 273
Google+ Communities, 46–47, 279–280
Google+ page
  building audience for, 273–274
  building circles, 273–274
  sharing, 273
Google+ stream
  interacting in, 271–272
  Manage Your Pages screen, 271–272
Got Milk page, 163–164
GoToWebinar tool, 312
GPlus.to website, 265
Graph Search, using in Facebook, 175–176
groups
  BigTent, 152–153
  building in social networks, 153–154
  forming, 151–152
  Google Groups, 152–153
  GroupSpaces, 152–153
  hosting services, 153
  management tools, 152–153
  Meetup, 152–153
  Ning, 152–153
  Yahoo! Groups, 152–153
GroupSpaces website, 152–153
guest posts, soliciting, 114
Gyft mobile platform, 293

• H •

Haller, Victoria, 118
Here On Biz app, using with LBS, 286
Highlight app, using with LBS, 286
HootSuite tool, 30, 34, 83, 89
  creating Twitter columns with, 203
  report, 38–39
  scheduling tweets with, 200
  using with LinkedIn, 259, 261
human touch, importance of, 22
humanizing brands, 12–14
humanizing in marketplace, adding to
    social media networks, 11
humor, sparking conversation
    with, 129–130

• I •

iContact e-mail marketing tool, 141
IFTTI tool
  scheduling tweets with, 200
  using with LBS, 292
image sources, 28
iMeet videoconferencing tool, 314–315
impact, analyzing, 81–82
incentives, creating, 73
incentives for sharing
  contests, 133–135
  discounts, 133
  freebies, 133
  providing, 132–136
Infusionsoft e-mail marketing tool, 141
Instagram, 54
  LBS (location–based services), 289–290
  posting frequency in schedule, 102
  using with images on Twitter, 188
  using with LBS (location–based services)
InstantConference tool, 312
interactions
  versus actions, 121
  analyzing on Facebook, 181–182
  attention spans, 39
  day of week, 39
  defined, 121
  determining value of, 35–36
  driving, 24
  information overload, 39
  metrics, 37
  moods, 39
  in online communities, 19, 146
  time of day, 39
  time zone, 39
  variables related to, 39
InterCall tool, 312
interviewing people, 114
iStockphoto website, 28
iTunes, downloading for podcasts, 306

• J •

JustTweetIt list tool, 204

• K •

kindness is king, 124
Klout tool, 83

• L •

LBS (location-based services), 64
  Apple's Passbook platform, 293
  Banjo app, 286
  ByteLights, 285
  checking into locations, 285
  comparing mobile marketing tools, 293
  connecting, 291
  deals driven by check-ins, 292–293
  discovering others nearby, 286
  explained, 281–282
  Foodspotting, 282
  Foursquare, 282, 288–289
  geocaching, 298
  geolocating, 297
  geotagging, 286–287, 297
  Google Wallet platform, 293
  GPS feature, 281, 285
  Gyft mobile platform, 293
  Here On Biz app, 286
  Highlight app, 286
  hybrid engagement, 298–299
  IFTTT tool, 292
  Instagram, 286–287, 289–290
  linking for integrated posts, 291–292
  making connections with, 284–287
  offers, 293
  online/offline engagement, 298–299
  Path, 282
  proximity, 286
  QR codes, 295–297
  SCVNGR, 282
  SMS marketing, 294
  Sonar app, 286
  Trover, 287
  using for promotions, 287–293
  Wyst, 287
  Yelp, 283
LBS account, setting up, 283–284
Lehmann, Lisa, 158
Likes, adding, 115

LinkedIn
  B2B (business-to-business)
    marketing, 245
  Buffer tool, 261
  business-minded audience, 56
  comments, 57
  Company Page, 57
  e-mail, 57
  endorsements, 246, 257–258
  engagement features, 245
  filtering news updates, 252
  frequency of engagement, 254
  going mobile, 259
  Help Center, 258
  HootSuite tool, 261
  InMail, 57, 246
  interacting with others, 254
  interactions through updates,
    251–254
  likes, 57
  messages, 246
  news feeds, 57
  number of users, 56
  P2P (Peer-to-Peer) marketing, 245
  personalizing invitations, 246
  polls, 57
  posting content, 253
  posting frequency in schedule, 102
  posting updates, 253
  profiles, 57
  reciprocal interactions, 246
  recommendations, 246, 255–257
  shares, 57
  start of, 56
LinkedIn Company Pages
  best practices, 251
  Careers section, 250
  connecting profiles to, 250
  creating, 250
  described, 249
  home page, 250
  Products section, 250
LinkedIn Groups, 46–47, 57
  discussions, 247, 258
  finding, 248
  forming, 258
  jobs, 258
  joining, 247–249

LinkedIn Groups *(continued)*
  managing, 258
  members, 258
  moderating, 258
  participating in, 248–249
  promotions, 258
  search feature, 258
LinkedIn profile
  activity, 242–243
  background, 243
  connections, 243
  editing, 244
  embedded presentations, 244–245
  enhancing, 244
  following, 243
  groups, 243
  photo, 242
  recommendations, 243
  setting up, 241–242
  snapshot, 242
  vanity URL, 244
LinkedIn results
  analytics tools, 261
  analyzing engagement, 260
  business benefits, 260
  connections, 259
  endorsements, 259
  inquiries, 260
  links clicked, 259
  mentions, 259
  recommendations, 259
  tracking interactions, 259–260
LinkedIn Signal, using, 252, 259
Listorious list tool, 204
live streamiing video, 315–316
Livefyre commenting add-on, 155–156
Livestream website, 316

• *M* •

Mabel's Labels, 72, 92, 344–345
Mad Mimi e-mail marketing tool, 141
Magisto mobile video, 316
MailChimp e-mail marketing tool,
    45, 140–141
ManageFlitter website, 193
Manestream Studio hair salon, 177–178

market research, engaging in, 16
marketing e-mail subscribers
    benchmark, 38
MarketMeSuite dashboard tool, 30
markets, tapping into, 15–16
Matilda Jane clothing company, 167–168
media, engaging with, 78
Meerman Scott, David, 80
MeetingOnNow tool, 312
Meetup website, 152–153
@mentioning, results of, 198
message clarity, importance to trust, 67
messages, 83–84, 148–149
messaging, 33–34
  branding documents, 34
  community policies, 34
  FAQ (Frequently Asked Questions), 34
  keeping consistent, 33–34
  paying attention to, 41
  rules of behavior, 34
  SME guidelines and policies, 34
  social media management tool, 34
  terms of service, 34
messaging map, 94–97
metrics, 36–37
mobile apps, 63–64
mobile devices, number of users, 63
mobile updates, receiving, 294–295
mobile video, 316. *See also* video
MomBiz, 349–350

• *N* •

negative feedback. *See also* complaints;
    responses
  acknowledging, 119
  addressing, 119–120
  apologizing, 119
  handling, 117, 119–120
  reviewing context, 119
  sharing, 119
negativity, managing, 17, 26–27
networks. *See* social networks
newsletters, 142–145
Ning website, 152–153
notifications, setting, 88–89
Nylabone, 348–349

• O •

online communications, being
    careful with, 21
online communities. *See also* communities
  action, 19
  adding value, 147
  appropriate content, 147
  courtship, 146
  deepening interactions, 146
  engagement, 146
  engagement guidelines, 147
  evangelism, 147
  explained, 18
  first impressions, 146
  first interactions, 146
  formation, 146
  forming, 146–147
  growing, 146–147
  honesty, 147
  infancy, 146
  interaction, 19
  kindness, 147
  organic ambassadors, 147
  participating in, 145–151
  prohibiting spam, 147
  reaction, 18
  superficial interactions, 146
online forums, 46–48. *See also* social
    networks
online marketing, engaging with media, 78
opinions, dealing with, 112–113, 128
Ow.ly URL shortener, 83

• P •

Paperlinks QR code scanner, 297
participation, setting ground rules for, 112
Path LBS (location-based service), 282
paying attention, 88–92
PeerIndex tool, 83
people. *See also* audience; customers
  attracting attention of, 13
  compelling to take action, 13
  convincing to do business, 14
  enticing, 13
  getting to talk, 20

  giving reason to return, 14
  putting faces to names, 12
PeopleBrowsr SME tool, 82
perks, offering, 41
personality, importance to authenticity, 68
pin feeds, getting noticed in, 222–227
pinbombing, avoiding, 227
pinning
  amount, 226–227
  effectiveness, 227
  finding people for, 226
  frequency, 226–227
Pinpuff tool, 220–222
pins, getting inspiration for, 224
Pinterest
  analytics, 220
  attracting attention, 228–229
  benefitting from integration, 233–239
  blocking pinning of images, 234
  business account, 212
  business accounts, 55
  Collaborates, 55
  Comments, 55
  comments, 217–219
  comparing to Twitter, 55
  contests, 135
  converting account types, 212
  conveying messages, 217
  Facebook pages, 238–239
  Facebook Timelines, 237–238
  Feedly RSS feed reader, 223
  graphics, 222
  group boards, 232–233
  growth rate, 54
  hashtags, 228–229
  iframe app services, 238
  increasing engagement, 228–233
  infographics, 222–223
  inspiring pinning images, 233–235
  interface, 56
  likes, 55, 217–219
  linking to Twitter, 235–236
  notices of actions, 220
  numbers, 219
  performance of pins, 220
  pin campaign, 220
  pinning images, 217, 223–225

Pinterest *(continued)*
  Pinpuff tool, 220–222
  pins, 55, 217–219
  Piqora tool, 220
  Popular category, 223
  posting frequency in schedule, 102
  posts, 55
  publishing text content, 55
  quantifying value of, 219–222
  Reachli tool, 220
  Repinly tool, 220–221
  repinning strategy, 225–226
  repins, 55, 217–219
  RSS feed reader, 223
  running contests, 230–231
  ShortStack iFrame app-generator, 238
  sweepstakes, 231–232
  tagging others, 229–230
  Threadless contest, 230–231
  tracking metrics, 219–220
  weekly summary, 220–221
  Wine Sisterhood sweepstakes, 231–232
  Woobox iFrame app-generator, 238
Pinterest boards
  accessing, 211
  arranging for effect, 216
  business goals, 213
  content-themed, 214–215
  event-related, 215
  keywords, 213–214
  names, 214
  setting up, 213–214
  target audience, 213
  topics, 213–214
  visual-themed, 215
Pinterest stream, de-cluttering, 225
Pinvolve application, 239
PitchEngine SMR tool, 80
plan, creating, 19
podcast audience, growing, 307–308
podcasts
  archiving, 60
  Blogcast FM, 309
  building audience, 305–308
  content, 305
  distributing, 306
  downloading iTunes, 306
  embedding, 60
  getting started, 305
  live streaming, 60
  publishing software, 305
  Rao, Srinivas, 309
  recording, 60
  SoundCloud software, 305
PodOmatic software, 305
policies, 34
Pollcode website, 113
Polldaddy website, 113
polling apps, using, 113
Porterfield, Amy, 178–179
posting online, trivial content, 27
posts
  paying attention to, 41
  scheduling on Facebook, 172–174
Pozner, Noah, 118
presence, demonstrating, 88–92
presence process
  establishing, 92–93
  message map, 93–97
press releases, 79–80
PressDoc SMR tool, 80
prizes, choosing for contests, 134
products, promoting, 114
promotions, using LBS (location-based
    service) for, 287–290

Qik website, 316
QR codes, 295–297
Quora Q&As, 151

Radian6 website, 34
Radicati Group, Inc. website, 44
Rafflecopter giveaways, 163
Rao, Srinivas, 309
reach
  explained, 87
  increasing via e-mail marketing, 143
Reachli website, 220
reaction in online communities, 19
reactive interaction, examples, 104
Repinly tool, 220–221

repinning strategy, using on Pinterest, 225–226
resources, considering, 86
respect, importance to customers, 18
response, importance to customers, 18
response rates
  measuring, 83
  URL shorteners, 83
responses. *See also* negative feedback
  assessing, 81–84
  expressing gratitude for, 91
retweeting, 190–191
  content, 115
  results of, 198
retweets, 15, 53
  boosting potential of, 197
  interpreting, 196
revenue, increasing, 108
reviews, getting from customers, 81, 108
rewards
  importance to customers, 18
  offering for action, 116–117
rules of behavior document, 34

● *S* ●

SalesForceMarketingCloud SME tool, 81–82
Scan QR code scanner, 297
schedule, setting, 100–104
SCVNGR LBS (location-based service), 282
Selective Tweets website, 207
sentiment, analyzing, 81–82
SEO (search engine optimization), 174–175
services, promoting, 114
sharing
  content, 15
  determining value, 132
  incentives for, 132–136
  quality content, 73
  with social network widgets, 154–155
ShopAlerts service, 294
ShortStack iFrame app-generator, 142
  using with Pinterest, 238
Shula, Don, 85–86
Shutterfly page, liking, 116–117
signature file, using with messages, 149
Simply Measured SME tool, 82, 87
skills, considering, 86

Skype videoconferencing tool, 313–315
smartphones, number of users, 63
SME (social media engagement). *See also* engagement
  basis of, 41
  changing consumer needs, 10–12
  considering, 10
  determining valuable interactions, 35–36
  explained, 9
  main goal in, 13
  process of, 10
  quantity vs. quality, 35
SME components
  action, 21
  audience, 21
  content, 21
  interaction, 21, 24
  outcomes and measurement, 21
  reaction, 21
SME downsides
  backlash, 31–32
  barriers to entry, 27–28
  distraction, 26
  inconsistent messaging, 33–34
  information overload, 28–31
  negativity, 26
  "time suck," 26
SME efforts, quantifying, 38
SME guidelines
  doing homework, 68
  experimentation, 68
  setting up, 68
  stating mission, 68
SME mistakes
  broadcasting only one's content, 338
  excessive automation, 338
  ignoring feedback, 339–340
  inconsistency, 339
  lack of planning, 337
  lacking personality, 339
  overuse of content, 341
  repeating, 341
  sharing only one's content, 338
  spamming, 340
  underestimating difficulty, 340
SME strategy, 26
SME tools, 81–82

SMM (social media management) tools, 90–91

SMR (social media release) tools, 80

SMS (short message service) marketing, 294

social engagement, importance of, 17

social media icons, adding to networks, 11

social media management tools, 34, 83

social media presence
    establishing, 27, 71–72
    quality of, 87

Social Mention SME tool, 82

social network widgets, 154–155

social networks. *See also* online forums
    building presence in, 14, 22
    displaying affinities in, 14
    engaging with, 50
    Facebook, 51–53
    Foursquare, 54
    Google+, 58–59
    Instagram, 54
    LinkedIn, 56–57
    Pinterest, 54–56
    popularity, 16
    promoting, 41
    statistic related to, 10–11
    Twitter, 53–54

social presence, demonstrating, 88–92

social sharing, 17, 20

social widgets, embedding in Facebook, 178–181. *See also* widgets

SocialBro tool, 110

Socialcam mobile video, 316

Sonar app, using with LBS, 286

SoundCloud podcast software, 305

spam, prohibiting in online communities, 147

Sprout Social tool, 83

SproutSocial dashboard tool, 30, 34

statistics, social networks, 10–11

stock.xchng website, 28

Storify website, 37

streaming video, 315–316

Studio Jewel page, 158–159

success
    leveraging, 41
    sharing, 107

Sumall.com site, 111

su.pr URL shortener, 83

SurveyMonkey website, 113

sweepstakes, 134–135

Sysomos SME tool, 81

• T •

tablet computers, number of users, 63

teleseminars, 310–312

terms of service document, 34

time investment, considering, 86

timing engagement, 102–103

TinyPrints engagement example, 16

Tout mobile video, 316

traffic
    benchmark, 38
    driving to Facebook, 171
    increasing, 106, 108

transaction metrics, considering, 37

transactions, benchmark, 38

transformation metrics, considering, 37

trend reporting, inconsistency in, 40

trending topics, tapping into, 126

trends
    observing in engagement numbers, 40
    paying attention to, 40

Trover app, using with LBS, 287

trust
    assessing, 81–84
    in brands, 71
    building, 22, 67
    contributing to conversations, 70–73
    of earned media, 70
    establishing guidelines, 68
    finding brand's voice, 70
    interacting authentically, 68–69
    message clarity, 67

Tweet grader website, 194

TweetDeck tool
    creating columns with, 203
    scheduling tweets with, 200

tweeting questions, 189–190

TweetReach website, 194

tweets
    adding headings, 196
    breaking news, 197

Buffer for scheduling, 200
crafting, 195–196
expressing gratitude, 197
HootSuite for scheduling, 200
IFTTT for scheduling, 200
keywords mentioned in, 89
limiting, 197
playing to emotions, 196
promoting others, 196
scheduling, 197, 199–200
shortening links, 195
TweetDeck for scheduling, 200
using hashtags, 196
Twellow list tool, 204
Twit Cleaner website, 193
Twitgoo, using with images on Twitter, 189
Twitpic, using with images on Twitter, 189
Twitter
    accessing on the go, 208
    adding to Facebook, 207
    API (application programming
        interface), 54
    attracting followers, 205–206
    avoiding humble brags, 187
    being authentic, 191
    being "present," 199–200
    benefit, 184
    Breaking News update, 184
    broadcasting, 185–186
    building connections, 201–204
    buttons, 205–206
    character limitation, 89, 183
    comparing to Facebook, 53
    comparing to Pinterest, 55
    creating columns, 201–204
    creating lists, 201–204
    DMs (direct messages), 53, 204–205
    Echofon tool, 89
    fast-moving conversations, 193
    focusing on passion, 192
    followers, 115
    HootSuite tool, 89
    Instagram for images, 188
    JustTweetIt list tool, 204
    knowing boundaries, 192
    listening on, 186
    Listorious list tool, 204
    ManageFlitter, 193
    master plan, 193
    @mention, 53
    mobile apps, 208
    number of users, 53
    posting frequency in schedule, 102
    promoting messages, 187
    real-time reach, 184
    @replies, 185
    retweets, 15, 53, 115, 190–191, 196–197
    search tools, 186
    searching bios on, 110
    seeking topics, 186
    sharing button, 206
    sharing interests, 185–186
    showing personality, 191
    topics to avoid on, 192
    TweetDeck tool, 89
    Tweets, 53
    Twellow list tool, 204
    Twitgoo for images, 189
    Twitpic for images, 189
    uploading photos, 188–189
    use of @ (at) sign, 198
    using period (.) with at (@) sign, 198
    visual hooks, 188–189
    WeFollow list tool, 204
    widgets, 205–206
    yFrog for images, 189
Twitter account, sweeping, 193
Twitter Counter website, 194
Twitter Favorites feature, 200–202
Twitter measurement tools, 194
Twitter stream
    being mentioned in, 186
    embedding, 206
    leveraging links, 196–198
    watching, 193

• *U* •

URL shorteners
    bitly, 40, 83
    Google URL Shortener, 83
    Ow.ly, 83
    su.pr, 83
Usenet newsgropus, 43
Ustream website, 316

• V •

Veetle website, 316
VerticalResponse e-mail marketing
    tool, 141
Viddy mobile video, 316
video. *See also* mobile video; YouTube
  analyzing impact, 333–334
  embedding, 331–332
  extending reach with, 330–334
  integrating, 331–332
  live streaming, 315–316
  popularity of, 313
  uploading on the go, 333
video crisis, avoiding, 33
video responses, taking advantage of,
    332–333
videocasting, 61
videoconferencing tools, 314–315
video-hosting sites, 316
Vimeo, 62
Vine mobile video, 316
viral video crisis, avoiding, 33
visibility
  increasing via e-mail marketing, 143
  maintaining, 124

• W •

webinars
  benefits of, 310–311
  versus teleseminars, 311–312
  tools, 312
websites
  AJ Bombers burger restaurant, 352
  AllFacebook blog, 157
  Angie's List, 80
  answering polls, 49
  Apple's Passbook platform, 293
  Audioboo app, 308
  Banjo app, 286
  benchmark for traffic to, 38
  BigTent, 152–153
  bitly tool, 40, 194, 259
  Blendtec, 350–351
  Buffer, 194, 200, 261
  ByteLights, 285

Cabot Creamery Cooperative, 347–348
Chirbit app, 308
Chobani Greek-style yogurt, 351–352
Citysearch, 81
Cone Cause Evolution Study, 135
Constant Contact, 45
Domino's Pizza franchise, 346–347
eBay Stores, 158
Echofon tool, 89
editorial calendar, 100
e-mailing site owhers, 48
engaging through, 48–50
enhancing for engagement, 154–156
Etsy, 158
Facebook Developers page, 180
Facebook Gifts, 158
Facebook Terms of Service, 53
feedback forms, 49
Flickr Creative Commons, 28
Followerwonk, 71
Foodspotting, 282
Foursquare, 282
Girls Crochet Headbands, 345–346
Google AdWords, 327
Google Alerts, 75, 88–89
Google authorship, 268
Google Groups, 152–153
Google Places for Business website, 80
Google Trends, 126
Google Wallet platform, 293
GPlus.to, 265
GroupSpaces, 152–153
Gyft mobile platform, 293
Here On Biz app, 286
Highlight app, 286
HootSuite, 30, 34, 89, 200, 259, 261
IFTTI tool, 200, 292
image sources, 28
Instagram, 188, 286–287
iStockphoto, 28
iTunes, 306
JustTweetIt list tool, 204
LinkedIn Signal, 252
Listorious list tool, 204
Little Pnuts, 106–107
live streaming video, 316
Mabel's Labels, 344–345
MailChimp, 45

ManageFlitter, 193
MarketMeSuite, 30
Meetup, 152–153
mobile video, 316
MomBiz, 349–350
Ning, 152–153
Nylabone, 348–349
Paperlinks QR code scanner, 297
Path, 282
Pinpuff tool, 220
Pinvolve application, 239
Piqora tool, 220
PitchEngine, 80
PodOmatic software, 305
Pollcode, 113
Polldaddy, 113
polling apps, 113
PressDoc, 80
QR code scanners, 297
Quora Q&As, 151
Radian6, 34
Radicati Group, Inc., 44
Rafflecopter giveaways, 163
Reachli tool, 220
Repinly tool, 220
Scan QR code scanner, 297
SCVNGR, 282
Selective Tweets, 207
sharing with friends, 49
ShopAlerts service, 294
ShortStack iFrame app-generator, 142
signing up for offers, 49
Simply Measured SME tool, 87
SocialBro tool, 110
Sonar app, 286
SoundCloud software, 305
SproutSocial, 30, 34
stock.xchng, 28
Storify, 37
Sumall.com, 111
SurveyMonkey, 113
teleseminar tools, 312
Trover, 287
Tweet grader, 194
TweetDeck tool, 89, 200
TweetReach, 194
Twellow list tool, 204
Twit Cleaner, 193

Twitgoo for images on Twitter, 189
Twitpic for images on Twitter, 189
Twitter, 89
Twitter Counter, 194
video hosting, 316
videoconferencing tools, 313–315
webinar tools, 312
WeFollow list tool, 204
Wildfire promotions, 163
Wine Sisterhood, 343–344
WiseStamp app, 44
Woobox iFrame app-generator, 141–142
Wufoo, 113
Wyst, 287
Yahoo! Groups, 152–153
Yahoo! Local, 81
Yelp, 80, 283
yFrog for images on Twitter, 189
WeFollow list tool, 204
widgets. *See also* social widgets
  +1 button, 157
  embedding, 154
  Facebook, 157
  Google+, 157
  Like button, 155
  LinkedIn, 157
  Pin It button, 155
  Pinterest, 157
  Shares, 155
  Tweet button, 155
  Twitter, 157
Wildfire promotions, 163
Wine Sisterhood, 343–344
WiseStamp app website, 44
Woobox iFrame app-generator,
  141–142, 238
word cloud, creating, 71
Wufoo website, 113
Wyst app, using with LBS, 287

Yahoo! Groups website, 152–153
Yahoo! Local website, 81
Yelp, 80
yFrog, using with images on Twitter, 189
Young, Lynette, 277

YouTube. *See also* video
  advertising options, 62
  annotations, 319, 329–330
  attracting viewers, 62
  beginning of, 317
  capturing attention of audience, 318–320
  community features, 62
  comparing to Google, 62
  creating playlists, 322–323
  interacting with community, 323–324
  maximizing subscriber base, 323
  no cost, 62
  number of users, 61–62
  posting frequency in schedule, 102
  SEO (search engine optimization), 62
  standing out on, 325–330
  thumbnails, 330
  tools, 62
  video content, 325–326
YouTube channel, optimizing, 320
YouTube metadata
  descriptions, 328
  explained, 327
  Google AdWords, 327
  keyword generation, 327
  tags, 328
  titles, 327

● Z ●

Zone Perfect fitness bar, 167–168